The Accidental Duchess

Born Emma Watkins, the Duchess of Rutland is the daughter of a farmer from Knighton, Powys. She worked as an estate agent, marketing properties in Worcester, and later as an interior designer. Today, the Duchess runs the commercial activities of Belvoir Castle, including shooting parties, weddings and a range of furniture. She has presented on various television programmes, including ITV's *Castles, Keeps and Country Homes*, appeared in an episode of *Alan Titchmarsh on Capability Brown*, and has produced a book about Belvoir Castle.

In 2021, the Duchess created a podcast titled *Duchess*, where she interviews chatelaines of castles and stately homes throughout the United Kingdom. In her podcast's first season, her interviewees included Lady Henrietta Spencer-Churchill of Blenheim Palace and Lady Mansfield of Scone Palace.

Watkins married David Manners, 11th Duke of Rutland, in 1992. The pair have five children.

Also by The Duchess of Rutland:

Belvoir Castle: A Thousand Years of
Family Art and Architecture

Shooting: A Season of Discovery

Capability Brown & Belvoir: Discovering
a Lost Landscape

The Accidental Duchess

From farmer's daughter to Belvoir Castle

THE
DUCHESS OF RUTLAND

PAN BOOKS

First published 2022 by Macmillan

This paperback edition first published 2023 by Pan Books
an imprint of Pan Macmillan
The Smithson, 6 Briset Street, London EC1M 5NR
EU representative: Macmillan Publishers Ireland Ltd, 1st Floor, The
Liffey Trust Centre, 117–126 Sheriff Street Upper,
Dublin 1, D01 YC43
Associated companies throughout the world
www.panmacmillan.com

ISBN 978-1-0350-0210-8

3 5 7 9 8 6 4 2

A CIP catalogue record for this book is available from the British Library.

Typeset by Palimpsest Book Production Ltd, Falkirk, Stirlingshire
Printed and bound by CPI Group (UK) Ltd, Croydon, CR0 4YY

Visit www.panmacmillan.com to read more about all our books
and to buy them. You will also find features, author interviews and
news of any author events, and you can sign up for e-newsletters
so that you're always first to hear about our new releases.

For Roma and John Watkins, my darling mum and dad

Contents

'Everything must change for everything to remain the same.'

Giuseppe Tomasi di Lampedusa, *The Leopard*

Prologue

MARCH 2001

WE WERE WOKEN that night, not by the storm itself, but by the children running into our bedroom.

'Mummy! Daddy! Water's coming in,' they chorused in more-or-less unison. It was around two in the morning, and I had been soundly asleep. 'The castle is flooding! You've got to get up!'

Helped by anxious hands and faces, I forced myself awake, got out of bed and fumbled my way into my slippers. We had only properly moved into this vast, multi-roomed, multi-towered extravaganza on a hill a few weeks earlier. I hadn't wanted to. I had been very happy in our marital home, which I had transformed from an un-loved regency house on the Belvoir estate into a version of the farmhouse where I myself had been brought up and where my parents still lived.

My childhood home, called – without a trace of irony – Heartsease, was in a hidden valley in the mythical border country known as the Welsh Marches, a magical place of

1

muscular hills and gentle valleys that was as different as could be imagined from the flat landscape that surrounded Belvoir Castle.

The original castle was built by the Normans shortly after the conquest. The name means 'beautiful view' in French, and the locals, who no doubt took a dim view of this un-English name, pronounced it 'Beaver', which is how it has been known ever since. Even though that first castle has long gone, the far-reaching views remain.

We had just finished decorating the drawing room in our private quarters – the part that the public don't see and which is much bigger than it sounds. The roof had been the first thing that we'd checked out, so – shock mixed with disbelief – I turned to my husband, bleary-eyed beside me:

'You stay and keep an eye on the girls,' I said. 'I'll go and take a look.'

Our three daughters, then aged eight, six and four, had been woken by the storm, and I could tell they were frightened. The castle still felt strange to them. They knew it as somewhere we would go on Sundays, to have lunch with their grandparents. They certainly didn't think of it as home. And as I followed them through a series of long, ill-lit corridors, I got a clear sense of why they found it so intimidating. The moonlight cast flickering shadows through the tall windows and, even as an adult, it was easy to imagine there were ghouls and ghosts lurking behind the long velvet curtains.

The girls had left the drawing room door open and I stood on the threshold and peered into the gloom without switching on the light in case the electricity was affected.

And while I could see that the room wasn't flooded in the Noah's ark sense – you didn't need wellington boots to cross the floor – water was nonetheless cascading down the newly painted walls. My heart sank. And then it struck me . . . Above this room was the library, which itself had been recently decorated by my mother-in-law, Frances, now the Dowager Duchess of Rutland. But it wasn't only the new wallpaper – it was the books, thousands and thousands of them, most extremely old, extremely rare, and irreplaceable. I knew that if I didn't do something quickly, we would lose them. Being dyslexic, I have never been a great reader, but this wasn't about me. It was about the family heritage.

I quickly ran back along the long corridor to what was once a butler's pantry but was now used by the cleaning teams to store basics, and I grabbed as many buckets and washing-up bowls as I could find, then handed them out to the girls as well as to David, who had followed us, though with only one arm that worked, his ability to help was limited.

'Put these on the floor wherever you can see the water coming in through the ceiling,' I said as I pulled on my wellingtons and threw my Barbour over my nightdress.

'Where are you going, Mummy?'

'Up on the roof,' I said, grabbing an umbrella. 'I need to find where the leak is.'

Belvoir Castle is made up of six towers and well over 200 rooms, with long corridors connecting them. The closest tower to where I imagined the water was coming in was Bellhangers. I knew there was no direct access from Bellhangers to the roof, so I went to the Flag Tower, found the key to the door behind the portrait of an un-named ancestor, and started up the stairs. There are ninety-eight steps from the ground up to the top, but I was on the first floor, so perhaps a dozen fewer, and then up and up, round and round the bare stone spiral staircase until I finally pushed open the door and emerged onto the roof, 450 feet above the ground.

The Flag Tower couldn't have been further away from Bellringers but as each tower is different I could at least identify it over the other side, and, clicking open the umbrella, I began to make my way around the castle walls, placing my feet as carefully as a cat. In fact, there are many separate roofs hidden behind the battlements, all of which are pitched, so to get from one to another, you have to scale rackety steps, first up to a ridge, then down the other side. Although I had a torch, it was useless until I found out where the leak might be. But I was up here now, and would need to do my best.

I inched my way round the ramparts searching for any sign of water. And then I found it: a great puddle in the gully where the slates sloped up towards the parapet. Gingerly I slithered down the slope on my bum, my night-dress already soaked through, my rubber boots acting as brakes. Something must be blocking the drain, I realized, and saw no alternative but to put my hand in the gutter and see if I could dislodge whatever it was. *Probably just soggy leaves*, I told myself. This was no time to be squeamish. But it wasn't leaves. I pushed my hand as far as it would go into the drain itself and eventually pulled out a dead pigeon. And when the water level didn't immediately start to go down, I put my hand in again and found a second. I tossed their sodden remains over the parapet to be disposed of by Belvoir's tribe of live-in rats. I felt no pity. I grew up on a farm where pigeons are the enemy, no better than vermin, their only use as target practice to be turned into pâté or pie.

Within seconds I saw that my DIY efforts had worked; the water was now draining away, and, job done, I squidged my way back along the acres of roof, my hair in rat-tails, then back down the spiral staircase, laughing out loud as I remembered something my mother had said when she realized that her son-in-law would one day be a duke and I would be a duchess.

'Just imagine!' she'd said. 'They'll be bringing you breakfast in bed every morning!'

Oh, the glamour!

Yes, my husband had inherited a castle, but behind the fairy-tale façade we were faced with jaw-dropping levels of debt, as well as battalions of rats, and staff who clearly preferred the former incumbents to us and our unruly brood of little people with their high-pitched voices and water pistols.

The children greeted me as a returning hero. The ceiling was no longer a waterfall, they informed me, but merely dripping. I decided I would worry about how to deal with the damage in the morning. Tucking the girls back up in their beds, I thanked them for their key role in the night's adventure, reassured them that all was well and turned off the light. Back in our room, I peeled off my wet nightdress, found a dry one and got back into bed, giving my already comatose husband a loving kiss.

By the spring of 2001, we had been married nine years. Only with the death of my father-in-law, in January 1999, had I been transmuted into a duchess – a title, it's fair to say, that meant more to other people than it did to me. But that night, as I lay there in bed, willing myself back to sleep again, the mantle of responsibility that now hung across my shoulders felt only too real.

Over the following twenty years there would be highs and there would be crushing lows, none of which I could anticipate. I wasn't the first young woman in the history of England's great ancestral houses to find herself chatelaine of a building she would never own. Just like the other duchesses of Rutland who had gone before me, whose vision had created the castle as it now was, I would simply be its custodian, the guardian of its future.

Chapter One

Heartsease

RADNORSHIRE, WHERE I grew up on the Welsh/ Shropshire border, no longer exists, having been incorporated into the county of Powys since 1973. But to the families who have lived and farmed there for generations, the idea of Radnorshire is as alive as it ever was – a liminal land, its way of life determined by history and geography.

England rolls into Wales quietly, green pastures dotted with lambs in spring, the boundary marked only by a change in the road surface. From the valley of the River Teme the land rises steeply, leaving behind the fertile farms of Herefordshire and Shropshire. Life for the farming community is tougher in Radnorshire than it is on the gentler English side, as orchards of cider apples give way to steep hillsides where only sheep can survive, and then only with difficulty. Although our farmhouse was less than 200 yards from the sign by the road that says, 'Welcome to Herefordshire' – and in fact our land now extends into all three counties – our identity as a family has always been firmly Welsh.

My parents met at a young farmers' dance when my mother was twenty and my father twenty-one, though it could have happened years earlier, as their fathers had known each other for ever. Jack Watkins – my father's father – and Eddie Davies, my mother's father – would see each other on market days in Knighton – and neither were averse to a little carousing when celebrating a profitable sale.

The landscape that formed the backdrop to my childhood had once been true border country, marked by a series of castles along Offa's Dyke, an 82-mile-long earthwork, said to date from the fifth century AD, built to prevent the marauding Welsh from raiding cattle from across the border. The remains of one of those fortified castles lies about half a mile to the south-west of our farm, though by the seventeenth century it had been totally reimagined as Brampton Bryan Hall, an elegant and extensive country house, set in an equally extensive park. By the eighteenth century, the once-notorious badlands of the Welsh Marches had become fashionably 'picturesque', where newly enriched factory owners from the Staffordshire potteries began eagerly buying up Radnorshire acres, building castellated houses with land-scaped gardens as country retreats. One of these – Stanage Park, designed by Humphry Repton in 1809 – was a ten-minute walk up from our farm, a hamlet known as Heartsease, just off the main road. Legend has it that the name was bequeathed by the famous Welsh hero Owen Glendower, who said his heart was set at ease when he crossed into Wales on returning from England. Another legend has it that the heart of Caratacus is buried there.

Our farmhouse itself was four windows across with an

off-centre front door painted white, its handsome eighteenth-century frontage of golden sandstone enclosing an older core. Around the cobbled courtyard were various farm buildings, and the pride of them all, at least to my mind, was the wood-framed long barn, dating back many hundreds of years, which grew gradually more dilapidated as I got older but which we regularly transformed into the most perfect space for parties.

I had an extremely happy childhood. According to my mother, I was the apple of my father's eye, and could do no wrong. I don't remember it quite like that, but Dad – John Watkins – had been an only child and his own father, my grandpa – Jack Watkins – had been rather harsh, leading to a stammer that affected Dad all his life. So, when he in turn became a father, he was determined to do better, throwing himself into his new role with the same passion as he threw himself into farming. Although it was my mother who gave me my bath at night, it was Dad who read me my bedtime stories until my eyelids grew heavy and I fell asleep.

Roma, as my mother was called, was a beauty. She had jet-black hair, pale grey eyes and golden skin, quite a contrast to the usually pallid Celtic complexion. Above all, she had a fantastic sense of fun and could have had her pick of any of the local boys. But her heart was set on John Watkins. In the end, it was she who proposed to him, or as good as. 'I'm off to Canada,' she'd said. 'So either make your move or I'm going.' The next day he proposed.

Roma was the perfect young farmer's wife. If she wasn't making jam or chutney or bottling plums she was sewing curtains or hanging wallpaper as smoothly as rolling out pastry. By the early 1970s, when another source of income was clearly needed, she did up two rooms in the attic, installed a bathroom, and opened up Heartsease as a farm-house B&B. My first job, aged about ten, was to act as waitress, going through the breakfast menu with the guests, carefully rehearsed by my mother.

'Cereals, fruit juice or grapefruit,' I'd recite. Then: 'Eggs – scrambled, poached or boiled.' Finally, following a long pause, I'd add, as if as an afterthought: 'Or a full cooked Welsh breakfast.' It cost Mum considerably less to do eggs, which came from our own hens, than to provide sausages, bacon and mushrooms and black pudding. Once breakfast was cleared away and the guests had departed, I'd help Mum strip the beds, remake them with fresh sheets and pillowcases, clean the bathroom and await the next arrivals.

My mother had a wonderful eye and sense of colour, and when she entered the flower-arranging section at the Young Farmers' annual show, no one else stood a chance. If that wasn't enough, she had an amazing voice and would regularly be asked to sing at weddings. But behind the laughter and the fun, there was a sad, if steely, streak in my mum. As the fourth child – and the second girl – in a family of five, she had never felt truly valued by her father. While Jean, the eldest, was undemanding and generally compliant, Roma and her father wound each other up. He saw her as wilful and headstrong. She saw him as controlling. In the mid-twentieth century, girls in Radnorshire's farming community were considered largely irrelevant and certainly not worth spending money on. And while Roma did go off to school – a convent, which she hated – it was for practical rather than educational reasons, their farm – Knill, the other side of Knighton – being so remote. She was a weekly boarder and would make the journey there and back on her bicycle. After leaving school, rather than being allowed to study music, which was her dream, she was packed off to secretarial college in Birmingham. What saved her, however, was having a mother who absolutely adored her: my grand-mother Muriel.

At the insistence of her father, my mother was christened Gertrude Naomi after her two grandmothers. However, Muriel got her way in the end by simply calling her baby Roma, and so she has remained. No one is entirely sure where the name came from, but it could not have been more appropriate: unusual, exotic and alluring, perfectly capturing her scintillating yet enigmatic personality.

Muriel's own mother – my great-grandmother, known as Blanche (having sensibly jettisoned her first name of Gertrude) – had been left a widow when comparatively young and brought up five children on her own. Yet, by sheer force of character and resourcefulness, by the time Blanche died she had managed to buy farms for each of her sons. What Muriel inherited was her mother's resourcefulness.

Muriel married well. And it was a love match. Eddie Davies was well-to-do – an only son with two sisters, Ida and Mary. Mary was the family beauty who married a small-animal vet with an up-and-coming practice in Birmingham – and Roma lodged with them when doing her secretarial course. They were well-off and Mary gave all her stylish hand-me-downs to Muriel – her sister-in-law –

who in turn bequeathed them all to me. Many were original 1920s flapper dresses. My absolute favourite was a black A-line number in crepe silk with diamanté decoration which I wore to all my early parties. The Davieses had a holiday house in Borth, a three-mile stretch of sand just north of Aberystwyth on the unspoilt Ceredigion coast and summer holidays there were a highlight of the summer.

As a young bride, Muriel kept hens who lived in mobile coops that would be wheeled around newly harvested fields so that the hens could feed on the spilled grain. When one patch was cleared, these coops would be rolled across to another patch. Every Thursday on market day my grandmother would ride (side saddle) into Kington to sell the eggs which were carried in baskets slung either side of her horse. But by the time I was born her old hen coops had found their way to the back of Heartsease, the hens they housed providing all the eggs we needed both for us as a family and the B&B.

My parents were both born just before the outbreak of war – my father in 1938 and my mother in 1939 – and as such they had childhoods that were dramatically different from those of their parents. Rural Wales was perceived – rightly – as a safe haven – and the moment war was declared in September 1939, women and children from cities deemed most at risk of bombing raids began to make their way to the west. The first wave to arrive at Heartsease between September 1940 and May 1941 consisted of evacuees escaping the London Blitz. After them came Polish refugees, until every spare room in our house had a family in it. Then, as Radnorshire's young men were called up, came the land girls and finally Italian prisoners of war to help work the farms.

There wasn't a farm in Radnorshire that didn't have evacuees, refugees or prisoners of war billeted on them. Heartsease, Knill or Stanage – there was no difference. We had several of the smarter families living in the house with us. The family of Brigadier John Hunt, who became famous for leading the 1953 expedition to Mount Everest, lived in one of our rooms. When he was knighted in 1966, he took the title of Baron of Llanfair Waterdine, a couple of miles away.

Italian prisoners of war didn't come to Heartsease – I don't think we had the space – but they were at Knill, the black-and-white farmhouse where Roma was brought up, in a valley the far side of Kington. Knill had no arable land, and so they farmed only livestock: Hereford cattle and Kelly Hill sheep from mid Wales. But the figure that dominated Roma's life at Knill was their housekeeper, Maggie, who turned up at Knighton's annual hiring fair shortly after the First World War when young Welsh girls would present themselves in their white pinnies, the pinny being removed once they were engaged.

'I hope you're not the sort who wants to change every year,' Maggie said in her strong Welsh accent. As it was, she stayed with the Davies family for forty-five years.

'She dedicated her life to our family,' my mother remembers. 'And when she died, we found £10,000 of those white five-pound notes, stuffed under her mattress.' These were first issued in 1945 and withdrawn in 1961, two years before I was born. Maggie had never had a bank account, and seemingly never spent anything. She would have been fed at the farm and her clothes would have been largely hand-me-downs. By the time of their discovery these notes were no longer legal tender, but the family were eventually able to reclaim the value back.

My own memory of Maggie was that, while Granny was Granny, Maggie was always quietly in charge behind the scenes. There was always a cohort of cats lined up by the window of her pantry waiting for the scraps she would give them. As for washing up, if you dared use more than a dribble of Fairy liquid (which had already been considerably watered down) then you'd be in for a scolding.

One job Granny never relinquished to Maggie was the milking. If the milk ever went sour, Maggie would give Granny a look, waggle her head and say, 'Ah, Missus, must be someone in love.'

When the Italian prisoners arrived at Knill, their dormitory was the storage loft of a semi-attached outbuilding reached via a narrow stairway that led up from the scullery, a stairway that also passed Maggie's bedroom. Although she must have been well into her fifties by then, she barricaded herself in every night, just in case . . .

As a young girl I would haunt that attic, which by then was crammed full of treasures that Muriel had collected over the years, rummaging through trunks of clothes belonging to Mary and other cousins. I once found a porcelain doll with a broken arm that Mum and I took to be mended at a doll hospital in Hereford on one of our shopping trips. Then there were the boxes of 'finds' Granny had bought at auction. Once her children had left home, she indulged her love of antiques and had a particular fondness for country house sales conducted by Russell Baldwin & Bright. She would always sit in the second row where she could catch the eye of the handsome auctioneer, bidding for job lots from stately homes that were going under the hammer. The brass knocker on our front door of Heartsease came from one of these sales, and every week I would fetch the Brasso from under the sink and polish it till it gleamed. One day Granny appeared with several boxes of parquet flooring for our hall which had to be stripped of their bitumen coating then sanded before they could be put down. The large mirror to the left of the front door was another of granny's finds. It had a shelf where Mum kept her bottle of Rive Gauche and she would give herself a quick spray and check her lipstick before going out. Facing it, next to a brass gong that would summon everyone to dinner, was a wonderful grandfather clock with painted country scenes on the front which I would have to wind once a week, always terrified I'd wind it too far. The sound of its *tick-tock, tick-tock* is one of the enduring sounds of my childhood.

Until the financial crash of 1929, the Watkins family had been tenant farmers on the Stanage Estate, but in order to pay death duties, the Coltman-Rogerses sold Heartsease to my grandfather outright. Although a social hierarchy still existed when I grew up in the 1970s, it was far less pronounced in farming communities than elsewhere. Squire and tenant alike had to deal with poor harvests, the fluctuating price of wheat or beef, while bad weather remained the ultimate leveller. And while shooting and riding to hounds are now considered 'country pursuits' designed for the entertainment of the rich, the reality is very different. Learning to shoot is a necessity in order to keep down vermin, or put down injured animals. As for hunting, there's nothing a vixen likes better than to take home a newborn lamb to feed her own offspring. During the war, our close Radnorshire community became even closer, and barriers that existed previously were broken down and a spirit of unity grew up between the classes. Grandpa's long-suffering wife Louie, for example, became great friends with Guy Coltman-Rogers' widow Stella, who had started out as an actress.

There are, of course, exceptions. I remember clearly walking up the long drive to Stanage, with Mum pushing her new baby in the pram. It was one of our regular walks, as we'd stop at an ancient oak, all gnarled roots, which were perfect for little feet and hands to clamber up to reach a 'seat' a few feet off the ground. Once safely balanced, I'd sing out, 'Birdies, birdies, where are you?' The words remained unchanged though the tune was more of an improvisation. I already loved singing, and would warble away to myself all the time, but this is my first memory of performing to an audience – albeit an invisible one – apart from my mother and my new brother William, then only a few weeks old.

One afternoon, shortly after our stop at the oak tree, a Land Rover pulled up. It was the owner of Stanage, the local 'squire' Guy Coltman-Rogers.

'Well, Mrs Watkins,' he said, as he climbed down. 'I gather you've pushed out another one.' Then, peering into the pram, he added, 'But goodness me, what an ugly little blighter he is.' From that moment on, my mother disparaged him at every opportunity.

William was born in 1965, and three years after that, Roger turned up. I had been the first little Watkins to arrive in September 1963, six weeks before the assassination of John F. Kennedy. This time there was no attempt to pacify grandmothers by giving me their names, even so there was still some dissent. My mother wanted to call me Emma, simply because she liked the name. My father had wanted to name me after an aunt who had done what few girls did in those days and pursued a proper career, leaving her Welsh home as soon as she could to train as a nurse in London, ending up as matron of a big teaching hospital. So a compromise was reached. I became Rachel Emma.

Although I was my parents' firstborn, I knew from early on that, as a girl, I would never inherit an acre of my beloved Heartsease. The farm and its assets would be split between my two brothers, and my father devoted the rest of his life to buying land and building up the business so that both his sons would eventually have their own farms. My future was equally set in stone. I would marry into a local farming family and beget more farmers. When I started going out with boys, the first question my father would ask was, 'So, Em, how many acres does he have?'

In this sense the Watkins family were no different to the Harleys who owned Brampton Bryan or the Coltman-Rogerses at Stanage. It didn't strike me as unfair; it was just the way things were. As for education, that was just something a girl did before she found a husband. William and Roger would get privately educated, just as Dad had been.

As for me, I was certainly not worth wasting money on. So at five I went to the local primary school at Bucknall, just over the river into Herefordshire. My father's goal for all three of his children, he said, was to turn us into upstanding citizens, but always laced with a great sense of fun.

Like all children brought up in the country I adored animals, from our working dogs, to the cats whose ostensible role was to keep down the rats but who also did duty as feet warmers in winter. And then there were the three cows that were all that remained of Grandpa's milking herd. He had hung onto these against Dad's wishes. He claimed it was because he wanted his grandchildren to have fresh milk every morning but more likely he simply found it hard to let go. Every morning at half-past five he'd come over from the bungalow he had built at the far end of a field called Dumbles. Milking done, he'd stomp over with a brimming bucket and deposit it, still warm and frothy, in our kitchen. Just the smell made me want to throw up. To this day I can't touch anything dairy unless it's been in the fridge for at least three days . . .

When Grandpa died, Dad got rid of the cows except for one Jersey, who had her own little shed where he would go and milk her every morning. He would sit on an upturned bucket and lean his head right in and push against her flank, then bring a bucket of honey-coloured foam across to the kitchen, which Mum would strain to turn into yogurt or churn into butter. Although I knew it was wonderful milk, rich and creamy, I still couldn't bring myself to drink it, especially when I could see bits of straw caught in the froth. It would never pass any health tests today and, if proof were needed, Dad caught brucellosis . . . But the B&B guests absolutely loved it.

I always adored our cattle – largely Herefords and Charolais – a suckler herd which Dad would bring on. This involved a lot of de-horning and de-bagging as it was called, which meant removing their balls. In the winter they'd be in the big barn, and in the summer they'd be put out to pasture and I would go up and join them on the hills and practise my singing for hours – like the birds in the oak tree, they were a very safe audience.

It turned out that I had inherited my mother's voice. Though the Watkins family were known throughout Wales as devout Quakers, a direct ancestor of my dad's, William Walter Watkins, allowed a house on his land near Pen y Bont to be used as a pub by the navvies who were building the railway, so in 1916 he was expelled. However, the Quaker ethos was still strong and my father would regularly read extracts to me from Thomas Walter Watkins's diaries. Now, however, we were firmly Church of England, at least on paper, and my mother was very active at Brampton Bryan Church, where my father acted as churchwarden. The Harleys who built both the house and the church were Puritans, followers of Oliver Cromwell, and the building reflects that sober outlook on life, which sat more easily with my father than the over-decorated churches elsewhere. But when it came to singing, they weren't that interested, and so I gave my first solo performance when I was seven at the Coxall Baptist Church, about a mile from Heartsease the other side of the Teme, where I sang 'There Is a Green Hill Far Away'.

What I wanted most in the world was a pony. Dad didn't like horses and wanted nothing to do with them. As far as he was concerned, they were for working the farm, and now that we had tractors, we didn't need them. Neither of my parents rode, yet I badgered and badgered and eventually he gave in.

Betty came to us from two valleys away. She had a white blaze on her forehead and had been black, but having done the rounds, was going a bit grey around the edges. Mum still remembers the morning she arrived, how I'd climbed up one of our gates, clambered onto her back and set off for the hills riding bareback because nothing had been organized in the way of bridle or saddle. In fact, she turned out to have very narrow withers, so even when we did get a saddle, it kept slipping, so I always rode bareback, with just a bridle.

From then on ponies were my life. If I wasn't at school, I'd be up at six o'clock, brushing her, feeding her, mucking her out, cleaning the tack and polishing the brass headband on her bridle until it shone. By the time my parents came down for breakfast I would have tacked up and gone.

I grew to know every inch of the land, woods, old drovers' tracks, following streams up onto bracken-covered hillsides until the whole of Radnorshire was laid out before me and then, on the horizon, the Beacons would beckon. Bad weather never stopped me. Rain or snow, I'd be out there, and in the summer months while my brothers fished, I would take Betty to cool off in the Teme.

My best friend Louise Davies lived just across the river and she was just as pony-mad as I was so we'd meet at the bridge, me on Betty, Louise on Noddy, and off we'd go, wherever we felt like, but usually Brampton Bryan Park.

Dad rented a steep 60-acre field on the upper slopes of Brampton Bryan Park where he grazed sheep, and Louise knew that all I wanted to do was to gallop up to the top and she would beg me not to. 'Let's just trot,' she'd say. Trot! I wasn't about to trot . . . and with one click and a kick of my heel, we were off, both our ponies racing up the hill, me whooping with sheer exhilaration, Louise clinging on for dear life.

The other place we would go was an ancient hill fort called the Knoll, the other side of the river. The land was owned by Louise's grandfather Bernard Davies, who had made a fortune in forestry. While Louise and her parents lived in this picture-perfect Georgian manor near the river, her granddad lived in a chalet-style house called Knoll End. At that stage in our lives, Louise and I were both devoted Donny Osmond fans, though our favourite song to sing along to was 'Long Haired Lover from Liverpool', which was actually sung by his younger brother Jimmy. Anyway, we'd put up a circuit of crossover jumps, called cavaletti, and go round and around flying over them singing this ridiculous song at the top of our voices, Louise on Noddy, a classic Thelwell grey, and me on Betty riding bareback. I only used a saddle at the Pony Club, where you had to.

I lived for the Pony Club camps at Pilleth, famous as the site of the Battle of Bryn Glas, where the Welsh forces of Owen Glendower defeated the English, led by Sir Edmund Mortimer. However, back then, it was probably more famous for its annual vintage car rally, and the B&B was guaranteed to be full that weekend. Here we learnt all there was to know about how to look after our ponies, from how to spot trouble before it became serious, to how to plait their manes. And, of course, over the years I made friends, one of the first being Arabella Lennox, whose family owned Downton Castle, ten miles or so across into Shropshire. And while Louise's family were well-off and lived in a lovely regency manor house, Downton Castle was on a different scale entirely. The first time I went there I remember asking Arabella if she ever got lost. She just laughed and said, 'Race you to the kitchen!' Although Stanage was just as grand, I'd never had reason to go inside, as there were no children there of my age.

Over time I came to realize that in essence these grand houses weren't that different from ours, they were just bigger. At Downton we would spend hours running along those long corridors, playing with other friends from the Pony Club. And once boys from the Young Farmers came along, we found that a castle was a great place to play hide and seek . . .

Brampton Bryan was another grand house that I was soon familiar with. Mrs Harley loved to go trapping with her ponies and she'd invite me along for company. Her children were all boys so she treated me like the daughter she never had, and once a week I'd be there, sitting in her bedroom chatting away, bringing her up to date with all the local goings-on as she changed into her jodhpurs.

In 1962, when my parents got married, my grandfather had handed over the running of Heartsease to Dad, but in reality he had been in charge for years because Grandpa had something of an alcohol problem. It probably started when he worked as a drover taking cattle from one farm to another in the early 1930s when money was short, when he'd be plied with drink at every farm he stopped at. He was still seen as a pillar of the community – high sheriff of Radnorshire no less. He died in 1973 when I was nine, and a few days before he passed away, I went to see him in hospital. He had always been a big pipe smoker and had a lump on the side of his lip which had now spread. It was cancer of course. Even though we all knew by then that he wasn't going to recover, nonetheless the death of a parent – or in my case a grandparent – is a shock. Even more of a shock was when Dad discovered the extent of Grandpa's debts. Although there was no mortgage on the farm, in his final years gambling had replaced the booze, and he would spend hours on the phone in his bungalow, black-and-white television flickering away in the corner, with the voice of racing, Peter O'Sullevan, providing the soundtrack.

Michael Sockett was the farm's mainstay. He had come to us through Muriel who told Mum she knew of this hard-working young man who was looking for a job. He was about ten years younger than my dad and he'd arrived when we children were very young. In fact I have no memory of the farm without him. It was Michael who had found Betty for me – she had been on a smallholding owned by his mother. After Grandpa died in 1973, Michael and his wife Ivy moved into his bungalow in Dumbles field.

Michael was a gentle giant. He loved nature and above all he loved Heartsease. He was a true gentleman of the countryside and no one remembers Michael ever saying a cross word to anyone during his entire life. My father might have cross words with him from time to time, but Michael never raised his voice in response. My mother adored him, though he would also drive her mad, striding into the kitchen just as we were having breakfast, us late for school, Mum in her dressing gown. He would barely even notice us as he stood at the bottom of the stairs and yelled up to my father: 'Come on, Boss . . . What about it, Boss? Time to get going!'

He had a phenomenal work ethic and made sure that William and Roger learnt the hard way, by dragging them out of bed if they didn't appear on time. He and Ivy eventually had two children of their own and when they left home Ivy looked after the elderly. Brendon became a gamekeeper on the Downton Castle estate where Arabella lived, while their daughter cared for disturbed children. Each in their way had a caring quality about them.

From the middle of August, I learnt to be careful about where I rode because the Glorious Twelfth marked the start of the grouse shooting season. Dad had a gun in a shoot called Beguildy and that shoot was one of the highlights of my summer holidays because I was given beating duties. By then, I had a new pony, Tina, while my brothers inherited Betty. We would get the two of them cleaned up and pile into Dad's old yellow Land Rover with the rackety old stockbox bumping along behind and drive up into the hills towards Brecon. It was an old Highways Agency vehicle which Dad had got cheap, probably because the colour did the opposite of blend in with the landscape. Once on the top of the moor we met up with all the other guns. And when everything was set, we riders would take up our positions and, at the signal, gallop through the bracken sending the grouse hurtling towards the guns. Once I remember Dad crouching down beside me and pointing out the most incredible bird circling above us that I had ever seen. Its outstretched wings must have measured almost two metres wide, and its tail was a deep fork.

'See that, Em?' Dad said. 'It is a red kite, a very rare bird, and you may never see one again.'

Little did he know . . . They were re-introduced not long after and although I still think they are utterly beautiful, I also know what damage they do now that the countryside is inundated with them.

As well as the Beguildy shoot, my parents organized a shoot of their own each year, sometime in the late autumn or early winter. It was called 'the Rat Patrol' after the Desert Rats who fought in North Africa in the Second World War, and was just for family and friends. The British were massively outnumbered by Rommel's Afrika Korps, so their mission was to harass and otherwise wreak havoc on the Germans, and we had a similar plan. We had been feeding and fattening up the pheasants on the Heartsease farm throughout the winter, then once a year it was time to reap what we had sown . . .

There was always a great atmosphere. Mum would have been preparing the shoot lunch for days, and the dogs raced around, knowing that something was afoot. This time there were no ponies involved. This wasn't grouse country; it was pheasants we were after. Of course, we had put down plenty of chicks of our own, but if birds from Brampton Bryan or Stanage chose to take flight with a healthy spread of tail onto Watkins land, well, we could hardly turn them back . . . This time our role as beaters was more traditional but, crashing through the undergrowth with Michael and Ivy Sockett, I'd pretend we were Apache warriors, about to go full pelt over the ridge, yelling our own individual war cries to draw the birds out of the woods and onto the guns that were waiting to pick them off. If I could have worn face paint and feathers I would have done.

Mum would pack a delicious picnic – the winter weather decreed hot food and so she'd give us hot sausages with mustard and mayonnaise, homemade soup and sloe gin that she'd made the previous autumn – and we'd wolf it down from the bonnets of each rusty Land Rover. Dad would always be tense, running around, barking orders, cursing everyone for being 'bloody idiots', especially those beaters who sent the birds in the wrong direction, away from the guns.

By the end of the day, our game bags would be weighed down with anything from between twenty to fifty pheasants. There were no losers. Everyone would go home with a brace of birds. Back home we'd hang them from binder twine in the scullery next to the kitchen and after a few days, when they were stinking to high heaven, Mum and I would spend hours plucking them, singeing the last of the stubble to make them table-ready. I could just about cope with the plucking, but gutting them was something I just couldn't face, so I'm afraid that was left to Mum. Once plucked and trussed, we'd squeeze as many as we could into the freezer. We'd be eating roast pheasant every Sunday for as long as they lasted.

There wasn't much in the way of organized entertainment in the area, so we made our own. Some people have the knack of throwing good parties, and an invitation from John and Roma Watkins would never be refused. Unless it was winter, the parties were held in the long barn, which would be transformed with lights, crepe paper, and whatever decorations the theme of the party suggested. A party was always an excuse for a trip to Hereford or Shrewsbury to browse over patterns and choose material for a new dress. As a young teenager I had long lank hair that did me no favours and Mum would encourage me to think about other ways of doing it to help me look my best. But however hard I tried, Mum always stole the show. She just shone. And then my father watched me like a hawk, checking out who I was dancing with – and always that same question at the end of the evening.

'So, Em, how many acres does he have?'

Chapter Two
Music and Movement

T HERE IS NO doubt that, if I were tested now, I'd be diagnosed as dyslexic. But fifty years ago, few people even knew the word, let alone what it meant. As far as everyone was concerned, Emma Watkins was 'slow'. Looking back, it should have been obvious that all wasn't as it should be and even my parents thought something was wrong. Basically, although I loved inventing my own stories and would recount them to Betty as we explored the hills of Radnorshire and beyond, I couldn't read, let alone write. It didn't help that the little school at Bucknell – so close we could walk there – was experimenting with the Initial Teaching Alphabet. Apparently it had been invented by Mr Pitman, the man who invented shorthand, and was equally complicated. Instead of twenty-six letters, there were a lot more – a special 'letter' for 'th' for example, another one for 'sh' and 'ch' and so on. But for me it was a disaster as it meant I had to learn to spell twice, first the ITA way, then the ordinary way. To make matters worse, both my brothers, both younger, were far more advanced than I was.

They hadn't gone to Bucknell but to the 'better' primary in Knighton, where they used the old-fashioned alphabet system – Janet and John – so in the end my parents sent me there too. Sadly, by then it was too late.

It wasn't just reading and writing that were a problem. Numbers were incomprehensible to me. Just like letters, they would jump around the page like fleas, never staying in one place and impossible to pin down, and the longer I stared at them the worse it became. Mum would get exasperated as, when counting to twenty, I would miss out twelve to fourteen. How could I do that? On the farm I had all kinds of responsibilities, so how come I couldn't even count to twenty? And while the polite term people used about me was 'slow', the word used by other children – including my brothers – was 'thick'. So I simply switched off, staring out of the classroom window through the mesh fence that cut us off from the playing field, and above them the soft blue-green of the hills, thinking solely of how long it would be before the school bell went and I could get out there. That I wasn't totally written off by the school (and everyone else) was thanks to my singing.

Wales is known as 'the land of song', not because the Welsh are naturally more gifted, but because they value the human voice. Some of that is down to history. The pagan tradition of storytelling in Wales goes back over a thousand years to the time of druids and bards, the itinerant poet-singers who composed and performed stories to a rural population hungry for heroes. By the nineteenth century, Wales might have been Christian, but it was a land of non-conformists, and the thousands of small chapels –

Methodist or Baptist – that served both scattered farming communities and the industrialized south – were poor. Organs or harmoniums were expensive, so the congregation made the music themselves with what they had, which is to say their voices – a tradition that has made Welsh male-voice choirs famous throughout the world. There is barely a town in Wales that doesn't have its own Eisteddfod, a celebration of music and poetry, where singers and poets compete against each other. I was probably seven when I entered my first Eisteddfod – either Knighton or Kington, I don't remember now, because from then on I would compete every year.

Whether we were typical or not, I don't know, but our two families – the Watkinses and Daviesses – were both very musical. One of Mum's brothers, Uncle Philip, played the piano and when we went over to Knill on Boxing Day for a big Davies family get-together, he would take his place at the keyboard and we children would all have to sing, and I was always the first to volunteer. Grandpa Knill, as I called him, would then give me the look I was familiar with, as he didn't approve of 'showing off'. But I couldn't stop myself. Apart from when I was out riding, I only felt properly me when I was singing. It was the same at Watkins family gatherings. All of us children had to do something – sing or recite a poem. So early on we got used to performing until it became as un-embarrassing as cleaning your teeth. Grandpa Jack (Watkins) had seven siblings. One used to play the piano and the others sang in harmony in the local church, and people used to say it was the highlight of the week, and probably the only time in the week when you got to meet other people.

Although my reading and writing did improve at Knighton, I was still a long way behind everyone else and as the Eleven Plus loomed, the exam which in those days decided if you went to Presteigne Grammar (which, to translate into Dad's language, meant finding a husband with enough acres), it became increasingly clear that I would fail, and therefore destined not for Presteigne but the secondary modern.

I knew that the boys would go to private schools. But I also knew Mum and Dad didn't have enough in the bank to educate me as well – they were struggling as it was.

But one day, without any great discussion that I was aware of, Mum, Dad and I got in the car and drove to Malvern, a town about an hour into England that had more schools than probably anywhere else in the country.

Thanks to a combination of mineral water springs and dramatic scenery – the Malvern Hills rise out of the wide plane of the River Severn like a benevolent sea monster – in the eighteenth-century Malvern had become famous as a spa town. The water that gushed out of St Ann's Well, halfway up the hill, was believed to have health-giving properties, and the rich were soon flocking in the hope of curing whatever ailments they were suffering from, while enjoying dramatic scenery at the same time. But the coming of the railway in the mid-nineteenth century led to thousands of day-trippers – workers from the potteries – which spoiled the exclusive atmosphere, so by the end of the century Malvern had ceased to be fashionable. The hotels and hydrotherapy clinics which had mushroomed over the previous hundred years became redundant and were soon being repurposed as schools. In this instance, the railway proved an unexpected bonus, as it meant that older children could get there on their own, waved off by their parents at Paddington and collected by school staff three hours later.

The school we went to see that afternoon was a prep school called Croftdown. We were taken on a tour and when it came to the dormitories, I noticed that each bed had a teddy bear by the pillow. Well, that did it for me. Mum didn't believe in teddy bears, so I had never had one. Maybe if I came here, I thought, then I could!

I was then ten years old, and the plan was that I would stay at Croftdown for a year to prepare for the entrance exam for Ellerslie, which took girls at eleven. A year doesn't sound long to a grown-up, but to an unhappy child it's a life sentence. As for the much-longed-for teddy bear, I didn't get one. Instead, Mum made me a sausage dog out of a red velvet dress I'd worn about six years earlier when I was bridesmaid to Lizzy, our mother's help who had arrived shortly after Roger was born. It had white rabbit fur around the collar and cuffs, and I absolutely loved it. But when these girls saw this homemade apology for a teddy, they just laughed, grabbed him and twisted his poor little body into a tight knot.

My sole crime at Croftdown was being different. I had been to the local primary school; they hadn't. I had a Welsh lilt to my voice; they didn't. And they, of course, had been at Croftdown since they were seven. I was this new girl who knew no one and had no idea how it all worked. I felt as if I had been wrenched away from everything and everyone I loved and thrown into a pit of snakes.

In fact, I did know one girl who was called Lucy and

whose parents lived in Knighton. But rather than becoming friends, we became arch enemies. Sport was one thing I positively enjoyed at school and, being tall for my age, I was picked for the netball team. Lucy was very competitive and, annoyingly for her, I was put at centre, previously her position. To show her displeasure, she pushed me against the wire around the court, so of course I pushed her back. She fell on the gritty surface and grazed her elbow and I was sent in to see the headmistress in her study.

Miss Portway-Fletcher resembled a squat, rotund brigadier and she made no attempt to hide her dislike of me. My punishment for 'causing' this 'rumpus' was by any criterion draconian. I was made to stand in the corner on the stairs, facing the wall, during all the free time for the next three weeks. To get my own back, I picked flakes of paint off the wall.

Part of the routine of Sunday was letter writing. In the morning we'd have church, in the afternoon we'd go for a walk on the hills, then in the early evening we'd go into the dining room carrying the leather writing case which had been on the list of essential equipment. Then, sitting on the wooden benches, we'd write to our parents. I saw no reason not to tell the truth. So my letters were largely made of sentences on the theme of 'I hate it here'. I told them about the hours I spent standing in the corner, not allowed to speak, and only because I'd pushed a girl who had already pushed me because she was jealous. It was rumoured that our letters home were censored, but it's hard to see how they could have censored that. A letter with two thirds of it crossed out would hardly inspire confidence in the parents!

At times I suspected my letters were never posted because Mum never seemed to refer to them in her replies. Instead, she did her best to keep me cheerful, writing to me about Tina and Janie, the little springer spaniel I'd pestered Dad to get me after his Labrador Beth had died, but that only made me want to howl even louder. So, in the absence of any other ideas, I decided to run away.

Malvern is built on the slopes of a hill which is surprisingly steep, so although a wall may be high on one side, it could be quite low the other, and I was adept at climbing. Walls and gates presented no challenge for a girl used to roaming wild.

Croftdown girls weren't usually allowed out on their own, but I had special dispensation to visit the dentist. I had a gap in my teeth so I wore a brace which needed to be tightened every three weeks. The gap had also left me with a lisp, so I had a speech therapist for that, repeating endlessly 'Six sizzling sausages' – or 'Thix thizzling thothajith' as it came out. One way or another I ended up going into the town quite often, so knew my way around. Most importantly, I knew which way to go for Ledbury. Once I was there, my plan was to take a bus home. I had just about enough pocket money saved up for the journey.

So, one lunchtime I scrambled through a bank of rhododendrons, then climbed over the boundary wall, then set off to the top road. It was obviously reckless. How did I imagine I would get back all the way to Heartsease, over an hour's drive away, with just a handful of small change? I didn't get very far before I was picked up by the police – hardly surprising given I was wearing the giveaway school uniform. Inevitably I was hauled up in front of Mrs Portway-Fletcher, who tore me off a strip, going on about what a great sacrifice my parents were making in sending me to Croftdown, how ungrateful I was, and how I didn't deserve to be there. She told me nothing I wasn't all too aware of already. She went on and on and I was convinced this was the lead-up to being expelled, which would have suited me very well. But I wasn't.

My feelings of guilt were outweighed by dreams of home and my second attempt was better planned. I waited for the weekend when I was wearing 'mufti' and this time made it to Ledbury by thumbing a lift! Only to be returned ignominiously to the school by the police.

Life at Croftdown was dominated by rules, mainly things you weren't allowed to do, while the things you could do had to be done at the same time as everyone else. Life on the farm had been so different and I began to realize quite how much freedom I'd been given, allowed to just go off on my pony into the wild, with nothing but a hunk of bread and some cheese.

However, as the weeks turned to months, I learnt that to survive I had to blend in, keeping my head down by mimicking other girls' accents and dampening down my own. Most importantly, I learnt that the way to be accepted was to find something you were good at, where you could shine. It didn't have to be schoolwork; it could be sport, which actually I enjoyed. As well as netball, I was captain of the high jump team. But it was team games I really enjoyed. The thing I really did shine at, however, without any real effort on my part, was singing.

Rather than Mum and Dad taking me to local Eisteddfods, it was soon my teachers who would accompany me, and before long I was being cast in lead roles in school plays, my first big part being Hansel in *Hansel and Gretel*, our end-of-year show.

We were allowed home once every three weeks, so Louise and I would arrange to meet and ride up to Brampton Bryan together and gallop up Dad's field and beyond. Just feeling the wind in my face was enough to make me forget the misery of school. However, all too soon the weekend would be over and the moment came when I'd have to get in Dad's car and, when we reached the main road, I'd turn my head to see Janie standing there, her tail hanging limply between her legs.

Towards the end of the year, a decision had to be made about my next school. Louise was going to Cheltenham Ladies' College, but she was clever, and Mum and Dad didn't think it was right for me. Lots of farming families sent their daughters to Ellerslie, so that was where I went.

One weekend, perhaps my first exeat since starting at Ellerslie, I went home to hear that Janie was missing. She had gone hunting with a sheepdog called Sydney. He had returned, but she hadn't. It had happened several days before – perhaps even a week – but Mum and Dad hadn't wanted to tell me over the phone, they explained. I was utterly distraught. Michael told me there was a new gamekeeper up at Stanage Castle who was proving rather zealous. He warned me that she had probably been caught in a snare. I spent the entire two days walking alone, calling her name, crisscrossing the estate. But nothing. That Sunday night on my way back to Ellerslie, my eyes were swollen with crying. I felt angry and guilty at the same time. It would never have happened if I had still been at Heartsease, if I had passed my Eleven Plus and gone to the local grammar school . . . She was never found.

Mum had been an active member of the Knighton amateur musical society for years – and she specialized in old-time music hall, dressing up in top hat and tails and swinging a cane. I'd been going with her to rehearsals ever since I could remember because I just loved it. My difficulty in reading was to some degree compensated by my memory, and it wasn't long before I knew all the words. 'I'm Burlington Bertie, I rise at Ten Thirty . . .' and 'I'm following in Father's footsteps, I'm following my dear old dad.' I knew dozens of them. My uncle Bev, one of Dad's cousins from Dolau, did a double act with Mum, and they'd sing, 'There's a hole in my bucket, dear Liza, dear Liza'. My all-time favourite was 'Ta-Ra-Ra Boom-De-Ay', and these songs were much appreciated by the girls in my first dorm, particularly with some of the words changed, like 'Ta-Ra-Ra Boom-De-Ay, my knickers blew away . . .' But the one they liked best was 'I'm Just Wild about Harry', and once we'd had lights out, we'd wait till the steps of the housemistress had died away and one of the girls would say, 'Go on, Emma. Sing "I'm Just Wild about Harry",' and so I would. I'd get up on the bed, strike the pose and sing away, 'I'm just wild about Harry and he's just wild about me.'

We might have been only eleven or twelve, but there was already a sense that at some time in the not too distant future, these feelings might apply to us too . . .

It wasn't long before boys began to properly feature in our lives. We'd talk about them incessantly and in year three came our first hotly anticipated 'social' with Malvern College, the pre-eminent boys' school in the town. By then I was fourteen and Mum had made a special trip up to London to see Auntie Marie who she'd been at school with and had brought me back a tiered skirt from Carnaby Street and a little waistcoat to wear on top. I thought I looked great. If I'd had an older brother it might have been different, but I had no experience with boys whatsoever. I don't know now what I expected to happen. So I just stood there, with as much of a come-hither look as if I was waiting for a bus. And while everyone else in my class seemed to be dancing, nobody asked me and I felt utterly humiliated.

What was it that these girls had that I didn't? Make-up, I decided. Make-up was strictly forbidden at Ellerslie, but it seemed that the socials with Malvern College were an exception. So I went out and invested in everything and caked it on. My 'look' centred on blue and green streaks of eye shadow and so much mascara I could barely see out. But it worked, if only to give me Dutch courage. I felt less inhibited in the presence of boys and started to go with other girls to the Bluebird tea rooms, favoured by the College boys. But they only had eyes for Sophie Cliff-Jones, a classic peaches-and-cream English rose.

Shortly before the second social was due to happen, I decided it was important to have a best friend. As usual, no one seemed interested in being friends with me, so I took matters into my own hands. There was a girl who'd recently arrived called Jackie Cox who struck me as a bit of a loner, so I wrote her a note which said, 'Dear Jackie, will you be my friend?' And she said yes. In fact, we were very different. She had a short blonde bob, whereas I had lank dark hair down to my waist, which I usually wore in two long plaits. I can't remember now what either Jackie or I wore on this occasion, but it clearly made no difference, because nobody asked either of us to dance. We were gooseberries, wall-flowers. However, towards the end of the evening when we'd been herded into a room which had been done up as a disco, a boy came up and asked Jackie to dance, and she accepted without a backward glance, leaving me stranded looking as if all I wanted in the world was to stand in that fake disco room, watching everyone else gyrating around to 'You Should Be Dancing' by the Bee Gees. Meanwhile, Jackie seemed to have disappeared, but right at the end of the evening, she emerged from who-knows-where and I saw to my alarm that something must have happened.

'Are you okay?' I asked.

She shrugged.

'But you've got marks all over your neck!'

'Shut up, Emma.'

'But what happened?'

'I told you to shut up.'

When she eventually explained, I was horrified. 'How could you ever let anyone bite your neck? What were you thinking of?' Later she explained that she'd been irritated by seeing Sophie Cliff-Jones going off with the coolest boy, so when this other boy had asked her to dance, she'd seen her chance and took it.

It seemed to me that there was a kind of natural selection.

The cool girls got off with the cool boys and vice versa. Jeff was a bit of a geek, and as much of a weirdo in his way as I was at that time. But he was a boy, and he seemed to like me, so we would meet at St Ann's Well and go for walks up on the hills, then we'd go down to the Bluebird and casually saunter in and he'd order two hot chocolates. And, geek though Jeff was, I will always be grateful.

It was around this time that I realized that the long-hair look I'd cultivated for years wasn't doing me any favours, so Mum took me to Ludlow to get it chopped off. The Ludlow hairdresser was a definite step up from the one in Knighton, and I opted for what I still think of as the Donny Osmond cut: shortish on the top and long at the back, and I've pretty much had a version of that ever since. Once I'd taken that radical step on the boy front, things began to improve and of course I was growing up and they did genuinely seem more interested in me. As a result, the friendship groups at school started to change. As a gap-toothed, lank-haired ugly duckling, I had been a member of the tribe of less-good-looking girls. Now, my status altered, I became part of Sophie Cliff-Jones's crew. When Sophie and I took to the tea rooms, she would sit there and look beautiful, like a swan placidly floating on a lake, while I did the talking for us both.

I grew up quickly in those early years at Ellerslie. At home, while I had been used to having the freedom of the countryside, Dad still kept us fairly cosseted. I remember going to see *Grease* in Hereford when it finally arrived there, but at the first hint of a sex scene, Dad marched us all out.

My sex education, if you can call it that, was limited if practical.

'You see that, Em?' Dad said, pointing at our bull mounting a heifer. 'That's as quick as it happens; you need to be careful of men.'

But that didn't mean I wasn't streetwise. One day, making my way back to school after tea at the Bluebird – inevitably a bit late – clutching a rolled-up umbrella as it had been raining, I was running along the top path when a man stepped out from behind a bush and stared at me. I stopped and stared back at him, but not at his face, because his flies were open and he was holding this pink thing that looked like a Walls pork sausage. I wasn't as much shocked as incredulous. Holding my head up high, I carried on walking, keeping my eyes fixed straight ahead, but, as I passed, I whacked him with my brolly where it hurt.

In the corridor I bumped into Miss Binion, who asked me why I was rushing in such an unladylike manner. So I told her. She went pale and was clearly very shocked, probably more shocked than I was. Because when you're brought up on a farm, sex, and which bits go where, is no great mystery. I might not have seen a man's private parts before, but I'd seen stallions being put to mares, and dogs would regularly hump quite unsuitable partners.

Mum's brother, my uncle Philip, had three children about the same age as us and we all got on like a house on fire. The holiday house in Borth, bought by Granny's sister-in-law, my great aunt Mary, was where we cousins would meet up during the summer holidays. Like me, Ruth, the middle one, adored riding, and from when we were about twelve, Uncle

Philip would bring her over in the Land Rover with her horse in a stockvan and after a night at Heartsease we would ride to their farm at Sennybridge, nine miles west of Brecon. It wasn't that far – perhaps forty miles by road – but we would take several days to do it. It wasn't about getting there, it was about the journey, about the adventure.

From our farm we'd go via Knighton and across the top of Radnor Forest – not a forest in the wooded sense but in the medieval sense of land set aside for hunting made up of moorland, high peaks and ridges. It is totally unspoilt and although we didn't know the history, it felt very wild and very ancient and I felt it had rich stories to tell. Sometimes in the early morning, coming across wild Welsh ponies quietly cropping, it felt quite mystical.

We didn't even take a map, but just followed our noses, crossing woods and streams, filling our water bottles from waterfalls, staying the night in pubs, where we were greeted more often than not with suspicion, the person in charge assuming we were runaways and so they'd insist on checking up with our parents. After all, we weren't old enough to go into a bar, let alone have a drink, and yet here we were asking for a room for the night. Like any adventure, it wasn't without its dangers. Once, early in the morning when we were tacking up, having led our ponies in from the paddock, I had just tied Tina to a cattle crush (a huge metal trap where you contain cattle before they're de-horned) before putting on her saddle and bridle, when she started backing up, and pulled this thing right over me. Luckily, I emerged completely unhurt – just a few bruises here and there. I had learnt early on that you had to get back up in the saddle and carry on.

Another year, we were going further afield. Dad had driven me up to Felin Fach where Mum's elder sister Auntie Jean lived, and Uncle Philip with Ruth and her pony met up with us there, then put my pony in with Ruth's and Dad drove off back to Heartsease. With both ponies now installed in Uncle Philip's trailer, we set off, with Ruth and me in the back of his Land Rover. We hadn't gone far and had just started going up a hill when Ruth and I realized something was very wrong. Both of us just started screaming, 'Stop! Stop!' The trailer hadn't been properly attached and was now careering back down the hill with our two precious ponies in it. Unbelievably, the trailer came to a stop in a hedge, the right way up, and they weren't even hurt. Uncle Philip was mortified. He checked them over, then put them back in the box and off we went.

I was growing taller which meant it would soon be time to swap ponies again, and one day Dad heard that a local farmer was selling a 14.2-hand mare, so we went to see her. She was beautiful, very dappled and a true grey. Her tack was immaculate, and it would all go with her, the farmer told us. Until now she had only been ridden by his son. Would I like to try her out? I put my foot in a stirrup and up I went, first we walked, then progressed to a gentle trot that became a canter until finally we were galloping around their paddock, jumping a hedge or two while my parents looked on. I turned her head and brought her back to where the adults were standing. My smile told them all they needed to know. The deal was done, and I was now the proud owner of Gay Lady. Tina was handed down to my brothers.

I remember that feeling of excitement on the day they

brought Gay Lady up to Heartsease in their horsebox. My stomach was filled with butterflies as I opened the tailgate and out she came, her coat gleaming in the spring sunshine. I wasn't a rider who was looking to develop my skills to become an expert, a top horsewoman, or to go into dressage. The days of careering round the Knoll were long gone. I wasn't as brave as I used to be when it came to jumping. Tina had taken to refusing and I'd lost my confidence. I had turned into what might be called a happy hacker. However, within moments of Gay Lady's arrival I saddled up and took her up all my favourite rides, through the woodland at Stanage Castle, across to Brampton Bryan, then next down to the river to see Louise. Noddy, her unadventurous Thelwell pony, was long gone, his place taken by Arabella – Bella for short. Bella was wild and flighty compared to Gay Lady, a complete turnaround from when we first rode together all those years ago, when she was the timid one. But other than that, little had changed. We'd still meet up on Dad's field in Brampton Bryan and gallop flat-out up to the top. There would regularly be some drama up there, like an adder in my path, or a ewe stuck in a fence, when I would turn Gay Lady's head around and ride to the farm to alert Dad or Michael Sockett. Now even Louise was prepared to go further afield, and her mum would make us a picnic to take with us on long rides, and we'd head up to the Radnor Forest, and sprawl among the prickly heather and pick winberries to eat with our lunch, but with O Levels looming I had less and less time and though I missed Gay Lady dreadfully, I hated to think of her out in the field with no one to ride her. I knew she really wasn't getting the exercise she needed and so I made no objection when Dad suggested I let Michael's daughter take her out. One weekend, when I was at home revising, Tracey had just saddled up and was in front of their bungalow when Gay Lady bolted, galloped through the open gate, onto the road and straight into the path of a car. Luckily, Tracey was thrown clear, and apart from a few cuts and bruises she was fine, but Gay Lady had broken her leg. We managed to get her into the cowshed where Grandpa had done the milking all those years ago, and Dad looked her up and down while I stroked her muzzle, whispering in her ear, 'It'll be all right, it'll be all right,' willing it to be true. Then, without saying a word, Dad came over and hugged me. And I started crying. I knew what was coming.

'Time to say your goodbyes, Em. I'll take care of her,' he said, and he kissed the top of my head, like he used to do when I was little. 'You go back into the house.'

Blinded by tears, I ran up the stairs to my bedroom and buried my head in my pillow so that I wouldn't hear the shot. Mum knocked on the door, but I just said, 'Not now, Mum. Not now.' No one could console me. I needed to grieve alone. Later, I heard Michael take the digger out into the field and dig a hole big enough to bury her.

I was terrified I would fail my O Levels, just as I'd failed my Eleven Plus. But this time I knew the consequences. I knew what it would do to Mum and Dad. I spent every available hour revising. There would be no more going to the Bluebird to flirt with the boys from the college. The night before every exam, after lights out, I would creep to the bathroom, go into a cubicle, shut the door and sit there on the closed lid and go through every page of my notes, imprinting every single one on my memory. It was the only method that worked for me.

I knew that I wasn't a complete failure. I'd got a distinction in all eight grades of my singing exams. I'd done piano up to grade 7 and learnt the guitar as well, though that was really only for fun.

On the strength of my music successes, it had been decided that I should try for a singing scholarship at the Guildhall School of Music and Drama. Of course, I was flattered. The idea of making a career as an opera singer was exciting. Dad was at best ambivalent, but he didn't want to burst my bubble and admitted later that, given the stiff competition, he considered that my chances were negligible. So that February, just after my mocks, Mum, Granny and I had gone up to London.

Mum was the only one of us who was used to being in London because she would come up regularly to see her friend Marie Powell-Blanche, who she'd known from convent school days when they were both rebels. Auntie Marie, as I called her, was incredibly glamorous. She had big blue eyes and blonde streaked hair, with possibly Italian blood. She always had a Hermes scarf and a designer handbag, and went in for exotic cars. She was an airhostess and looked after first class. Make-up was a big part of the beginning of her day and she was always immaculate. Auntie Marie was a constant presence in our lives and I knew her really well. I think Mum saw in her what life might have been like if she had gone to Canada and not married Dad.

Granny and I had never been on the Tube, and we wasted

no time in chatting to the passengers sitting next to us or opposite, just like on the buses at home, not knowing it wasn't the done thing. 'We're off to the Barbican,' Granny informed anyone within earshot. 'Emma's got an interview for a scholarship there!' Sharing the achievements of her grandchildren was what Granny did. It wasn't about showing off, it was the way she had devised of inspiring all fourteen of us with just a hint of competition.

What strikes me now is how naive I was. I had no idea of how prestigious the Guildhall was. Hundreds of hopefuls were being interviewed for only a handful of places, and it had been made very clear to me that I had to get a scholarship, or it was a no-go. I was blithely unaware of how unlikely that was, and so when I emerged from the interview room and Mum asked me how I got on, I said it was fine, that I'd breezed through and there was no doubt in my mind that I would be offered a place. Perhaps my optimism was infectious, because that was exactly what happened.

Chapter Three
Innocent Abroad

DAD WAS ADAMANT. At sixteen I was far too young to live in London on my own, and it wasn't going to happen. If I was still set on this idea of becoming an opera singer, then I would have to wait two years until I was eighteen. That was plenty young enough, he said. To his great surprise, I think, the Guildhall agreed to hold over my scholarship.

I cried when I got my O Level results later that summer. I'd left school not knowing if I would go back, if I would ever see it or my friends again – girls who, against all odds, had become true friends. But the rules were clear: only girls who did sufficiently well at O Level could come back to do A Level. And although I failed Maths – no great surprise to anyone – I passed all the rest – eight! – which came as a surprise to everyone, including me.

So I went back, and those last two years were by far the happiest of my time at Ellerslie. I wouldn't have missed them for anything. Of all of us, only Sophie and I failed to make prefect, but we chose to see it as a badge of honour rather than a snub.

Gone were the petty rivalries between us, that silly business of who was pretty and who wasn't. Gone was the fascination with boys we'd had when we were sixteen. At eighteen it was more like 'Oh well' – possibly helped by the fact that now we had regular lessons at the College and just saw them as equally vulnerable and confused as we were.

By chance, the sixth-form corridor gave onto a road that led directly up onto the hill, so had easy access from Sophie's bedroom window, and they didn't appear to check up on us as such.

Having lessons with the College boys was fun, not least because we had male teachers who we could ogle. I remember one particularly handsome young man who taught us Geography. In the Geography class I also met Toby Tarplet, who sat near me. He was a day boy who lived in the country somewhere between Malvern and Worcester and he was just plain naughty.

He would come to school on his motorbike and we would arrange to meet on the top road. I'd climb out of Sophie's window and go to the appointed place and time, then we'd swing around the Malvern hills, me riding pillion. It was as if, finally, I had found freedom.

As for Jackie, she had turned out to be extremely clever and hardly had to revise at all. After our exams were over but before we got our results, her parents very sweetly asked me to go on holiday with them to a Greek island not far from Corfu. A few weeks before we were due to set off, I wrote to her dad Andy who was a doctor. I had always been a bit worried about my weight, but now that I realized I'd be stripping off in public – particularly as I knew Jackie's brothers would be among the watchers – I decided I needed help, and who better to ask than her father? So, I wrote setting out my predicament and asked if he could prescribe me a pill that would do the trick. He wrote back saying there was nothing wrong with my shape, that I was absolutely fine as I was. So that told me.

Being on holiday in Greece with the Cox family was a big thing. I loved Jackie's parents and I think they thought I was quite 'out there' and a good foil for their daughter. We drank ouzo and did Greek dancing with local boys after dinner with the family at a restaurant right on the edge of the sea, and I felt nearly delirious with happiness. Being on your first holiday without parents is a lovely feeling.

I passed Geography with a B. In Music I only managed a C. A Level Music is much more technical than people realize and involved a lot of maths, and that's probably what pulled me down. As for Religious Education, I had only taken it because it was seen as an easy option. Not easy enough it seems. I failed. But I now had two A Levels to my name and as far as Dad was concerned that was good enough, and in September I started at the Guildhall.

Louise and my life had intertwined since we were children and, after finishing her A Levels at Cheltenham, she had got a place at the Central School to study drama. Our parents had always got on and had even shared research on the various boarding schools they were considering. With us both now studying similar subjects in London, our parents decided we should flat-share. We ended up in a room on the Brompton Road, between Harrods and the Natural History Museum. Harrods had been a name to conjure with when I was growing up. Auntie Marie spoke of it with reverence and Mum never threw away a Harrods carrier bag, so anywhere in the vicinity of this legendary emporium was by definition glamorous. The room itself was tiny and depressing, however. It had two single beds pushed against the walls, which had peeling wallpaper, and we were directly above a 24-hour convenience store.

The room across the corridor was shared by a girl called Becky, who was also at the Guildhall where she was studying the clarinet, and a dancer on the hugely popular *Benny Hill Show*. She was always coming back with presents she'd been given by fans. To supplement her income, she said she had a side-line in pole dancing! To us two innocents from the Welsh Marches, that sounded intriguing – neither Louise nor I had ever heard of this kind of dancing. So, one night, she invited us to go along. Just the idea of a nightclub in Soho was glamorous, but from the moment we went through the door, I knew it was a hideous mistake. By then it was too late to back out, however. At least it was incredibly dark, so nobody could see these two innocents sitting on the front row, puce with embarrassment. We sat through it until our flatmate had been on but the moment we could escape we did.

Although I had danced and flirted with a few of the young farmers in our area, I had never experienced that heart-pounding, dry-mouthed delirium of falling in love. But that changed the moment I set eyes on Robin. He was eighteen, the same age as me, and we were on the same course. He was quite simply the most beautiful man I had ever seen, with electric blue eyes that seemed to pierce my soul. I would surreptitiously follow him around, peering from behind concrete columns, before turning hastily away every time I caught his eye. Then on one momentous morning he suggested we have lunch together at a nearby Italian salad bar. I couldn't believe my luck. Who needed farmers when you could have a Greek god? I am known for having a conspicuously healthy appetite, but that day the last thing I could think of was food, so I just picked at my salad and tried to calm my racing heart.

'Darling Em,' he said. 'You are an absolute delight and I hate to have to tell you this, but I'm afraid you're barking up the wrong tree.'

I had no idea what he was talking about and the expression on my face must have shown it.

'Dancing at the other end of the ballroom?' he suggested, as if that would make it clearer.

Finally, he leaned across the table and said, 'You see, I'm fonder of the male variety.'

Words like homosexual were never used at Heartsease, and if there were any gay men among the young farmers in Knighton, their closet doors were still firmly shut. To say that we stayed friends sounds like a cliché, but it was true and indeed we are close friends to this day.

The Guildhall was tough. Sight-singing was a nightmare. It was like reading all over again; the notes would go up and down the page like iron filings in the grip of a magnet. Singing in a foreign language was, to say the least, a challenge. I memorized a repertoire of about twenty-five songs, but present me with something new – particularly in German or Italian, where I struggled with the pronunciation – and I was lost. As for scales, it's hard to imagine anything more boring. The truth was that I had never really had to practise before, and now it was essential. I could see that my teachers were really struggling to know what to do with me. At the Barbican I was surrounded by raw talent, and I didn't have it. Once a week we would sing in the auditorium and everyone would comment and that was agony. In order to hold a note long enough, we learnt to develop our breathing using our diaphragms, known as the Alexander technique. I never got it. I didn't want to put in the leg work. I began to see that I would never rise above the chorus.

And did I really want to be an opera singer anyway, travelling from country to country, never staying in one place for more than a few days? That wasn't the life I'd envisaged for myself. What I wanted was a farmhouse with an Aga and a brood of children running around. So, I decided to leave. I stayed until the end of the year because it seemed churlish not to, but once the decision was made there was no turning back, no change of heart. I wrote to my parents to tell them and that was that.

I knew that I couldn't just slink back to Radnorshire and carry on as if nothing had happened. I would stay in London and find a job. Although I didn't have many saleable skills, I did have some. I could drive, for example. I had always helped my mother around the house, from making the B&B beds to cooking the breakfasts, and I knew that a magazine called *The Lady* had classified ads, so I tried there and got taken on as nanny to a wealthy Argentinian family with two children who lived in a large house on the borders of Fulham, near Chelsea football ground.

The mother, it turned out, needed more looking after than her offspring. Once I'd ferried the children to their smart school in Knightsbridge, I was required to race back to the house to make the señora breakfast in bed. The petrol gauge on the old Renault that came with my job was broken, so the only way to keep track of how much fuel there was left in the tank was to count the miles. One day on my way back from the school run, the engine spluttered to a halt right outside Harrods. I thought of what Auntie Marie would think and I was mortified. The uniformed doorman just looked on with disdain and did nothing to help. Luckily, a kind policeman helped push this rust bucket around the corner while around me vans hooted their disapproval.

It was not a happy time, and I filled the emptiness I felt inside with food. It wasn't all bad. The children themselves were lovely and the parents were happy enough to let me take them down to Heartsease where, even if only for a few days, they could enjoy the freedom I had had when I was their age. Whatever career I eventually carved out for myself, I decided, I wanted to live in the country. So, I looked into studying land management and found that I needed the dreaded Maths O Level that I had failed at Ellerslie before I could even apply. This time I would do it, I decided. I enrolled on an evening course and somehow managed to get through and in 1984 I opened the precious letter of acceptance from Southampton College of Higher Education.

In those days land management was a very male environment, and there were just two girls on the course. Without planning it, I had found myself surrounded by men who wanted to live their lives on the land. In other words, this was the perfect place to find a potential husband.

John Walder was tall, dark and handsome and, unlike the other alpha males I came across in Southampton, he had seven sisters, so he knew how to talk to girls. He was kind, thoughtful and fun.

Although my mum had been severely disappointed at my decision to abandon a career as a singer, my father was delighted and had no hesitation in inviting my new boyfriend down to the farm. For the first few hours after our arrival, the two Johns got on very well, until the moment boyfriend John brought out a brand-new CD player he had been given for Christmas. Up until then, music had been on cassettes or LPs – long playing records. CDs were very new and didn't feature in everyday vocabulary, certainly not in Radnorshire. Dad took one look and decided it was really a machine for playing blue movies. He wasn't about to allow pornography in the house, he said, and without ceremony threw my boyfriend out. As a proud Protestant, he was naturally suspicious of Catholics like John anyway, and his final words as he showed him the door were that he wasn't going to stand by and watch his only daughter being 'polluted' by this 'muck'. So, no surprise that that relationship didn't last.

Although I enjoyed my time at Southampton, any course of higher education involves considerable reading, and land management was no different. The problems I'd faced at school showed no signs of going away. Essays were torture and quite simply I was finding it hard to keep up. It wasn't that I didn't understand the concepts; I just couldn't express what I knew on paper. I felt as if the world was closing in on me. So, in the second summer of my degree, I applied to Camp America, an organization that places foreign students in holiday jobs, either in summer camps or families. I opted for nannying, looking after three children just outside Boston, in a beautiful house near the beach. The parents were high-flyers and were out at work most of the time. As jobs go, it was hardly onerous. I mostly looked after the youngest child of what I now knew was a second marriage, and we spent the day playing in the extensive garden and swimming in their beautiful pool. In the evenings, I would help cook supper.

The older two from the first marriage were in their late teens, not much younger than me, but definitely more worldly. After leaving the Guildhall I had been in self-sabotage mode and had taken up smoking, something I had never done before. Unbeknown to his parents, the elder son grew weed on his balcony, and one day he rolled a joint and handed it to me. It was not much different to cigarettes, he said. The effects were instantaneous and I was absolutely terrified. Here I was supposed to be looking after the children and now I was away with the fairies. How could I be so irresponsible? I was so ashamed, I jumped into their red Subaru and drove to the other side of Boston, pulled into a Dunkin Donuts drive-thru and ordered the biggest box I could find in an attempt to soak up the poison. I never touched weed again.

At the end of the summer I returned to England to discover that I had failed the taxation module of my land management course and would need to repeat the entire year. I decided I'd had enough, informed the college of my decision to leave and went back to Heartsease. While I helped Mum hang wallpaper in the attic rooms, she made a list of things I might do.

A friend of a friend of my parents ran an estate agency in Worcester and was persuaded to take me on to learn the business. I started at the bottom – on a salary of £2,700 per annum – and would spend all day measuring up houses. It was too far to commute from Heartsease, so I rented a room in a goat farm a little way out of the town. After a few months I was given more responsibility and began to show prospective buyers around and negotiate sales. I wasn't that enamoured with the job, however, and started to make mistakes. One day I advertised a house for £10,000 more than it was worth and the boss summoned me to the office and threw the phone at me for having lost him a sale.

But at least my social life was looking up. I had found my young farmer . . .

Peter was eight years older than me. He was very traditional, and yet also extremely capable and forward-thinking. He was usually to be found on his tractor, and perhaps he reminded me of my own father. He didn't hide the fact that he was looking for a conventional kind of wife, and for about eighteen months I thought that person was me, because for reasons I now cannot understand I had become completely besotted with him.

To anyone involved in that world – which includes farmers – Cheltenham races are the highlight of the racing calendar. It's very social – the kind of event where you dress up and drink champagne. So, when Peter asked me to go with him and join up with a group of his friends, I was very excited. I bought a new outfit for the occasion, complete with hat, and was convinced that his asking me was a sure sign that he was about to propose. Among the friends we were meeting up with was one of his former girlfriends. She had a particularly strident voice and even though I was chatting to someone else, it cut through any conversation like a rusty knife.

'Are you serious about this one, Peter?' she asked him.

'Oh no – but she's a lot of fun!'

I had no idea if he meant it or if it was just a bit of banter, but either way it made no difference. I had been humiliated and, without saying a word, I walked out of the enclosure, through the car park toward the exit, where I approached cars queuing at the roundabout with my thumb out saying, 'Hereford?'

The next day a large bouquet of flowers arrived with a note saying 'Sorry', but I never spoke to him again.

It was time for a change. My brothers and I were going skiing in Switzerland in January and that inspired me to register with a budget chalet company called Bladon Lines. If I was out there already, I might stand a better chance of getting a job as a chalet girl, even though I had zero experience.

First, however, we had Christmas at Heartsease, which was always a very special time. I'd look forward to it with as much excitement now I was well into my twenties as when I was a child and woke at six o'clock to the magic of a stocking weighing down my bed. This year was different, however. On Boxing Day morning, my grandmother got out of bed at six, as she had done every day of her life, had a bath, and then apparently suffered a massive heart attack. It was a terrible shock. Hers was the first dead body I had ever seen, and as I looked at her, lying in her bed, her hair spread out on the pillow, it seemed impossible that this amazing woman, who had so much energy, who had brought five children into the world, could just leave it so suddenly and so quietly.

The funeral was held at Knill Church a week later and everyone was still in shock. Her death had come completely out of the blue, so none of us was prepared. As for the skiing trip, we talked about cancelling it, but Mum said no. Life had to go on. And she had Dad. It was our parents who had encouraged us to take up skiing and we had all learnt at the same time, including Mum and Dad, on a family holiday in the Italian Alps. So, waving our sad good-byes, and with Roger driving, we set off.

My premise had been right. I checked in with Bladon Lines as soon as we arrived in Switzerland and found I'd been accepted. So, once our holiday was over, William and Roger dropped me at the airport where I was due to meet the company rep. Looking back now, it's a wonder she didn't reject me on the spot. I was wearing white sixties platform boots and a sparkly ski jacket more suited to a disco than the ski slopes. If this wasn't enough, I was also carrying a large bag of novelty animal hats. At least that proved a talking point. 'A friend made them,' I explained to the rep, a slight girl with blonde hair. 'He thought I could sell them to guests.'

The first thing Nicola, the rep, did when we arrived at the resort was to introduce me to the girl I would be sharing a room with. While I looked like I was auditioning for an Abba tribute band, Jenny had more of a soulful poet vibe. She was wearing an overstretched yellow jumper and was sitting on the bed knitting, with no make-up and short dark hair, the kind of person you might find communing on Glastonbury Tor. My first thought was: I can't share a room with this girl.

I learnt later that Jenny had precisely the same thought and had immediately gone down the corridor to Nicola's room and said, 'I can't do this. I can't share a room with this girl.'

Our home-from-home was a sixties block above a disco and we realized early on that there was little chance of getting any sleep. All the Bladon Lines girls were based there, and it was clear that I was different from them in more ways than my dress sense. For one thing, I was older. For another, I was a long-time rule-breaker, while they did things by the book.

The chalets where we would work were two miles away at the other end of the village. There were seven in all, arranged around a kind of courtyard. Each chalet had two chalet girls and the jobs were shared. While one did break-fast the other prepared lunch and so on. Although Jenny and I were very different, we soon discovered we shared the same overall philosophy, namely that if we spent all day cooking, we weren't going to improve our skiing. As for the matter of freshly baked cakes as promised in the brochure, I worked out we could bake a week's worth on Saturday changeover days, put them on the balcony outside to freeze overnight, then de-frost one each morning and no one would be any the wiser.

Our bible was the Bladon Lines recipe book. Although the brochure promised cordon bleu cookery, in reality it was rather more basic: lasagna, sardine pâté, turkey and hazelnuts, crunchy-topped pork chops and seafood crumble. The strangest recipe of all was Monkey's Delight, which was bananas wrapped in ham, then doused in a cheese sauce. It was surprisingly popular. Jenny proved brilliant with puddings, and my speciality was starters.

It didn't take long for the other chalet girls to catch on to our bending of the rules. They wondered how we could stay out at the disco until 3 a.m. and yet contrive to be on the slopes by 10.30 a.m., having prepared all the food for the day. They complained en masse to Nicola that we weren't baking our cakes fresh, and one Saturday morning she turned up and, spotting seven cakes lined up on the balcony, promptly threw them into a bin bag.

We never knew from one week to the next who our clients might be. There could be families, groups of friends, or people who had booked separately. These were the most time-consuming, as you had to play at being a 'mine host' to bring the group together.

All-male parties tended to suffer from wandering hand syndrome, which was when a wooden spatula came in handy, and men also tended to exaggerate their prowess on the slopes. One group of burly builders from Southampton told me that the runs near the resort were too easy, and could I take them to a black run? I was often asked my advice on this kind of thing – it was part of the job – so I agreed. They were great fun and quite larky but when we eventually got up there, they had a change of heart and point blank refused to go down. I wasn't a brilliant skier but I had done this run and knew that its bark was worse than its bite and assured them they could do it. But no. And then – disaster. We got back to the lift only to discover it had closed ten minutes earlier. The only way down now was on skis. The only easy run was to Verbier, on the other side of the mountain. So, as there was no alternative, that's what we did.

Once down in Verbier the trouble really started. Round Mountain, as our village was called, was miles away and the only way to get there was by taxi, which was expensive. Verbier was a much smarter resort and just as I was negotiating with the taxi driver, I heard someone calling out my name. I turned round to see a girl from Ellerslie called Polly Kottler. She took no notice of my group of builders and proceeded to tell me that a whole group of girls I knew from Pony Club were here in Verbier. Until then, the builders had considered me 'one of the lads', but with Polly talking about Pony Clubs and dorms, with every second word being 'gosh', 'fab' or 'super', they saw me in a very different light. Not only did they make me pay for the cab back to the chalet, claiming it was my fault, but they made me wait to cook dinner until 11 p.m.

Nicola quickly forgave me for the frozen cakes and as the season went on, we would arrange to take days off together and go skiing further afield. We turned out to have a lot in common: we both had two younger brothers; our mothers were both 'lookers' who played golf and bridge; and we both adored our fathers.

'What are you going to do when you leave here?' she asked me a few weeks before the season came to an end.

'I don't really know,' I said. And I didn't. The idea of going back to being an estate agent held no appeal. But what else was there?

'Try Page & Moy,' she said. Nic came from Leicester, and Page & Moy was a Leicester-based travel company that specialized in guided coach tours around Europe.

'But I don't know Europe,' I protested. 'I've been to a Greek island for two weeks and that's it!'

She said I shouldn't worry. I was a quick learner, so I just had to 'gen up' a bit beforehand and I'd be fine.

Easier said than done. Because if I couldn't read at speed – which I couldn't – the idea that I could just 'gen up' wasn't going to work. But if Nic thought I could do it, perhaps I might try . . .

Another consequence of not being able to read is that you develop an ability to bluff. So that, at least, I was good at. Take Paris. As the coach made its way into the centre of the city, I saw we were heading towards a seriously impressive, massive arch in the middle of a massive roundabout. 'What's that?' I asked the driver. He gave me a quick look to see if I was joking. I wasn't. 'The Arc de Triomphe,' he said. Drivers were my life-saver. With their help I managed to bluff my way around Amsterdam, Bruges and Cologne.

One of my fellow guides was a Welsh girl called Gwen, and we did a deal. While she answered guests' questions about local history, I organized quiz nights and keep-fit classes. It was on a trip to the Rhine that I made my biggest mistake. The site of the Battle of Arnhem was our last major stop other than a quick toilet break on the motorway before getting the ferry back to Britain. It was only when we reached the port that I realized we were missing three passengers and I had no idea where they were. I had no option but to call my boss at head office.

I had committed the cardinal sin of group travel, the one rule that had been drummed into us from the start: you count them out and you count them in. I had no choice, he said, but to send a minibus back to the motorway service station, which was the last place anyone remembered seeing them. They were found milling around wondering what on earth had happened to their coach.

'How you got away with that, I will never know,' Gwen said when I told her afterwards. Because, miracle of miracles, I hadn't been sacked. 'When you have children,' she added, 'you'll be the kind of mum who leaves her kids in the supermarket.'

Even though I was now twenty-five, I remained incredibly naive. My fitness classes were a great success until, during a tour to Germany, one of the women had a heart attack and, although rushed to the local hospital, died. I couldn't understand it. We had only been doing a very gentle routine from a book I'd bought in W H Smith for exercises for the over-50s.

I was interviewed by the police but, as I didn't speak a word of German, I couldn't understand what they wanted. I was then called by head office. 'They need to see your fitness instructor certificates,' they said. It never occurred to me that I needed any . . .

Chapter Four

Dashing Away With a Smoothing Iron

JEREMY HOPE WAS someone I had sold a house to in Ross-on-Wye and so had seen first-hand how he and Mary, his wife, had transformed what had been a rather bland interior into something wonderful. And one day, shortly after I had returned to Heartsease and was thinking about what to try next, Jeremy phoned.

The Hopes ran an interior design company in London and a woman they'd worked with a few years back called Janet Baker had recently moved to Herefordshire, he said.

As her children were now all at school, she wanted to go back to work and had wondered if they had ever thought of opening a branch of their design business outside London. In fact, he said, they had been thinking on very similar lines. But, Jeremy said, if Janet were to do it, she would need someone to help her. And that was the purpose of his call. Might I be interested? It would take some time to set up, he explained, but I could spend a month or so working with them in London so he could train me up.

I had always loved the whole idea of texture and colour

and how to 'create' a room. Granny's 'finds' that I would rummage through in the Knill attic included hangings and curtains, and bell pulls and pelmets she had bought at country house sales run by Russell, Baldwin & Bright.

Sometimes good things just fall into your lap, and this was one of those times. It turned out Janet lived in a village called Eardisley, just eight miles south of Kington, no more than ten minutes from Heartsease by car, and barely a mile from Croase Farm, a little black-and-white Herefordshire fruit farm that Dad had bought the boys. I drove over to see her and we got on instantly.

Mum and Dad were bemused at this sudden change of direction. As far as they were aware, the closest I had come to interior design was helping Mum hang wallpaper.

'Jeremy says he wants me to go to the London shop for six weeks to learn the ropes,' I said, 'so presumably he knows what he's doing. After all it's his money.'

By the end of the month, I was sleeping on Auntie Marie's sofa in her flat in Cathcart Road in Chelsea. The Hopes' shop was only ten minutes' walk away and sold a mixture of real antique and reproduction furniture. I took to it like the proverbial duck to water. Learning how a room is built up layer by layer was fascinating. I saw it was like putting on a show. Get the basics right and then have fun. I learnt how to create mood boards, how different fabrics and looks went together. I learnt the importance of putting together a good team, finding the best curtain maker, upholsterer, carpet fitter, chatting them up, getting them working as you wanted them to. And then learning a decorator's dark arts, like how to weight curtains for example.

It was like opening a door into a different world. We would go into Queen Anne houses that hadn't seen a fresh coat of paint for half a century and help to transform them.

My training complete, I returned to Herefordshire – not to Heartsease, but to Croase Farm. By the time I got to Janet's in the morning, her children would have already left for school and she had been out for a ride.

The houses that we were bringing life back into were often black-and-white timber-framed buildings that were typical of Herefordshire. We'd re-do the bed trimmings for enormous four-posters, working with Jacobean tapestries to colour-match curtains. Many people just lacked the confidence to make changes, but once they trusted our ability to interpret what they wanted, they would recommend us to friends, and that was how we grew our client list. The only problem was distance. The business was based in Ross-on-Wye, thirty-seven miles to the south, which meant at least an hour's commute each way for both Janet and me.

So we made the decision to go it alone. Between us we now had the experience and, as the plan was to work more locally, we wouldn't be trespassing on the Hopes' home turf. As for premises, we could base ourselves at Janet's farmhouse. We invested in the business 50/50 – a fitting home, I decided, for the small legacy Granny had left me in her will.

Between us we had enough contacts to get going. Mum was a natural networker and before long she was spreading the word that we were open for business. We didn't mind how small the job was. As long as the client was happy with the results, we felt confident that word of mouth would do the rest. In terms of who did what, we played to our strengths. Janet looked after the business side, while I focused on sourcing materials and keeping up with new trends and decorating techniques, while both of us built up our contacts. I never went anywhere without our cards and a tape measure. We called ourselves Eardisley Park Interiors, after Janet's beautiful Queen Anne house, which her husband had bought after moving from Bristol.

Since bumping into Polly Kottler in Verbier, she and I had kept in touch. One day she phoned and decided her mother Susie needed new curtains. Would I be able to do them? Polly was now working in Worcester and was living in Susie's lovely Georgian vicarage outside Pershore near Evesham. It had enormous bay windows and it wasn't something she felt competent to do herself. She'd be sure to make a mistake, she said. So, I went over to measure up, which involved getting a stepladder because the drop was so long.

I had found a brilliant curtain maker called Jenny in Eardisland, a village halfway between Kington and Leominster, and when I told her the client was set on a Laura Ashley fabric, she wasn't best pleased. The quality of the material simply wasn't good enough, Jenny said. The poles were complicated as it was. The shape of the window meant they had to be curved.

Anyway, the day came when the curtains were ready, and Jenny and I drove to Susie Kottler's house with them loaded into my car. Bulked out with thick interlining to make up for the poor quality of the fabric, and then rolled up and protected by a thick plastic covering, they were exceptionally heavy, and it had taken three of us – Jenny, me and the carpenter – just to carry them into the house. So, once again, out came the stepladder and up they went. And then, as I stood back to admire the work, I felt my heart sink to my stomach. Jenny was still up on the stepladder.

'They're too short,' I said.

'They can't be!' Jenny said in alarm. 'I double-checked against your measurements! I know I did!'

'It's not you, it's me,' I said. 'I'm useless with numbers. I must have made a mistake.'

I was mortified that I had managed to mess up something so basic.

'By how much, Emma?'

'About four inches . . .'

There was then a horribly long silence before she spoke.

'I think I'll just be able to do it, but you're going to have to tell her.'

Luckily, because of the extra-long drop, we had allowed for especially deep hems, and there was just enough fabric to lengthen them. But it was a steep learning curve. From then on, I would always measure everything three times. By luck we had had enough fabric to alter them, but what if we hadn't? And what if it hadn't been cheap Laura Ashley but expensive French silk brocade . . . It didn't bear thinking about.

It was an exciting time for the Watkins family. A few years previously, Dad had decided to expand into large-scale chicken farming, and one thing chickens need is copious water, which doesn't come cheap. So, ever aware of the maxim 'Take care of the pennies and the pounds will take care of themselves,' he brought in a water diviner to find out if there was water on our land before we started sinking bore holes. In fact, the diviner identified several places we could try. Anything to do with animal feed needs to be tested, and so it was sent to be analysed. It turned out it wasn't simple spring water; it was water rich in trace minerals as it came from an aquifer. No one in the family is now sure who was the first to suggest we bottle it, but somebody did, and the rest, as they say, is history. Within weeks, William had taken out a patent on the name, and Radnor Hills Spring Water was born. It took time to bring it online, but, thirty years later, it is now a global brand.

As for Janet and me, we were up and down to London, visiting wholesalers, sourcing materials, and generally finding our way around, both literally and metaphorically. During our first year, we went up to Earls Court for Decorex, the annual trade fair for interior designers. Each night we would return to our room at the Farmers' Club, overlooking the Thames in Whitehall, our bags bursting with samples, our heads brimming with ideas. On the last day, we visited the stand of Cole & Son, the luxury wallpaper manufacturer, who proudly bear the accolade: 'By Appointment to Her Majesty the Queen'.

We had recently opened an account with them and Christopher, the son, had suggested we make ourselves known to him during the fair. He was flamboyant and chatty, and I liked him instantly.

'I'm having a small dinner tonight at home,' he said. 'Nothing too formal. But if you're not doing anything else I'd be delighted if you could come.'

Janet was already having dinner with friends, but I was

free. 'I'd love to,' I said, and he handed me a card with his private address.

Janet and I continued going round the stands, but I found I wasn't concentrating. I felt surprisingly jittery, thinking about what I should wear, and what time I should arrive. Christopher was clearly quite smart, I decided. He had said 8 p.m., but getting out of Earls Court at rush hour was a nightmare. And I then had to drive to the Farmers' Club and change . . .

It was just as I feared. Janet and I set off in my brand-new little Peugeot 205, but it was gone 7.30 by the time we arrived back at the club. I had packed a suitable dress just in case, but hadn't thought to hang it up, and as it was linen it was very creased and in dire need of an iron. We could probably ask the housekeeper, Janet said, but there just wasn't time. Christopher had made clear this was where he lived, so he was sure to have an iron, I decided. I'd do it there.

From the A–Z I saw that The Boltons was a lozenge-shaped 'square' between Earls Court and Chelsea. As this was roughly the way we had just come from, I made good time. I can't remember now what I'd been expecting, but these were clearly very grand houses, double-fronted in white stucco. They even boasted small drives, unheard of in central London. I pulled up outside, grabbed the carrier bag with the dress, crunched over the shingle, and rang the bell marked Cole. It wasn't one house, I now realized, but had been split up into flats. I said my name into the intercom, a voice came back, 'Ground floor, on the left,' and I was buzzed in. Compared with the pristine marble entrance hall, the flat looked just what it was: a bachelor pad, slightly shabby at the edges and cluttered with boxes and sample books of wallpaper. In the narrow hall there were riding boots with mud still on them – nothing like I had expected. Even more surprising – I seemed to be the first guest. Well, I thought, at least that meant I'd be able to iron my dress.

'I'm just in the kitchen, sorting out the ice,' I heard Christopher say from somewhere out the back. 'I won't be too ticks. Just go through. David will keep you company.' So, I wandered through to the room just visible through an open door to see a vast table laid for about twenty and one young man standing by the mantelpiece, a huge marble affair covered with invitations. The young man must be David, I surmised, and mumbled an awkward hello. I then called out to the disembodied voice in the kitchen, 'I don't suppose you have an iron I could borrow, do you, Christopher? I'm afraid I need to iron my dress.'

'Of course. In the basement flat,' he called back. 'Out of the door and left down the stairs. You'll find an ironing board and an iron there.'

So, I smiled at David and then headed out of the door into the hall as instructed, clutching the carrier bag with my dress. When I heard footsteps behind me, I looked back and saw it was David. He had clearly been here before and went straight to a cupboard where he found an ironing board, and then to a small kitchen and, with the air of a magician finding a rabbit in a hat, held an iron aloft. While this was going on, he chatted easily, saying he was hopeless with ironing and always got someone else to do it. Briefly I wondered who that someone else was.

There was something very easy about his manner. I didn't know him from Adam, but I felt perfectly comfortable taking my dress out of the carrier bag and getting going. As I ironed, he asked me how I knew Christopher, what I was doing in London, and where I lived.

'Radnorshire,' I said. 'It's on the—'

'Welsh Marches. Yes, I know.'

I was surprised. Hardly anyone knew where Radnorshire was, not least because it hadn't existed in any official sense since 1973.

'And you?' I asked. 'Where do you come from?'

'Leicestershire,' he said, watching as I ironed.

The dress I'd brought with me was turquoise linen with spaghetti straps, tightly fitted with a peplum at the waist and quite fiddly to iron.

'You've missed a bit there,' he said, pointing out a crease, and I laughed.

'As you can see, ironing is not my forte.' Above our heads we could hear that guests were starting to arrive, so he said he'd see me upstairs and left.

By the time I had changed, put a comb through my hair and gone back upstairs, the flat had filled with people. I had expected everyone to be smartly dressed, but there were several who had clearly come straight from playing tennis. Just like David, they knew exactly where to go and dashed downstairs to have a quick shower.

Christopher was the perfect host, guiding me by the elbow, introducing me to this person and that, and when he disappeared back to the kitchen, David sought me out and did the same. He seemed to know everyone. It would have been very easy to feel intimidated, but somehow I didn't. It was all very easy and friendly and I was reminded how humiliated I had been at Cheltenham races and how different this felt. It also felt invigorating to be in a room with such interesting people.

As for dinner itself, there was nothing daunting about it whatsoever. Just a smoked salmon starter, followed by a pheasant casserole. In terms of the food, I could have been back at Heartsease, I thought with a laugh. Nothing about it felt like it was a grand London dinner party – not that I knew what that was – but at least it meant I could properly relax and enjoy myself.

My companion of earlier in the evening was seated at the far end of the table, but when I looked up I would regularly catch his eye. He had interesting, rather hooded brown eyes the colour of toffee, and I felt as if he were studying me, but with a definite twinkle. He was one of those people who always seemed to be smiling. As the evening wound to an end, David came across and asked if we could share a taxi. I told him I had come by car.

'Even better,' he said. 'I was hoping you might give me a lift to Seymour Walk. It's not that far, but as you may have noticed I've got a bit of a gammy leg and I'd rather not walk unless I have to.'

'Of course,' I replied.

We said our goodbyes to Christopher, then got into my little Peugeot. The conversation flowed easily, with David saying occasionally, 'Turn right here, turn left here,' and it obviously wasn't very far at all, because within less than four minutes he said, 'We're here,' and I stopped outside a narrow house in a cul-de-sac. I imagined we'd have a little chat before he got out and I drove back to the Farmers' Club. But no. Without warning, David suddenly lunged towards me in the darkness. Until then I'd felt totally comfortable, but although I sensed there was a definite attraction, I hadn't been expecting this, and I immediately pushed him away.

'We shan't be having any of that!' I said, sounding like a proper Miss Prim. 'I barely know you!'

As a one-time chalet girl, I was used to men behaving badly – it came with the territory – but I certainly hadn't expected it of someone like him. A goodnight peck on the cheek is one thing, but this was way more than that. I mean, we had only just met!

'I've got a long drive tomorrow. I've got to go,' I said.

Without saying a word, but looking suitably chastened, he got out of the car then handed me his card. I didn't give him the satisfaction of looking at it and did a three-point-turn and drove away.

Every Friday evening, my brother and I would sit down in the kitchen, open a bottle of wine and chat about what we'd done over the past seven days. We might share the same house, but we often didn't see each other from one week to the next. Both of us now ran our own businesses, so there was always plenty to talk about. I naturally told him about the previous night's dinner party and showed him the business card David had given to me.

'David Manners, Marquis of Granby, registered firearms dealer,' he read out, then handed it back.

'You want to stay well clear of him, Em. He either runs

a pub or he's a gun-runner. Possibly both – one a front for the other.'

William was clearly miffed and had no problem showing it. Over the last few years I'd been involved off-and-on with a chap called Richard. He was from a 'good' Herefordshire family and William was convinced we were 'a good match', largely I think because he and Richard got on well with each other.

Richard was an auctioneer. He was very bright and a real larger-than-life character who everyone loved, with a quick sense of humour and people were spellbound when he was conducting a sale. He put me on a pedestal and spoiled me rotten. I loved his brain but I think he was too nice. Looking back, I don't think I found him enough of a challenge.

David, on the other hand, had certainly piqued my curiosity, and perhaps William realized this, which was why he was being surly.

We had just poured ourselves another glass of wine when a white van came bumping up the pot-holed track that led to the house, and William and I watched as it came closer, assuming it must be lost, because nobody came to Croase Farm except us or our friends. Finally, it pulled up outside, and through the window we saw a frazzled driver get out. He came to the door and William went to answer it.

They exchanged a few words that I didn't hear, then I caught 'You're going to have to help me with this lot, mate.' A few minutes later, the most enormous bouquet of red roses came through the door, and somewhere underneath them was William.

'But who are they from?' I asked.

(*top left*) Elizabeth,
5th Duchess of Rutland,
by George Sanders.

(*top right*) Kathleen,
9th Duchess of Rutland,
known as Kakoo, by
Dame Laura Knight,
1933, with her bulldog
Johnny at her feet.

(*bottom right*) Violet,
8th Duchess of Rutland, by
Sir James Shannon, 1890.

My father-in-law, Charles, 10th Duke of
Rutland, at the coronation of Elizabeth II.

Jack Watkins, high sheriff of
Radnorshire – my father's father.

Muriel and Eddie Davies –
my mother's parents.

David with his father and mother at the
christening of his baby brother, Robert, who
died of leukaemia aged two and a half.

A studio portrait of the Watkins family, with William in the bow tie.
My dress was green and cream with a ribbon down the front. Mum had
to stop me dressing Roger up as a girl as I had really wanted a sister.

At the back of Heartsease with my first pony Betty.

Me aged sixteen, on the brink of womanhood. The dress was from Laura Ashley. It started as a bridesmaid's dress and was given new life after I cut off the ruffle at the bottom.

On Gay Lady at the Knighton Show, working hunter class. I remember being very annoyed as I had forgotten my gloves.

Home for the weekend from Ellerslie – spending time with my second pony Tina and her first foal.

Chalet girls a go-go. Nicola and me larking around in fancy dress at the end of our stint with Bladon Lines at Haute-Nendaz in Switzerland. I am wearing a puff-ball skirt and pink leggings.

Our official engagement photo – my gorgeous antique ring prominently on display – taken in front of the lake beneath the castle. My Donny Osmond-style hair was a great improvement on the lank locks I'd had previously.

My hen night with Theresa my soon-to-be sister-in-law who organized it all. I am wearing my 'lucky' dress, the one I wore the evening David and I met. On the left is Linda Freeman who I shared a flat with in Ross-on-Wye.

Dad arranges my train before we head out onto the cannonade below the castle for the speeches. Behind him, dressed in blue, is my mum. Looking on is David's Uncle John.

Proud Dad, even prouder daughter, on the stairs leading to the forty-acre landing en route to the chapel.

My romantic empire-line wedding dress was a nod to the 5th Duchess. The incredibly long veil, seen here pooling on the carpet, was held in place by the Rutland tiara, which arrived under armed guard.

Watkins family on the left, Manners on the right. Back row (*left to right*): Roger, William and Dad, then, next to David, his best man Charles Welby, the Duke and Eddie, David's brother. Sitting down (*left to right*): David's half-sister Lady Charlotte (Lottie) and Mum in blue next to her. Then, the other side, Frances, the 10th Duchess, and Theresa, my sister-in-law. Taken in the Regent's Gallery in front of the Mortlake Tapestry.

'You tell me, sis.'

'They'll have to go on the dining room table,' I told him. There certainly wasn't room in the kitchen. I now saw that they came complete with their own huge bucket of water. There must have been 200 of them.

William handed me the card that had come with them, with 'Emma Watkins' written on it. So, not a mistake, then. I opened it up and my heart gave a little flutter of excitement.

> *Very sorry for upsetting you last night.*
> *I would love to meet you again. David.*

William clearly noticed the smile that spread across my face.

'Hmmm,' he sniffed. 'Not only does he own a pub, he's obviously also stupid with money.'

Less than half an hour later, the phone rang.

'Have they arrived?'

It was David.

'You're mad!' I said. 'And yes, they have, and thank you! But how did you get my address? How did you get my number?'

'Ever heard of somebody called Christopher Cole?'

He wanted me to describe the exact colour of the roses, and to take a photograph and send it to him. He asked me to check that the stems had been crushed, and if they hadn't been, he was insistent that I do it.

'What – all 200 of them?' I said. By now I was laughing, and whatever irritation I'd felt at the 'liberty' he'd taken the night before had evaporated. I wasn't used to men making such an effort to impress me, and clearly that's what he was trying to do.

We chatted on for about half an hour, and it was like talking to an old friend that I'd known for years. When I finally hung up, I could see William was not impressed, and he became even less impressed as the days went on and David called again and again. My brother would walk past glaring as I clung to the phone, laughing as David told me some funny story, or I told him about the house I'd visited that day, and what I was proposing to do to revamp it. Unlike most men I'd met, he seemed genuinely interested in what I did, and over the days that followed we chatted for hours.

'Who is this bloody guy?' William muttered under his breath by the end of the second week.

'He's someone who actually listens to what I have to say,' I retorted. 'And is genuinely interested. Unlike some people, he doesn't see me as a useless scatterbrain.'

It turned out that David knew our quiet corner of the world quite well, as he was often buying and selling antique guns in the area.

'I should warn you,' I said, 'that my brother is highly suspicious of you. He's convinced you're less antique-gun dealer than gun-runner! And as for the pub, what's that about?'

'What pub?'

'The Marquis of Granby. It says so on your card.'

At that, he burst out laughing. 'Do you know why there are so many pubs called the Marquis of Granby?' he asked.

I didn't. So he told me about an ancestor of his called the Marquis of Granby who had fought during the Seven Years' War.

'There were no pensions in those days, even for returning soldiers, so he gave every single one of his men cash out of his own pocket. And many of them bought pubs and named them after their benefactor.'

'So, this general, he was some kind of relation of yours?'

'Way back, but yes.'

And I didn't give a second thought about this ancestor from 300 years ago.

Although always intended for my brothers, when Dad first bought Croase Farm, he had rented it out to students, and it still felt very much like a student house. William and I each had our own rooms, and now we had another two students living with us – friends of William's from Newcastle University, from where he had just graduated. I don't remember now if they were being paid, or if it was just something they were doing as part of their thesis, but they were researching into possible products to do with mineral water, as well as things like branding and packaging, so we had bottles all over the house. There was already interest from McDonald's, while Mum was doing market research at motorway service stations. When buyers turned up, she always made it feel like a proper family gathering, which it was. One day the senior buyer from McDonald's arrived for lunch, and so we were all there, doing the 'family business' thing, and because I felt I wasn't really contributing much, during a gap in the conversation I said to this very senior man: 'So, Mr Blank. What do you see yourself doing in ten years' time?'

There was a horrible silence, and everyone stared at me and suddenly I realized just what I'd said. My diplomatic skills clearly needed practice.

Meanwhile, David and my relationship – because that's what it felt like, even though we'd met just the once – showed no sign of running out of steam as his phone calls became part of my routine. And it was lovely knowing there would be someone to chat to at the end of a busy day. At some point I mentioned I was driving up to a friend's wedding in Yorkshire in August.

'Perhaps you could drop in and have lunch on your way back,' he said.

Why not? I thought.

His instructions on how to get there were, as usual with David, very precise, and I followed them to the letter, leaving the A1 at Grantham then taking narrow country lanes, through villages called Harlaxton and Denton, until I reached Woolsthorpe. This part of England was a complete blank to me. The only name I recognized was Melton Mowbray, home of pork pies. Then, suddenly, at a break in the trees, I saw this enormous citadel rising out of the otherwise flat landscape. Stanage was a minnow in comparison, and I found it difficult to keep my eyes on the road. I was spellbound by this fairy tale castle topped with turrets and towers, jutting into the skyline. It was utterly mesmerizing. I checked the notes on my lap and, yes, I was on the right road. His address was the Old Saddlery, so presumably a converted stable block. Moments later, I came across the white gates that David had mentioned and turned left into the castle grounds. I drove along the driveway, the castle staring down from the top of the hill, searching for the round riding ring. Then, there it was, the Old Saddlery, an unremarkable stone building around a courtyard. I parked in the shade and, minutes later, David came out to meet me.

'You made it,' he said, big eyes, big smile.

By now I was used to his voice, but to see him standing beside me I was instantly reminded of the man I had met at Christopher's dinner party, and my heart did a little flip inside.

'Come in,' he said, 'lunch is almost ready.'

An attractive middle-aged woman was standing expectantly at the top of the stairs.

'This is Mrs Pacey, my housekeeper,' he said, and we smiled and shook hands. I was a bit nonplussed, as I'd assumed she was his mother.

'David, your guest must be thirsty after her long journey. Perhaps you'd like to get her a drink.' She might not be his mother but there was a definite closeness there that I thought was rather endearing.

Everything in the flat was immaculate. After a much-needed glass of water, he poured us each a glass of wine. He was exactly as he'd been at our first meeting, asking me questions, genuinely interested in the wedding I'd just come from. When Mrs Pacey brought in lunch, I was surprised. Instead of a salad, or something else that would have been appropriate for a hot summer's day, we had over-cooked roast beef, mushy vegetables and gravy. It reminded me of the food we'd had at Ellerslie. David seemed to love it.

'Mrs Pacey has been my housekeeper for years,' he said once she was out of earshot. 'She's a godsend as there are things I find impossible to do because of my arm.' He went on: 'It's been partially paralyzed since birth. I've had fifteen or sixteen operations since I was a boy. Numerous muscle transplants to try to get this hand to open.' His leg, I now realized, was part of the same thing.

'I'm so sorry,' I said, not quite knowing what to say. But suddenly I saw a different side to him, imagining how much this sweet, gentle man had had to endure growing up, missing out on so much, all the rough and tumble of being a boy. He was very open about it all; there was no shame, no secret, but I was moved nonetheless that he had told me.

After lunch we went for a walk, and it was obvious he was having trouble putting on his boots. 'Here, let me help,' I said.

But he batted away my offer.

'If I need help, I'll ask for it,' he said.

We went for a wander down the lane surrounding the castle, and I asked him who lived there.

'My parents,' he replied.

At first, I didn't know whether he was joking. I was still getting used to his sense of humour, so I said nothing but decided to call Christopher when I got back home.

I had a long drive ahead of me – about three hours – so I left at about five and Mrs Pacey came down to see me off. I thanked her for lunch.

'I look forward to seeing you again very soon,' she said before leaving David and me to say our own goodbyes. This time it was me who leant in towards him and gave him a kiss.

'Next time, you should come for the weekend,' he said as I got in the car.

'That sounds nice,' I said. I smiled, gave a quick wave, then, putting the car in gear, pulled out into the road and headed for home.

Chapter Five

Well, Has He?

'JUST WHO *IS* David Manners?' I asked Christopher Cole the next morning when I called him. I was sitting in the kitchen at Croase Farm, fiddling with the telephone cord, feeling very confused. If I was thinking of getting involved with David – and on the way back from Belvoir I'd decided that I was – then I had to know what I was letting myself in for. 'For example,' I said, 'do you know that his parents live in a castle?'

'Of course I do.'

'So, they're millionaires, then.'

'Not exactly . . .'

'What do you mean, "Not exactly"? Do they own that place or are they just renting a flat in it?'

'They own it as much as anyone does in their situation.'

'What situation?'

'You mean you genuinely don't know who they are?' Even down the phone I could hear the disbelief in Christopher's voice.

'If I did, we'd hardly be having this conversation.'

'They're the Duke and Duchess of Rutland.'

I took a breath. David's parents – a duke and duchess? And Rutland? Belvoir was in Leicestershire. I didn't get it. 'But, Christopher, his card says David Manners. No mention of Rutland.'

'Manners is the family name. David will stay David Manners until his father dies and he accedes to the title. Until then, as the eldest son, he's the Marquis of Granby.'

Oh right . . . as if that made it better.

Later that week I popped over to see Mum and Dad. I knew Mum wanted to hear all about the wedding I'd gone to in Yorkshire as she knew the groom, the friend of mine responsible for the novelty hats I had taken to Switzerland. Also, I'd decided the time had come to tell them about David. Christopher had given me a brief rundown, but I still found it hard to square that with the charming and self-effacing man I'd had lunch with a few days earlier and who I was becoming interested in. My father, of course, asked the inevitable question.

'So, how many acres does this David have?'

For once I had an answer guaranteed to stop him in his tracks.

'Around 17,000,' I said. 'Give or take.'

Two weeks later I was back in Leicestershire. By then I'd had time to let it all sink in. Wikipedia didn't exist in 1990, but Hereford public library had provided the basics about Belvoir and the Dukes of Rutland. For example, that the current castle was the fourth to be built there, and that the site had been given to someone who had fought at William the Conqueror's side at the Battle of Hastings. It wasn't a direct line, so from time to time the title and lands had passed to cousins etc., but even so . . .

Strange though it was, I felt much more comfortable knowing what to expect, and when I walked up the stairs to be welcomed by Mrs Pacey, it really did feel like a welcome. David had invited some local friends over to dinner, but when I offered to help, he said that wouldn't be necessary and that Mrs Pacey was in charge. And I remember thinking, *Let's hope it's not overcooked beef again . . .*

The first person to arrive was Terry Woods. David and Terry had met years before at the art gallery where they had both been working when David was in his early twenties. Although Terry had been married – in fact he had two children – he had subsequently come out and now had a male partner. At first, I sensed he was giving me the once-over, checking that I wasn't a gold-digger, or the aristocratic equivalent. But there was always so much fun and laughter whenever he was around – he was like a modern-day court jester, always ready with a quip and good at diffusing difficult situations – that very soon I felt completely at ease.

As more of David's friends began to arrive, I could easily have felt overwhelmed, but, Terry having decided I was a good egg, they seemed to take their cue from him. Lady Sarah McCorquodale, for example, the sister of Diana, Princess of Wales, was there with her husband. Charles and Suzanna Welby were neighbours who lived on the adjoining estate. Suzanna was completely mesmerizing. Incredibly tall and exotic, like an ultra-glamorous Cruella de Vil, I was spellbound by her.

'I've never met anyone like you before,' I said with my usual tact when we were introduced. 'You're unbelievable.'

She laughed and from that moment on took me under her wing. I could never have imagined then that we would become lifelong friends.

Although I didn't find these people threatening – they were simply catching up like any group of old mates – I decided to make for the kitchen and ask Mrs Pacey if there was anything I could do. When I'd arrived, she'd told me to make myself at home, so that's what I was doing. At home, or with close friends, I'd wander into the kitchen and offer to help, even if the offer was turned down. However, David had followed me and, taking my elbow, guided me back to the sitting room, saying, 'Mrs Pacey has everything under control. That's not for you to do.'

David had done everything he could to include me, specifically introducing me to everyone as his girlfriend. But was I sufficiently committed yet to introduce him to those I loved as my boyfriend? As I drove back to Croase Farm on Sunday evening, I decided I was. That night, when he called to check that I'd got back safely, I suggested that he might like to come down to Radnorshire. 'Though, I warn you, you'll have to meet Mum and Dad,' I said. 'But if you're up for that . . .'

It was October by the time we found a weekend that would work for us all. By the time Friday came, Mum was in full hostess mode. As for the idea of meeting a marquis . . . she could barely contain her excitement. Out came the best china. Out came the Silvo and the Brasso and we covered our ancient oval dining-room table with newspaper to protect it while we polished and gossiped in time-honoured mother-and-daughter fashion.

I doubt that David had any idea of the trouble my parents had gone to. But just as Mum was determined to be the perfect hostess, so David was determined to be the perfect guest. Dad had chosen a lamb from his prize flock in David's honour to have for dinner and, sitting round our newly polished table, he recounted the history of the Watkins family. Although I'd heard a lot about the Manners' family history by then, I had never said much about my own, because it seemed so tame in comparison. But that evening I heard things that I had never heard before, including stories about Mum's family, the Davies of Knill, and David was fascinated. Dad in turn was fascinated by what he told them, some of which I already knew but the majority of which I was hearing for the first time, about the Belvoir archives, for example, that contain journals, bills, accounts and most importantly letters going back generations. Nor was the conversation limited to history. Dad hadn't forgotten the 17,000 acres, and this time he got to hear it confirmed first-hand. But, as to farming at Belvoir, this wasn't David's area of expertise. A farm of that size needed a team of professionals to manage it, though he was clearly excited about a new combine harvester that had recently arrived and was looking forward to taking it out, he said.

At which, Dad launched into the Wurzels' 'I've Got a Brand New Combine Harvester'. When the laughter had died down, David said, 'You'll have to come and see it when we get you up.'

'I really like your young man,' Mum said as she and I

washed up after lunch. 'He's such easy company and is obviously completely smitten with you.'

That Sunday, after church at Brampton Bryan, my parents had a few people back for drinks. While this was something they often did, the Coltman-Rogerses of Stanage or the Harleys of Brampton Bryan weren't usually included. They would only get asked for the big drinks party we held every Christmas Eve. But it isn't every day your daughter comes home with a marquis in tow, so on this occasion they were invited.

The one person whose reaction I had been nervous about was William. He had been so disparaging about David – not least because of his gaffe about the Marquis of Granby being a pub. However, he turned up for lunch with his girlfriend Jane and within minutes he and David were getting on like a house on fire.

David and I were now very clearly an item, and we would spend alternate weekends at the Old Saddlery and Heartsease. Dad would take David out to check up on his sheep – Kerry Hills and Mules – or his Herefords, with Lottie my liver Labrador jumping up in the Range Rover beside Dad's collies, and as the weeks went by it was clear that David was becoming really interested in just what it meant to run a farm on your own.

David meeting my parents was one thing. My meeting David's parents was quite another. But within six months after that never-to-be-forgotten dinner party in London, I was invited to stay at the castle for a shooting weekend, and I was both excited and terrified, while David was simply nervous. By now I was used to his friends and, although at first I'd imagined we had nothing in common, it turned out we did. Like them I had been to boarding school, I had had a pony since I was about seven and we were the same generation: we listened to the same music, saw the same films, watched the same television programmes. None of the above was going to apply to the Duke and Duchess.

The fact that it was a shooting weekend made things easier. While I don't shoot myself, shoots were part of the farming calendar in Radnorshire, and so very much part of my life, from the Glorious Twelfth when the grouse shooting season began, to the infamous Rat Patrol.

David had given me precise directions about how to get there. But, inevitably, nervous about being late, I had left plenty of time, in fact rather too much, so it was early afternoon on a Friday in November 1990 when I passed through the white gates as instructed.

Up close, Belvoir Castle is huge. The first hurdle was locating the front door. Eventually I found it tucked away on the garden side of the house, away from the main portico and the staff entrance. So, naturally, I rang the bell. And heard nothing. Not the sound of it ringing inside nor the reassuring clatter of footsteps. After a reasonable amount of time, I pressed it again, this time keeping my finger firmly on the button in case there was a loose connection.

Eventually it was opened by a heavily built, tall man in pin-striped trousers, waistcoat and tailcoat, the stereotypical butler. He could have come straight out of a 1950s horror movie. He was like Dracula without the teeth.

'You called?' he said.

'I'm sorry,' I said. 'I thought perhaps the bell wasn't

working. I'm Emma Watkins,' I added, extending my hand, which he glanced at disdainfully. 'I'm here for the shooting weekend.'

'You're far too early,' he said, though he stood aside and ushered me in.

Outside was bright sunshine, while inside it was cold and dark. Without another word he picked up my suitcase and set off up the stone spiral staircase.

While the staircase continued to wind upwards, he stopped at the first floor and I followed him in silence down a long, wide corridor, lined with oil paintings – mainly portraits dating back centuries. Finally, we arrived at what I realized must be the private drawing room. A fire was lit, and there were fresh flowers on a central table. Silently the butler indicated I should sit on a bright red sofa. When he left, I took the opportunity to look around. The room itself was huge – soaring ceilings, four double-width windows at least twice my height, small tables covered with silver-framed photographs, a card table and paintings hung one on top of the other covering the walls.

I got up to look out at the amazing view but then suddenly froze. Immediately behind where I had been sitting, a woman wearing a tweed skirt was lying on another sofa, eyes closed, clearly having a doze. Although David had shown me photographs of his parents, this was the first time I'd seen his mother in person. Even asleep she managed to look glamorous, immaculate 'done' hair, and fully made up with red lipstick. I returned to my sofa and sat there wondering how long it would be before she woke up. In front of me was a covered ottoman strewn with books and magazines, so I picked up one on gardening and ten minutes later was startled when she walked round the sofa towards me.

'You must be Emma,' she said as I stood up. 'I'm Frances.' Then, crossing to the fireplace, she rang a bell.

'Tea, please, Horton,' she said when the butler appeared. Then she sat down and motioned me to do the same. 'So lovely you were able to come, Emma. David has one shoot a year, you know, just like our other two, Edward and Theresa.' Then we made small talk – my journey, the weather – the hope that it would stay fine for tomorrow with the wind in the right direction – until tea arrived. After a suitable interval, the Duchess rang the bell again. 'I'll look forward to seeing you later,' she said. Then Horton reappeared to show me to my room. My suitcase had already been taken care of by the housekeeper, Mrs Plowright, he explained, as we started back down the long corridor to the same spiral staircase, up several twists to the floor above, and then along another wide corridor, this time in the other direction. He told me that Mrs Plowright would be along shortly.

The pink bedroom, as it was called, was huge, with windows looking south over a wide valley. There were no other houses or villages as far as I could see, just miles and miles of parkland, rising to a ridge of low hills. Although we were one floor up, the ceilings were just as high. As for the bed, you needed a chair to get into it.

A two-bar fire was plugged in beside an ornate dressing table, which just managed to take the chill off the room. The dressing table had all the country-house essentials: aspirin, Alka-Seltzer, a box of tissues. As for my suitcase, there was no sign. However, when I opened the chest of drawers looking for a hairdryer, I discovered it was filled with all my own clothes, neatly folded and separated into categories. They must have been unpacked by Mrs Plowright, I realized with horror, and my cheeks burnt at the thought of her seeing my old undies.

As if by telepathy, Mrs Plowright then appeared and showed me where everything was, including my bathroom, which was the other side of the corridor, she explained, one of a row of three that appeared to have been tacked on as an afterthought. It was tiny, with the loo immediately on the right, placed on steps like a throne, while the bath was down several more steps to the left. Finally she said if I needed anything ironed, I should ring the bell.

As I was staring out of the window contemplating the glorious view, I heard the click of the door and seconds later a voice I recognized.

'Boo!'

'David!'

Relief flooded through me and I rushed over and held him in my arms.

'Everything okay? You haven't been eaten by ogres or assailed by ghosts?'

'Not yet . . .'

First, he took me though the schedule. We were going to be about twenty-two for dinner, he said. Mainly friends of his, eight guns and their wives or girlfriends, as well as us, Lottie – his half-sister Charlotte, daughter of his father's first wife – and her boyfriend Lol, who lived in a house on the estate, and of course his parents would also be there.

The dress code for this evening was casual, while Saturday night, he said, was black tie.

After enjoying a luxurious deep bath – dressing gown and bath salts provided – I got dressed. Mum had bought me a fabulous pair of cobalt-blue suede trousers which I wore with a shiny Frank Usher silk blouse. David came to get me at a quarter to eight to take me down. His mother was very strict when it came to timing, he explained. It was all to do with the staff. You needed to look after them. If you started late, you ended late, and that wasn't how things were done. We were going down early as he needed to be there to greet his guests.

I had met a few of them before, including an old girlfriend of David's and a couple whose names I don't now remember whom I'd met when we'd gone to Ascot earlier in the summer. As for the Duke himself, he was exactly as you would imagine a duke to be, tall and very distinguished looking and completely charming to everyone. But my real fascination was the staff, because I'd never been to a dinner where you were literally waited upon. There were three butlers that night. The head butler was called Nailor. It turned out my old friend Horton was the under butler – his principal job being to keep the various fires going, as well as deputizing in Nailor's absence, which was how he had happened to open the door to me. The chauffeur was also on butler duty, as he always was when there was a big party to look after. When the butlers weren't doing anything else – while we were eating – these three stood there like waxworks, their hands behind their backs. They never spoke unless they were spoken to, and even then, the responses were minimal. I began to understand why Horton had appeared so remote. It was simply what he'd been taught.

I was fascinated by how everything was done. Meat was carved before it appeared in the dining room, and when the platter was offered (always from your left), you either accepted or declined with an imperceptible shake of the head – though I found it impossible not to smile and say, 'No, thank you' – then the butler would pass to the next person along. A minute or so later you'd be offered vegetables. And so it went on. As for conversation, you talked to the person on your right first then to the person on your left. No matter how tedious (or fascinating) the conversation might be, ignoring this rule was 'bad form'.

Once the pudding course was over, Frances walked down the table and touched each girl on the shoulder. This was the sign to stop whatever we were doing and leave the men to their port, brandy, cigars and chat (political or risqué) while we girls 'withdrew' to the drawing room where we had assembled before going into dinner.

Once furnished with our coffee – the butlers again; female staff being relegated to the kitchen or bedrooms – Frances went round noting down on a little pad how many of us wanted breakfast in bed. Not so different from our B&B I thought, except there were more decisions to be made: Eggs, what sort? Poached, fried, scrambled or boiled. Bacon? Toast? Brown or white. Tea: China or Indian? I had no idea there was more than one sort. Then what newspaper did we want, and would we like early morning tea? And what time . . . This all seemed far too tricky, so I opted for breakfast in the dining room.

I slept surprisingly well – probably the result of drinking more than I was used to – and woke the next morning excited for the day ahead.

The dining room table, which the night before had been sparkling with glass and silver set against gleaming mahogany, was now covered with a damask tablecloth with fresh flowers in the middle. Breakfast itself was laid out on the side, kept warm in chafing dishes, and you helped yourself. Each person was allocated their own silver butter dish, with two curls of butter. It was the same with the toast, cut wonderfully thin and presented in individual silver toast racks. Tea – China or Indian – also arrived in its own individual pot, and there was hot water in silver ewers if you needed a top-up. You even had your own salt and pepper. But by now, fascinating though this all was, I was desperate to get outside and join the shoot and crack on with the day, because that was the one part of this weekend that I understood.

I'd been told that David was a good shot, but I hadn't realized quite how good. I stood beside him and was completely blown away, watching in awe at how he managed his gun with such limited use of his right arm and hand. He somehow cocked it onto his right arm and had immense control.

Sporting shotguns have two barrels, and the aim is to kill two birds at more or less the same time, one with each barrel, before the gun is reloaded. That morning David got seven 'Rights and Lefts' on the trot. *Bang, bang,* two dead. He was obviously chuffed that I'd been there to witness this fantastic display. I'd heard that he was a deadeye dick, as the Americans say, but I had never imagined he could be as good as this.

I don't shoot and have never wanted to. What I enjoy most is being involved, crashing through the undergrowth, as a beater. Beaters are very often estate workers – and there is a wonderful camaraderie among them. At the same time, they're incredibly competitive. They loved being with David because they knew they'd done their job well. To spend a day driving birds on to guns that miss is disheartening.

After elevenses, which, exactly like at home, was consommé laced with Worcestershire sauce, sherry or sloe gin, served with hot sausage rolls, I asked David if he'd mind if I went off with the beaters. Not at all, he said, and pointed me in the direction of the gamekeeper, called Big John, who he said would look after me. Big John spoke with an accent that was quite different from anyone else on the estate and as we walked towards the woods, he told me he'd spent 'thirty years below ground and thirty years above ground', having started as a fifteen-year-old down the pit in the Yorkshire coalfields. He was – and still is – a truly wonderful man and I felt privileged to be part of his team. I was very impressed at how they did it – quietly, just beating wooden sticks on tree trunks – rather than yelling like hyenas as we did at home.

At Heartsease, a shoot lunch was basically a picnic, when a Land Rover would pull up, the tailgate would come down and you just tucked in with everyone milling around. At Belvoir, it was a proper sit-down meal. We were taken back to the castle in the gun bus, then ushered into the private boot room, where the guns took off their Barbours and boots and changed into their smart shoes, all the while chatting about each other's birds, and how many 'Lefts and Rights' they had managed, while we girls went up to our bedrooms to powder our noses.

At dinner the previous night I'd been faced with an artichoke, which I had no idea how to deal with, so I'd watched how other people managed before attacking it myself. Today's trial-by-food was bits of bone swimming around in a sauce, a dish called osso buco. Another first, another mystery. With sticky toffee pudding, however, I was on firmer ground. Finally came the cheese course: a whole wheel of Stilton wrapped in linen. Instead of cutting it with a knife as we did at home, here it was dug out with a silver scoop, like a spoon with sharp edges and the sides turned up. Under EU law – even after Brexit – Stilton has PDO status, which means it can only be made from milk from a restricted geographical area. Four of the six licensed dairies are in the Vale of Belvoir, and one of the farms provides milk for the Colston Bassett co-operative, and so cheeses are specially made for the castle. It is quite a delicacy and, in my view, utterly delicious. But what fascinated me most that day was the array of biscuits on offer. At home, we just had Jacob's Cream Crackers.

Unlike other meals at Belvoir, a shoot lunch always has a sense of urgency, as everyone is keen to get back to the line for the next drive. The day ended with a duck drive, and we were taken in the gun bus to two small lakes close to the castle. The guns were dropped off one by one around the edge, while David stood in the middle of the bridge where the lakes joined. By this time the sun had disappeared and night was closing in. As the birds were driven – mallard and geese – and the guns shattered the silence, foxhounds in the Belvoir Hunt kennels nearby the castle began to howl – an unnerving sound if you aren't expecting it, which I wasn't. Then, as the whistle rang out ending the shoot, the dogs – Labradors and spaniels – swam out to retrieve the wild ducks and geese that had landed in the lake and Big John set out in a little rowing boat to pick up those they had missed.

It must have been five when we arrived back at the castle and the fires in the drawing room were blazing. At one side a table was laid out with the most sumptuous tea: hot crumpets, cucumber sandwiches and, best of all, potted shrimps that you spread on hot toast – tiny brown curls packed into spiced butter, which I found totally irresistible. I ended with the most amazing coconut cake, steeped in honey and liberally covered with fluffy white icing.

You always feel totally stuffed after a shooting weekend, because food is such a big part of it. That afternoon was no different and I felt like going to sleep, but David reminded me that we needed to be back in the drawing room at 8.00 for dinner at 8.30. At about a quarter to eight he came to find me. His mother had put him in the blue dressing room next to me, but the communicating door was firmly locked. Frances had strict ideas about not sharing rooms. She was a devout Catholic, and while the rest of the family went to the local church at Bottesford, the Duchess went to Mass every Sunday in Grantham (Lincolnshire) or Melton Mowbray (Leicestershire).

For dinner that night I had brought a dress of Mum's,

short – just below the knee, and made of black silk taffeta. The moment we arrived downstairs, however, I felt distinctly underdressed. Frances was resplendent in floor-length green silk and an emerald necklace that emphasized the colour of her eyes, and she looked absolutely stunning.

She and the duke made an exceptionally handsome couple. He was then in his seventies – Frances was his second wife – but was still immensely attractive, tall and distinguished with a definite twinkle in his eye, and it was clear where David got his easy, sociable charm.

For men, black tie can mean exactly that – a dinner jacket worn with a black bow tie – but in country houses, it generally means a smoking jacket if you have one. These are elaborate affairs made of silk velvet and come in various colours, often with a flamboyant lining. They have shawl collars with frog fastenings rather than buttons and they are usually worn with embroidered slippers.

David's slippers had been handmade by his mother, meticulously stitched in green needlepoint with a black 'G' for Granby, and under the 'G' was a ducal coronet. The design was her own and she had approached the Royal School of Needlework to get it translated into a pattern. While I know she absolutely adored David, she didn't wear her heart on her sleeve. Yet she had clearly put so much love into making these beautiful slippers – they had taken months and months – no one could doubt the strength of her affection.

Compared with the previous hectic day, my first ever Sunday at Belvoir was very relaxed. A late breakfast was followed by a tour of the castle for those people in the party who hadn't been there before, which of course included me.

We did all the state rooms which the public sees, but also the private side of the house. Apart from the main entrance, with wide shallow stairs leading up to the state rooms, all the other stairs at Belvoir are spiral and looked – at least to my eyes – exactly the same as one another. I was completely overwhelmed, as anyone would be. The numbers were staggering: five towers, twenty-two turrets, fifteen staircases and literally hundreds of paintings, on every wall – grand rooms, bedrooms, bathrooms, main corridors, back corridors, storerooms, attics. As for the overall number of rooms, the figure was certainly over 200, although nobody has ever counted them.

The main event, however, as always at Belvoir on Sunday, was lunch. It began at a quarter to one with a Bloody Mary, or, as Horton put it, brandishing a large jug of murky-coloured tomato juice: 'Bloody or Virgin, madam?' I had no idea what he was talking about. Then came lunch itself, truly delicious roast beef and Yorkshire pudding. By this stage we all knew each other really well and the atmosphere had an end-of-term feel to it. As for the meals, Frances always did incredible *placement* to ensure no one sat next to the same person twice. She kept notes on every aspect of the weekend. Not only who sat where, but what was eaten, which bedroom they were in and who else was in the party, so that, when it came to the next shoot, the same people wouldn't be invited together. She would even try to put them in different bedrooms. Shooting weekends were Frances's forte. She did it in a wholly military way and it was quite a spectacle.

Between weekends, David and I would speak every day

on the phone, me in the kitchen at Croase Farm, he in his kitchen in the Old Saddlery. By now it was February and one night, following a bad storm, our phone line went down. So, not wanting to miss our nightly chat, I drove to the nearest telephone box and stood in the dark, putting coin after coin into the slot.

We were in the middle of discussing something totally inconsequential when, out of nowhere, as if he'd suddenly remembered he'd forgotten to put toothpaste on a shopping list, he said, 'Oh, the other thing is, will you marry me?'

I pressed the receiver closer to my ear, unsure what I had just heard, and then I laughed. What else was I going to do?

'I can't believe you have just asked me to marry you over the phone,' I said. 'That's appalling, David. What happened to the bended knee? Where's the chivalry?'

Then he laughed too and we quickly moved on. But after I'd hung up, I drove back to Croase Farm in a state of elation mixed with confusion. I'd had no indication that he was planning to propose, and so I hadn't had a chance to think whether I might accept. But was it a proposal or a joke? Either way, it wasn't something I was likely to forget, and that tingle of excitement kept coming back.

The following weekend we spent in Belvoir, and as always, Terry the jester joined us for lunch. 'Well?' he said turning to David. 'Have you asked her yet?'

Then he turned to me and said, 'Well, has he?'

At this point I decided the table needed clearing.

The rain of earlier in the day having stopped, David suggested a walk. We got in the car and drove beyond the castle to the Spring Garden as it's called, which was then carpeted in snowdrops with a few early daffodils coming through. We followed the winding path up to the Moss House, one of the earliest follies in the garden, made of gnarled wood and looking as if it belonged in a fairy tale. We'd been there before – it was a regular haunt – so I sat down on the rustic bench and expected David to join me and enjoy the view. He didn't. He just stood there looking nervous.

'Well, put quite simply, Em, I really would like us to get married.'

I said yes and, feeling stupidly, deliriously happy, we skipped back to the car to break the news to Terry, who of course was waiting with a bottle of champagne ready to pop.

'Now all you need to do is ask my father,' I said.

Of course, that wasn't strictly true. I was twenty-eight, perfectly old enough to make my own decision, but I thought it would please my dad. And that evening, rather than go back to Croase Farm, I drove straight to Heartsease and told them the news. They were absolutely delighted, although I swore them to secrecy, saying that I'd told David he had to ask Dad first, but from then on they kept a bottle of champagne permanently on ice.

'You never know, he might do it this weekend,' Mum would say, preparing one of David's favourite dishes, firmly believing that the way to a man's heart was through his stomach.

Yet three consecutive weekends came and went – and nothing.

I got to the point where I almost believed I'd imagined the whole thing. Then late in March, we had a full house because David and Terry and an impossibly glamorous American friend of theirs called Wilma were coming down for the local hunt ball. It was nearly midnight by the time we got back to Heartsease. Dad loved it when we were all there, and he was still up and determined to enjoy a good chat, though Mum had already gone to bed. I said I was going up too, bid everyone goodnight and said I'd see them in the morning. I had just reached the landing when I heard Terry clear his throat and say, 'Look here, David. Have you got around yet to asking John for Emma's hand in marriage?'

I stood stock still. There was a brief silence when I heard a floorboard creak, and then, standing in the dark on the stairs, as I had so often done in my childhood, eavesdropping on my parents talking with their friends, I listened as David asked my father for his permission to marry me.

I dashed up to Mum's bedroom, just in time to hear Dad shout up: 'Roma, you'd better come down – and bring that bottle of champagne in here!'

Chapter Six

Welcome to the Family

S UNDAY LUNCH AT the castle always felt incredibly special to me, almost like going to the theatre.

'You need to tell them, David,' I said, one Sunday in May 1991, as we walked arm in arm up the drive. 'If you don't, it's going to leak out from somewhere and that would be embarrassing for everyone.'

That Sunday seemed the perfect occasion. Unusually, it was just Charles and Frances and us. However, as lunch progressed, I could sense that David was becoming increasingly nervous. Then, as we walked back to the drawing room for coffee, thinking about where we were going to take our places, like actors emerging from the wings, unsure of their marks, David suddenly turned to his father and said, 'Papa, could I have a word with you in your study?'

I knew what was coming and sat on the red sofa, like a coiled spring.

'Whatever needs to be said can be said amongst us all,' he said.

And then out it came.

'Quite simply, I'm going to marry Emma,' David announced. For a brief moment I felt a wave of panic wash over me, but then my father-in-law's face broke into a smile.

'My dear boy, that really is wonderful news,' he said, and went over to David and clapped him on the shoulder. 'Many, many congratulations!' Then, turning to me, he said, 'Emma, my dear, I am truly delighted. Welcome to the family.'

Frances, who was sitting next to me, took my hand in hers. 'Really marvellous news. Thrilling. And now you and I must get to know each other.'

I was astounded. Although Charles had always been very approachable, I'd felt that Frances had kept me at arm's-length, albeit in the nicest possible way. 'I suggest we meet up one day in town,' she said. 'Lunch at Claridge's would be nice, don't you think? I'll ask my secretary to arrange it.'

At that time I had no idea what Claridge's was. I'd heard the name, but had somehow imagined it was a smart department store, like Harrods, but in a different part of London.

It turned out to be a prestigious hotel just off Bond Street. I had decided to buy a new dress for the occasion and for some obscure reason thought I might find something in Marks & Spencer on Oxford Street. So, I caught the 6 a.m. train from Hereford, then a bus from Paddington to Marble Arch. First call M&S, and then on to Selfridges next door, where I bought an umbrella made by Christian Dior as it looked like rain. Outfit complete, I changed in the ladies. Only when I emerged did I catch sight of myself in the mirror. My heart sank. The dress I had bought was navy with matching buttons and I realized I looked exactly like an air hostess . . .

Everything about Claridge's oozed glamour. Entering the lobby was like finding yourself in a 1930s film where at any moment Fred Astaire and Ginger Rogers would come gliding across the black-and-white chequered marble floor. I walked over to the concierge and said that I was meeting the Duchess of Rutland. At the mention of her name, his demeanour changed. 'Of course, Miss Watkins,' he said. 'Please follow me. Her Grace is waiting for you.'

The dining room was equally intimidating. Not only because it was without doubt the smartest restaurant I had ever set foot in, but it would be the first time I had spoken to my prospective mother-in-law without David by my side, excluding the first time when I found her asleep on the sofa.

Within seconds a waiter was hovering. 'A bottle of the Pommery, I think, James,' the Duchess said as she lit a cigarette and then offered one to me. 'I think the occasion warrants it, don't you?' She was dressed from head to toe in cream silk and looked as if she'd stepped out of the pages of *Vogue*.

The champagne arrived as we inspected the menus. Taking no risks, I ordered exactly what she did. And then we started to talk, woman to woman. The first half of our lunch – mozzarella and tomato salad – was devoted to David. She told me how it had been a very difficult birth. Nerves in his right arm had been damaged, which had led to partial paralysis. As a result, life had been hard for him as a little boy. Not only was he limited as to what he could do, but he'd had to endure operation after operation. In a subtle way she was telling me that there was more to marrying David than just marrying David. That marriage to David came with responsibilities. My view then was that every marriage has responsibilities. As to what those responsibilities might be, she didn't spell out and I didn't ask.

She looked at me so earnestly and so intently I could see that her eyes were welling up with tears, and that just made my own emotions overflow, and my own eyes began to well up. 'I love him, Frances. Nothing else matters to me. I just want to be with him.' And, for the second time since we'd known each other, she put her hand on mine.

From then on, the atmosphere eased, and she told me about the death of her second son Robert, who died of leukaemia when he was only two. The more I heard, the more tragic it became. Because it wasn't only Frances's loss – terrible though that was – it was David's loss too. Losing his baby brother when he was only four, with all that he was going through anyway, it didn't bear thinking about.

Once we had finished and the waiters had cleared away and we were waiting for coffee, the conversation changed tack.

'So, tell me, Emma,' Frances said. 'Have you and David had any thoughts about dates?'

I told her we were thinking about later in the summer, perhaps September, around the time of my twenty-ninth birthday. At this she looked genuinely shocked.

'But, my dear girl, that's far too soon! I think you should be looking at a year's engagement at the very least. There's so much to plan and simply not enough time. Next year will be better. June is such a lovely month for a wedding; the rose garden at Belvoir will be in full bloom.'

Only then did I realize she was talking about us being

married at Belvoir! I didn't know what to say. Weddings are always hosted by the bride's family. It was there in black and white – or rather in gilt on vellum – on every wedding invitation I'd ever received: Mr and Mrs So-n-So request the pleasure of Miss So-n-So at the wedding of their daughter etc. etc. I was my parents' only daughter and Mum had been planning my wedding since I was born. She had spent decades doing the flowers at Brampton Bryan Church. Just the previous evening she'd telephoned to say that she'd spoken to a company in Knighton about the marquee for the back lawn and that she'd had a wonderful idea about how to decorate the font.

As for my dream of marrying a farmer, while the identity of the bridegroom would change, my vision of the wedding itself never did. I would be married in Brampton Bryan Church. All three of us Watkins children had been christened there. Grandpa was buried there. Granny's funeral had been held there. But sitting there in Claridge's with my future mother-in-law, I didn't say a word. Was it cowardice? I still don't know to this day.

In the train on my way back to Hereford, I thought of what life must have been like for Frances as a young mother. The Belvoir nursery was presided over by Nanny Webb, who had been nanny not only to her husband Charles but to Charles's father before him. And now she was to take charge of David. Three generations of Dukes of Rutland. No one was going to question the wisdom or otherwise of the old nanny who everyone adored. Inevitably Frances would have felt undermined, and it would have made natural bonding between mother and son much more difficult. And then the tragedy of Robert . . . It was no wonder she could seem remote.

When Mum asked the next morning how I'd got on and what my future mother-in-law had had to say, I told her only half the truth. 'Frances expects us to wait,' I said. 'So it looks as if this year is out. It'll be next summer at the earliest.' And perhaps that was all the Duchess intended. To give me time to have second thoughts. Time to work out whether this was really what I wanted. After all, if you're going to be married for a lifetime, what's another year? I was impatient because I had found my man and just wanted to get on with our life together. But I now think that Frances was right. As for my own mother, I loved her and I wasn't prepared to be the one to break her heart. Someone would have to do it eventually, but it wouldn't be me.

Once the announcement of the marriage appeared in *The Times* and the *Daily Telegraph*, and the engagement photographs were taken, David Manners, Marquis of Granby and Miss Emma Watkins of Heartsease, Knighton became officially engaged and the Manners family went into action.

David's Aunt Ursula, known as Ursie, threw a family party in her grand house in Kensington Square where the entire Manners clan of aunts, uncles and cousins assembled to take a first look at David's intended. To me this lunch felt like a moment of truth, make-or-break time, so I wore my lucky outfit – the same turquoise linen dress I'd worn to Christopher Cole's dinner party, two years earlier.

There wasn't a family engagement ring as such, so David and I went to Grays antique market in Davies Street and chose one together. It was beautiful. A hoop of two sapphires and three diamonds, five stones which in my head stood for I. Will. Love. You. Always. I did then, and I still do.

In London, thanks to Janet, I became a member of the Farmers' Club, which meant that we could stay there when we were in London. Although David had been a member of the Turf Club in Carlton House Terrace for years, it was very old-fashioned and unmarried couples were not permitted.

We were soon being inundated with invitations, and the occasion I remember most clearly, and which felt like a turning point, was the Historic Houses Association AGM.

In order that I should look the part of a marchioness-to-be, David took me shopping and bought me a beautiful taffeta dress with a needlepoint jacket to go with it decorated with hunting scenes. He loved taking me shopping because he loved having me on his arm, looking my best and showing me off to his friends.

That evening was the first time I had felt completely at ease at one of these dos. People were both welcoming and wonderfully eccentric. There was Robert Brudenell of Deene Park in Northamptonshire, who had been at school with David, and Simon and 'Scruff' Howard of Castle Howard in Yorkshire. However, the most eccentric of all was Benjamin Slade, whom I happily informed reminded me of Del Boy. He wasn't affronted because he had no idea what I was talking about, having never watched *Only Fools and Horses*. Everyone was so warm; it was like finding a new family. So many characters and every one of them fun. I began to see that, if I looked the part, I could play the part.

What was becoming very clear was that, in contrast to everything I had imagined or been told, real aristocrats were the opposite of snobs. They were not remotely bothered about who your forebears were, or whether your family had come over with William the Conqueror, or if you were an eleventh cousin twice removed of Her Majesty the Queen. Only two things mattered: how interesting you were and how much fun you were.

Meanwhile, in Herefordshire and Radnorshire, the news that a local girl was marrying into the English aristocracy was hailed as a Cinderella story. I knew it wasn't the case, but from time immemorial there's been appetite in the British public for those kinds of stories, be they rags to riches – making a fortune from nothing – or tales of high romance across the social divide. To some degree we've all been brought up on them. They're about the possibility of transformation. And the idea that a future duke had plucked me from the milking parlour fell perfectly into that category.

One evening David and I were invited to dinner at a smart Kensington restaurant to which some of his former girlfriends had also been invited. At one point during the evening, I went to the ladies, where – from the privacy of a cubicle – I overheard a couple of these girls commenting on David's fiancée.

'I suggest we call her the Dairy Maid Duchess,' giggled one, a suggestion that was received with a gale of laughter. After that I decided that attack was the best form of defence and took great pains to talk about the farm, about cleaning out the chicken sheds, and de-bagging the cattle. I was not ashamed of who I was, or where I came from. And I would be the author of my own portrait. David had taken me as I was, and they would have to too.

Meanwhile, advice was pouring in from every quarter:

'You simply must have your wedding list at Peter Jones.'

'You simply must get your dress at Tatters.'

'You simply must get Pulbrook and Gould to do the flowers.'

'We simply must meet your parents,' the Duchess announced one Sunday lunch. 'I will write and invite them to come to a shooting weekend.'

The morning the letter landed on the doorstep at Heartsease, I was in the kitchen having breakfast before going off to measure up velvet hangings for a four-poster bed in a house near Ludlow.

'Did you know about this, Em?' Mum asked. I had to admit that I did. 'You could have warned me,' she admonished.

I countered with, 'I thought you'd like the surprise!'

By this time my parents had heard a good many of my stories about life at Belvoir, the conventions and codes of behaviour etc., but when Mum asked whether I thought we should get Dad a smoking jacket, I said no. Smoking jackets were far from universal and a dinner jacket would be fine.

However, this forthcoming visit was a great excuse for Mum and me to go shopping together, always a great treat when I was growing up.

A few years earlier she had made friends with a stallholder at the weekly market in Hereford who had great clothes, mostly German brands, and she was a regular customer. When she wanted something a bit different or a bit special, that's where she'd go. At some point this woman told Mum that she ran a wholesale business based in a warehouse in Ross-on-Wye and offered to give her a trade card. This warehouse was where my cobalt-blue suede trousers and silk shirt had come from that I wore for the first evening of the shoot. It was where my 'lucky' turquoise dress came from that I was wearing when I first met David. So I said, 'Mum, let's just go down to Ross!' I loved going there. With row upon row of wonderful clothes, sometimes at less than half price, it was like Christmas, Mum and I going up and down the rails fingering beautiful fabrics, hiding in corners trying things on while trying to look like buyers.

So that's exactly what we did. And she bought a casual-but-smart outfit for the first evening, a country-house outfit for Saturday, a drop-dead gorgeous outfit for Saturday night, and gosh did we have fun. Dad said he didn't need anything new and that he was all right as he was, but Mum bought him a pair of new pyjamas anyway. As always, Dad took everything in his stride. Nothing fazed him.

However, as the date approached, questions from Mum began coming thick and fast.

'So what do we call them?'

A simple enough question perhaps, but I honestly still didn't really know. On that first visit they had asked me to call them Charles and Frances, but the staff called them 'Your Grace'. Others, I noticed, just said 'Duke' or 'Duchess'. The whole business of upper-class etiquette was a total mystery to me.

So, in November 1991, six months after we'd announced our engagement, Mum packed her finery and, just as I had done a year earlier, set off with Dad for a shooting weekend at Belvoir Castle.

Just like me, they were put in the pink bedroom with the

little bathroom across the corridor with its quaint arrangement of loo, bath and basin. When I walked up from the Old Saddlery that afternoon to see how they were settling in, Mum said she was surprised they didn't have an 'en suite'. I explained that the plumbing in the castle was a complete nightmare, hardly surprising given it was well over 100 years old. As for how they should climb into the bed, I moved a couple of chairs just as I had done. At least now I knew why beds in castles were so high. 'It's to avoid the draughts,' I explained. When the castle in its present incarnation was built, there were only coal fires, which also explained the bed hangings, because bedrooms in these grand houses were always freezing.

On a visit to Haddon Hall that summer (the other Rutland house in the Peak District), Frances had given me Diana Cooper's marvellous memoir *The Rainbow Comes and Goes*, which covers her early life growing up in Belvoir and Haddon as the youngest daughter of the 8th Duke of Rutland, though in fact her biological father was Henry Cust, MP for nearby Stamford in Lincolnshire, as well as being a well-known womanizer.

Diana Cooper (she had married Duff Cooper, later ambassador in Paris) was a great society beauty as well as an actress. She was born Lady Diana Manners in 1892, so grew up in the heyday of the Edwardian country house, a way of life that would come to such an abrupt end with the outbreak of the First World War. The Manners family were then immensely wealthy. They not only had Belvoir but also Haddon Hall, where they would decamp for the summer. Rich though they were, however, only the main rooms at

Belvoir were heated. The corridors, stairs and everywhere else were freezing, to the extent that Diana tells how from autumn onwards, black woollen capes were put in every bedroom which you would don whenever you left your room, to go to the drawing room, say, where everyone would huddle around the fire, and then the capes would go back into service for the return journey.

It wasn't just the immediate family who lived in the castle back then. The tradition of looking after poor relations who had fallen upon hard times continued well into the twentieth century. In fact, David's father was an embodiment of the term *noblesse oblige*, which demands that those with a position in society have a responsibility to look after the less fortunate. But David was always frustrated at how soft his father had been. And while he continued to believe the aphorism 'with great privilege comes great responsibility', he became exasperated when Charles would bail out relations – also privileged – who themselves had acted irresponsibly, leading directly to their financial woes. And these bailouts would be called on all too frequently and cost the estate a fortune.

The weekend my parents came to Belvoir was a great success.

David and I didn't join them for dinner that first evening, but I said I'd see them at breakfast and we'd then go on to the shoot together. In fact, because I was so anxious to know how everything had gone, as soon as I woke up I went straight to their room.

'You won't believe what your father's done,' Mum said the moment I walked in. Dad, I couldn't help but notice, was looking distinctly sheepish.

'He got out of bed to go to the bathroom across the corridor, and coming back got confused about which door to go in and walked into the Duchess's bedroom instead! And what's worse, he'd refused to put on those nice new pyjamas I'd got him and was just wearing his old vest and nothing else. So there she is, fast asleep, and at three in the morning she wakes up to see this stranger, standing in front of her with everything hanging out. It's a wonder she didn't scream blue murder!'

As for the night before, it had been a triumph, Dad said. 'Your mum stole the show, she really did.' Later Mum told me that, just before going down, she'd had an attack of nerves. 'And I said to your father, "I'm sorry, John, but I just can't do this." And he looked at me, and said, "Roma, I have never seen you look more beautiful. So put your shoulders back and we're going down."'

Dad took to the Duke immediately, and when Mum was introduced to the Duke and Duchess of Bedford, she couldn't have been more excited. Charles Chelsea, as we called him, Viscount Chelsea, later the Earl of Cadogan, was totally smitten, Dad joked. 'He couldn't keep his eyes off her!' They were all about the same age and Dad even admitted to feeling jealous when, after dinner, Charles Chelsea chose to partner Roma at bridge. David's father didn't play but Frances was very keen and would always find out who played among her guests so they could sit down for a rubber or two after dinner. Dad was relatively good, but Mum could hold her own against anyone and they had been commandeered to make up a four.

That weekend, the thorn that I had been unable to grasp

following my lunch at Claridge's was dealt with by Frances. She and Charles persuaded my parents to accept that we wouldn't get married in Radnorshire. Dad – who as the father of the bride would be footing the bill – had been convinced by Charles's argument that he would save money by not having to hire a marquee. Mum and Dad would still be the hosts – the invitations would still go out in their names – but the wedding itself would be held at Belvoir rather than at Heartsease.

Even so, Dad was determined that they should see where their future daughter-in-law grew up, and David's parents readily accepted Mum and Dad's invitation to spend a weekend at Heartsease.

I can't remember now how long it was before they actually came – I think around a month. Just enough time for my mother to update the parts of the house that she didn't consider up to scratch. The main bugbear was the bathroom. The one on the landing used by the B&B guests was far too small for a duke and duchess, she said. So, we would just have to lose one of the bedrooms. So my old bedroom was stripped of its purple wallpaper and honeysuckle curtains and painted a neutral shade of peach. I admit I was sad to see it go. I had chosen it all myself – my first foray into interior decoration – when I was about thirteen.

There was to be a smart dinner party, and Mum's cleaning lady was deputed to come in to assist in the kitchen and to help serve. There was a real sense of 'we're all in this together'. Even Michael Sockett was infected, asking every time I passed him in the yard, 'So, we've got the Duke and Duchess coming this weekend, is it, Em?' However, once they did arrive, he was so starstruck that he lost the power of speech.

For a few days before their arrival Mum was busy in the kitchen preparing scallops, beef Wellington and sherry trifle. There was also a cheeseboard with grapes and port. Dad even joined the Wine Society to brush up on his vintages.

Finally came the moment when the brown Rolls-Royce glided to a halt in front of the house. Frances emerged carrying what looked like a pillow. I stood there in amazement and thought, *Does she think we don't run to pillows in Wales!?*

Mum took it all in her stride. She told me later, 'It's probably just the one she prefers.'

As they approached the front door, David stepped forward to greet them – he had arrived the night before. It was hard to believe that it was barely a year since he himself had first seen the farm, but his excitement was palpable. Heartsease was a place he had come to love and he couldn't wait to show his parents everything. It was really touching.

And so the weekend began: Dad putting everyone at their ease, Mum bringing in tea and Welsh cakes, and being rewarded by seeing them all disappear. Every so often Mum and I would escape to the kitchen.

'So, how do you think it's going?' she'd ask.

'Really well.'

'Sure?'

'Sure. You have absolutely nothing to worry about, Mum,' and I'd give her a big hug.

It was still well before Christmas but early in the shooting season, and so my father had arranged a shoot for David's parents at Powys Castle and had invited some of their more 'respectable' friends. Although our own shoot was perfectly good, he wanted to give them a flavour of Wales beyond Radnorshire.

We were up and awake early next morning for the hour's drive across to Powys, opting for the scenic route. None of us had been there before, and in hindsight it would have been far easier to have had the shoot at home, although I must say Dad was a lot more relaxed than he was on the shoot days ordinarily, and afterwards we had lunch inside the castle itself.

Back at the farm, Frances was happy to muck in, clearing away plates and taking them out to the kitchen. On one occasion, much to my mother's horror, I saw her standing at the sink getting stuck in to the washing up wearing a pair of Marigolds.

On Sunday we had planned to go to church as usual, but when Mum found out Frances was Catholic, that was abandoned and Dad took them on a tour of the farm instead, proudly showing off his herd of Herefords as well as his chicken houses – just as he had done with David the year before.

Again, in a re-run of David's first visit, the Coltman-Rogerses and the Harleys and some other local notables came for pre-lunch drinks. It turned out that Stella Cumber, from Brampton Bryan Manor, had been on the same cruise as Charles and Frances, while Mrs Harley and I reminisced about the days when she and I would go pony trapping.

At one point during lunch, Dad said, 'You must be very disappointed that David isn't marrying an aristocrat.'

Frances immediately put down her fork and looked horrified: 'Don't forget, John, that I am bog Irish,' she said.

It was never the Duke and Duchess who questioned whether I was the right sort of woman for their son. I remember getting terribly frustrated when my cousins asked if I was equipped for the job of being David's wife and moving in those circles.

The most common question I was asked, by both them and others, was, 'Do you think you'll be able to cope?'

'What's there to cope with?' I would reply.

I knew full well that people only ask if you can cope if they don't think you will. I had been immersed in David's world now for some time, and I truly didn't know what the big deal was. David and his parents were basically like everyone else, with their own problems and worries, who happened to live within an extraordinary set of rules and customs – rules and customs I was getting closer to understanding day by day. David certainly never gave any indication that he doubted me. If anything, I seemed to give him more confidence than he gave me.

But my wider family remained unsure, and I remember Dad's cousin, Uncle Bev, saying, 'You're not going to change, are you, Em?'

I felt that they feared they were losing me to this unknown world, and that I needed to assure them I would remain Emma Watkins at heart.

Mum and Dad shone in any circle and that in itself had given me confidence since I was knee-high to a grasshopper.

At seven I had sung a solo at Coxall Church. I had performed in countless Eisteddfods. At drama school I had held my own with singers and actors whose talent was unquestionable. I had blagged my way around Europe persuading coachloads of tourists that I knew what I was talking about.

Looking back now, it strikes me as uncanny that, completely without planning it, I had somehow managed to accumulate skills that, over years to come as chatelaine of Belvoir, would stand me in very good stead.

Chapter Seven
Dearly Beloved

THE YEAR OF our long engagement, David and I spent several weekends at Haddon Hall – the family would always spend August there – and this was a wonderful way of understanding how they used these buildings. Just as their ancestors had done, they would entertain their friends with grouse shooting on the moor, and trout fishing on the River Lathkill, because this way of life had been going on unchanged for generations. Slowly it was dawning on me that the faces staring at me haughtily down the centuries from their gilt frames were not simply historical figures or names in the tourist guide, they were David's ancestors, some of whose physical characteristics and traits of personality he carried in his DNA.

One painting in particular set me thinking. I had always been drawn to an amazing portrait of a young girl with masses of curly blonde hair that hung in the private dining room at Haddon but hadn't really questioned who she was. However, while reading Diana Cooper's memoir *The Rainbow Comes and Goes*, I suddenly realized that this was her: Lady

141

Diana Manners as she then was. And looking at her eyes in this portrait, I could see that they weren't the eyes of either Violet her mother, the 8th Duchess, let alone the Duke, but the blue eyes of her biological father, Henry Cust. And that began to raise all sorts of questions. How did Violet feel when she realized she was pregnant with a child that wasn't her husband's? Did the Duke, David's great-grandfather, know? Looking at those eyes, it's hard to imagine that he didn't. Yet he brought her up as his own and she bore his name and the title that went with it, which undoubtedly changed the course of Diana's life. What is clear from her memoir is that this wasn't about averting scandal or what he saw as his duty; he absolutely adored her and cherished both her unusual beauty and her artistic talent. That portrait and her memoir were the beginning for me. Through the Manners women I was starting to unravel the story of the castle. It was like putting together an enormous jigsaw and just like with any jigsaw, you had to start somewhere, so I started with her.

Haddon Hall, a fortified manor, is possibly the most romantic house I have ever seen. Unlike Belvoir, which was re-built in the early nineteenth century, it is still very much a medieval building, which grew organically from its beginnings in the Middle Ages, through the early modern era, until its blossoming under the Tudors. It has remained unchanged since 1703, when the 9th Earl of Rutland became the 1st Duke and moved to Belvoir, leaving Haddon largely abandoned. It was only in the 1920s that the 9th Duke, David's grandfather, recognized its importance and he and the Duchess, born Kathleen, known by the family as Kakoo, spent a lifetime restoring the house to its former glory.

What makes Haddon Hall truly romantic, however, is the story of how it came to be in the Manners family at all. Thanks to an advantageous marriage in the twelfth century, it came into the possession of the Vernon family. Four hundred years later in 1563, the daughter of the house, Dorothy Vernon, fell in love with Lord John Manners of Belvoir. Dorothy's father, Sir George Vernon, disapproved of this young aristocrat. Dorothy was nineteen, and while marrying without your father's consent wasn't illegal then, she risked being cut off financially. So why did he object? She certainly wasn't too young – in *Romeo and Juliet*, written thirty years later, Juliet is only fourteen. Perhaps it was that old stumbling block: religion. The Manners family were Protestants whereas the Vernons were staunchly Catholic. Or perhaps it was simply that as a younger brother of the 3rd Earl of Rutland – and thus unlikely to inherit anything – John wasn't seen as a good enough match for Dorothy, who was an heiress thanks to Sir George's personal wealth. But true love will out and, nothing daunted, the pair eloped. A little bridge over the river – known now as the Dorothy Vernon bridge – is said to be the one they escaped by, and from all accounts they lived happily ever after.

Then, twenty-four years later, fate intervened and the 3rd Earl died without a male heir, so his younger brother John acceded to the title, meaning that Dorothy became the 4th Countess of Rutland, and she arrived at Belvoir, bringing Haddon Hall with her.

Gradually I was beginning to realize that these had been

real living people, people not too different to David and me. To go against her father's wishes showed extraordinary bravery. These young people's love for each other must have been so intense. There was so much at stake, and yet they took the risk . . . Where did they go to tie the knot? To a renegade priest as Romeo and Juliet had done? And these people were David's direct ancestors . . .

Over the years books and plays – and even an opera – have been written by those intrigued by Dorothy's story. And now it was sending me further down the road to discovery about the women who have been fundamental to the history of both the family and Belvoir itself.

Every morning, whenever we were at Haddon, the family would all troop down to the Dorothy Vernon bridge carrying old-fashioned fishing nets on long poles kept expressly for the purpose of catching crayfish. I have to admit that this required no great skill and we'd eat the morning's haul – bucketfuls – for supper that evening. However, skill was certainly needed to use the fly-fishing rods David and I had been given as a wedding present by the Haddon Estate. Although I'd grown up only a few miles from the Wye, that for much of its length marks the Welsh/English border, I had never been interested in fishing, whereas my brother William was obsessed by it. Now was my chance to discover the appeal. Sadly, the Haddon ghillie spent many frustrating hours on the Lathkill trying to teach me to cast, but to no avail. The chief quality would seem to be patience, which I don't have.

Haddon Hall had been restored in a totally authentic way by David's grandfather, which led to a few inconveniences.

Like every building of this antiquity, embellishments or upgrades dating from different eras were added as and when they became necessary – because of an expanding family, say – or simply when money became available. The result of so many different levels is steps everywhere. Due to the fragility of the original panelling, there was no central heating, so you were reliant on your electric blanket and plug-in electric fire for any kind of warmth. As for hot water, there was a huge ancient boiler which required considerable coaxing and whenever the family were there, Horton would come up to take charge of it, stoking it every morning.

There wasn't the same upstairs/downstairs arrangement at Haddon as there was at Belvoir, so the atmosphere felt much more relaxed. The tiny kitchen was used by everybody. It was dominated by a big table in the middle where the housekeeper, Mrs Whitaker, would sit, and there always seemed to be someone standing at the sink washing up. I remember one day Charles coming in, opening a drawer and taking out this massive wooden spoon – two feet long at least – and Mrs Whitaker saying, 'For goodness' sake, leave that alone! . . . Your Grace.' Witty, as she was always known, was very much the old-fashioned housekeeper, with a proper rope of keys around her waist. She had a natural air of authority and you messed with her at your peril.

One day, she passed me an envelope. In it was a photo taken at her first school – she must have been aged about eight, with two long pigtails. And there, among the other faces of pupils staring out at me from fifty years ago, was a great tall boy, a head taller than everybody else, who I instantly recognized as my dad! It turned out that Witty had grown up on the Stanage estate and knew Dad really well. As to what her father did, I never found out, but the likelihood is that he was working in the forestry department.

It was at Haddon that I first got to know David's sister Theresa, who was almost exactly the same age as me. When Theresa entered a room, it was like a window had been flung open and the temperature changed; energy flashed around her like a lightning rod. During the 1980s she was the lead singer in a band called Business Connection, described as hard rock meets punk. She was a human dynamo and you couldn't help but be swept up by her. We got on like a house on fire, so when she said, 'You simply must let me organize your hen do!', my answer was a loud, 'Yes please!'

In the early 1990s, hen parties weren't as common as they are now, and I was absurdly excited as I had no idea what it actually entailed. Theresa most certainly did, but she refused to divulge details and determined that it would be a surprise. Being embraced with such gusto by my future sister-in-law felt enormously special.

Finding a date that everyone could make wasn't easy, but eventually we settled on an evening in May, about a month ahead of the wedding on 6 June. My 'hens' included Sophie Cliff-Jones and Jackie Cox, representing my Ellerslie days. Then, from my estate agent era, Philippa Evans-Bevan and Linda Freeman, who I shared a house with when I was working in Ross-on-Wye. Last but very far from least was Nicola Smith, my Bladon Lines rep. Representing the Rutland side was the dynamo herself, and David's half-sister Lottie.

The evening started with a drink at the Manners' family

flat in Belgravia, and everyone was in a high state of excitement. Apart from Sophie and Jackie, who obviously knew each other, they all came from different stages of my life, and it gave me enormous pleasure to see how they immediately got on. The first surprise was when a white stretch limo was spotted through the window waiting in the road outside. In we piled, to find glasses and champagne, suitably chilled, waiting for us in the back. The great thing about champagne, Theresa explained, as the limo pulled away from the kerb, was that you didn't need a corkscrew.

We already felt like celebrities, and whether the plan had been for us to vaguely swoop around the streets of London, opening the windows and shouting raucously at passers-by, or whether the chauffeur genuinely got lost, I will never know, but eventually we turfed up in a restaurant called Monkeys in Cale Street in Chelsea, where Nicola and I fell about laughing wondering if their signature dish would include bananas, ham and cheese sauce . . . Towards the end of the evening, when we were all definitely the worse for wear, a bronzed Adonis appeared to ribald laugher and saucy looks. Light on his feet and heavy on the oil, he boasted tight blonde curls such as you might find on a Greek god, or more prosaically a Chippendale. I managed a giggle so as not to spoil the fun, but actually I felt really quite shocked and just relieved that he didn't actually strip.

We rolled back to the Farmers' Club at around one in the morning. By turns giggling and saying *Shhh*, we rang the bell marked night porter and tried to attract the attention of someone inside, while listening for the rattle of the lift which might indicate we had been heard. When we'd set off earlier in the evening – teetering on high heels and already tipsy with excitement – the concierge, a rotund Irish woman with a soft Galway accent and dyed red hair, had made clear that she would stand for no nonsense and on no account could we turn up after midnight and expect to be let in. So, as we waited for someone to open up, it occurred to me that it was like a drunken re-run of my arrival at Belvoir for that first shooting weekend, except that when the door finally opened it was by a dishevelled night porter wearing a moth-eaten jumper over tartan pyjamas rather than the magisterial figure of Horton.

Inevitably there was a last-minute crisis. David had asked Terry to be his best man, but Terry was quite a delicate soul and it was simply too much for him. At one dinner party he got so drunk that he staggered outside and told the assembled paparazzi that he was 'absolutely never going to be best man to David Manners', and then went on a rant, sounding off about everyone in the family. We were obviously mortified at this drunken outburst, but then, to add insult to injury, the Duke banned Terry from the castle, so David was left without a best man. Luckily, his neighbour Charles Welby needed little persuasion to take his place. I was doubly delighted as it meant I had the ultra-glamorous Suzanna Welby as support behind the scenes.

While the best man's speech is supposed to add humour to the proceedings by taking the groom down a peg or two, the job of the family friend is to describe the bride in glowing terms while shedding light on her background. Because of the high-profile circumstances of the wedding, our family friend had to be someone who could cope with making a speech in front of 500 people. It so happened that we had the perfect person in the shape of Simon Gourlay. Not only was he our immediate neighbour – he had moved into Hill House Farm a few years before I was born – but since the 1970s he'd been very active in the NFU and had recently completed five years as president, and indeed was now Sir Simon.

The Gourlay family had been in our lives ever since I can remember. The sons from his second marriage were roughly the same age as we were, and after the Knighton school bus picked us up from outside the farm, it would wander up the hill until it reached the top where the three Gourlay boys would get on. They were quite off-beat, definite free spirits, and their father was the same. He had also had a son with his first wife. Her parents were doctors and they lived halfway between us and Knill, where my mother was born, and they'd ask their friends' children over to play with their grandson, as otherwise he was on his own. In their garden they had old farm machinery – tractors and steam engines and suchlike – that we used to clamber on, so simple but providing hours of fun, and throughout our childhood we'd go over at least once or twice a week.

A few days before the wedding, I said a tearful goodbye to Lottie my Labrador and to Heartsease itself, along with the hills and valleys that had made me. My old bedroom was now known as the Duke's bathroom, and I thought of all the history the house had seen, including my dad being born in the front room. Of course, I would come back, but deep down I knew it would never be the same.

Then Mum, Dad and I set off in their new Range Rover

for Belvoir. Every so often Dad would break the silence by turning to me and imparting some fatherly advice.

'Don't share too much with people, Em. Try to keep your head below the parapet. This sixth sense you have, it's not something that everyone understands.'

During the time I was working with Page & Moy, rushing around Europe attempting to speed-learn essential facts about each country's heritage, I'd had a feeling in the pit of my stomach that something was wrong. In the days before mobiles, calls to and from anywhere abroad were impossibly expensive, so I rarely phoned home. But that morning I did, to be told that my younger brother Roger had been involved in a car crash.

As we drove across Herefordshire and Worcestershire, a journey I had taken so many times since my first visit to the Old Saddlery to meet the mysterious young man I'd taken a shine to at a London dinner party, Dad talked about the importance of trusting my instinct and not automatically taking what people said at face value. Until I had a very clear idea of who I could trust, he said, I should be wary; I should keep myself guarded.

The day before the wedding, the Duke and Duchess hosted a party for all the farmers and tenants on the estate. In many ways, this was the high point for Dad, as he spent the entire afternoon chatting about farming to people whose experiences of working on the Belvoir estate were on the one hand so different to his, and yet the similarities were there too. When I spoke to him that night, he told me that he had been very touched when Charles had taken him to one side and assured him that I was in safe hands and that he didn't need to be anxious about me. 'I am also convinced that she'll do a good job,' he'd said. 'As you yourself know, John, Emma has exceptional qualities, and I promise you they won't go unrecognized.'

For practical reasons, most of the wedding arrangements had been left to my mother-in-law. But when it came to my dress, that would be entirely my decision. Whether I would have had the same style had we been married at Brampton Bryan, I don't know. Possibly not. But ever since my first visit to Belvoir, I had been drawn to the portrait of the 5th Duchess which hung at the top of the main staircase. At first, it was simply because it is a stunning portrait of a beautiful young woman that brilliantly captures the period. But the more I learnt about her, the more Elizabeth herself began to get under my skin.

Lady Elizabeth Howard was the daughter of the 5th Earl of Carlisle. In April 1799, when George III was on the throne and Britain was at war with America, she married John Manners, the 21-year-old Duke of Rutland. She was eighteen. And here I was, two hundred years later, about to step into her shoes, aged twenty-nine. Although my dress wasn't a copy of the one Elizabeth wears in the portrait – mine would be off the peg – nonetheless she was my inspiration. The 'look' I wanted was regency, but where to find it?

Obviously, I had never gone shopping for a wedding dress before and had no idea even where to start. Several people – including my mother-in-law-to-be – had suggested Tatters in Chelsea, close to Seymour Walk, where Frances had a house and where I had dropped David off that night we first met. Further along the Fulham Road was Amanda Wakeley, one of Princess Diana's favourite designers, so I started there, but ended up finding the perfect dress in Tatters after all.

For years Mum had said that, being short in the waist, empire-line dresses worked well for me. And this was everything I was hoping for. I had an obsession with lace, and while the band under the bust was in crepe satin, the skirt was lace over silk, while the sleeves were also lace but minus the lining and ended in a V over the wrist, giving a slightly medieval look. The train was manageable, though the veil (to be held in place by the Rutland tiara) was ridiculously long. As for the bridesmaids, I continued with the regency look and they wore tight little bonnets and carried baskets of flowers. They could have stepped straight out of the pages of *Pride and Prejudice*.

On the eve of the wedding, David slept at his flat at the Old Saddlery and I stayed in the Wellington Room at the castle, so called because Belvoir was big enough to keep a suite of rooms at the disposal of the Iron Duke, and this was his bedroom. It is still decorated with the same Chinese wallpaper that he would have looked at as he went to sleep. As for Mum and Dad, they were just down the corridor in the Pink Room – at least this time there was unlikely to be any confusion over bedrooms.

The first knock on the door that morning was Mrs Plowright with breakfast. Then came Mum, who read out some telegrams. At around 9 a.m. Theresa floated in, and afterwards Auntie Marie, Mum's airhostess friend who would be doing my make-up. We helped her get set up, moving the furniture around to make the most of the light. The biggest question mark of the day was the weather. Would it hold? At nine o'clock it was still overcast, but as the day wore on it cleared, much to everyone's relief.

I knew from my days singing at Eisteddfods that the longer you have to wait before you 'go on', the more nervous you become, and that morning the hours seemed to tick by very slowly until I felt at risk of getting overwound, just like the grandfather clock at Heartsease.

The wedding was due to start at 3 p.m. Over 500 had accepted (700 invitations were sent out) but as the chapel could only seat 150, most would only attend the reception. About 2 p.m. the Rutland tiara arrived from London under armed guard. It's so valuable it's kept in a vault and I hadn't even tried it on. Luckily, I have bouncy hair, so getting it pinned on was comparatively easy. By now fully kitted out in their wedding outfits, Mum and Auntie Marie left to check up on the bridesmaids who were assembling downstairs. Then, after a last long hug with my dad, looking exceptionally debonair in his morning suit, we made our way down. Here and there I recognized members of the staff, for once their usually impassive faces wreathed in smiles. I even spotted Horton.

Mum was waiting on the 40-acre landing with the bridesmaids. Auntie Marie had already gone in. After arranging my train and the veil, she gave a squeeze of my hand, then turned and walked into the chapel, the last guest to take her seat. Then the music began . . . Dad and I looked at each other, and he said, 'Okay, Em. This is it.' I took his arm, and in we went.

The chapel was jam-packed, extra rows of chairs fitted in where they could, as well as the two galleries full to bursting. And then came a moment I will never forget: as if on cue, a sea of smiling faces under a kaleidoscope of hats turned round to watch us proceed down the aisle. Ahead, to the right of the communion rail, David and his best man Charles Welby were waiting.

The service was conducted by the Belvoir chaplain, Anthony Clayton, but I remember little of what he said after 'Dearly beloved, we are gathered here . . .' and I looked at my own dearly beloved and he looked at me. When it came to our vows, I could barely speak. Once I had filled huge spaces with my voice, now it was no more than a bat's squeak. David was nearly as bad; somehow he managed to stumble over 'With all my worldly goods I thee endow', and a giggle rippled through the congregation. As for the music, Frances had organized the choir from St Wulfram's Church in Grantham and they were wonderful, but the most moving moment came during the signing of the register, when my Uncle Owen, one of Mum's cousins, sang 'Oh for the Wings of a Dove'. Uncle Owen wasn't like Mum physically – he was slight with red hair – but he had all the Davies musicality and this wonderful tenor voice. On the Manners side, Charles's sisters, Aunt Isabel and Aunt Ursie, were spellbound, while Isabel's daughter Lindy was in pieces. Belvoir was like a second home to her, as she was born in 1941 and, with the country at war, she and her brother had spent their early childhood in the nursery ruled over by Nanny Webb. Though Lindy had held her 21st-birthday soirée at Belvoir, her wedding was in

Westminster Abbey, where she married the Marquis of Dufferin and Ava, who was one of the first high-profile casualties of AIDS. David Hockney went on honeymoon with them, driving across America in an open-top Cadillac. In the sixties and seventies she had been a major player in the London art scene. She was passionate about art, and was mentored for several years by Duncan Grant at Charleston. As for her parties, they were legendary.

The reception was held in the Regent's Gallery, named following the Prince Regent's visit over the new year, 1814/15. Originally, as the name implies, it had a balcony overlooking the chapel, but David's great-grandmother, Violet, decided to replace the balustrade with a wall of mirrors. It's exceptionally long anyway – 131 feet – but the mirrors mean that, when you're in it, it appears double that length.

The walls are hung with Mortlake tapestries which Theresa thought would make a good backdrop for the wedding photographs, and she was right. Everything at this point was a bit of a rush. The photos needed to be done quickly so that people could start coming in for the champagne and canapés. David and I went to the top of the landing where the guests were announced by a Master of Ceremonies outfitted in red. Without him I don't know how I would have coped. I knew hardly anyone, and I had little hope of remembering even people I had in fact met as I was so keyed up. It was obviously different when the Welsh relations arrived, but there I was faced with a different problem in that I had to stop myself giving a hug to each and every one. It was as if I was on stage: I was wearing a costume, so I felt I had to act in a way that was appropriate to the role.

And then, as if by ducal command, the haze lifted and the Master of Ceremonies invited guests to assemble in the garden, it being time for speeches. Close family, together with Simon Gourlay and Charles and Suzanna Welby, went out onto the cannonade, a wedge-shaped structure above the lawn like a thrust stage, where Susanna's hat completely stole the show. It was like a flying saucer made of woven straw above an equally dashing outfit of chiffon pink silk.

Simon made the perfect speech – less about me and more reflecting our family's love of Radnorshire and the life we led there. The best man's speech raised a laugh when Charles admitted that he wasn't first choice. What he didn't say, but which I thought he might, was how there had been a last-minute scare when David lost the wedding ring, which subsequently turned up in his trouser pocket. The ring was made from a nugget of Welsh gold, and a gunsmith that David knew had introduced him to a goldsmith in Birmingham who turned it into a simple band.

Tables for the wedding breakfast had been set up both in the Ballroom and the State Dining Room the previous day. Now it was the turn of the Regent's Gallery. And while the speeches were going on outside, inside a military operation was underway to quickly set up and lay the tables.

Just before we took our places, I had a very special moment with my brother, captured for all time in a photograph that, even now, gives me goosebumps when I see it. We had lived together at Croase Farm for seven years and although both of us were fiercely independent and our temperaments were like chalk and cheese, we had become very close. When we were children, I was happiest out on the moors riding my pony, whereas William was happiest fishing and he would stay out for hours, just casting his line over and over again, or tying intricate flies made out of feathers and fur. I don't remember now exactly what he said – possibly nothing more than, 'Oh, Em' – but as I looked into his eyes it was as if he knew that I had entered another world. At the same time, however, I felt he had a great sense of pride in my decision.

No wedding day is complete without dancing, and ours was no different. A stage had been set up in the big bay window in the Regent's Gallery and we danced to Lord Colwyn's Band. This is not a made-up name like Screaming Lord Sutch – Anthony Hamilton-Smith really is the 3rd Baron Colwyn (and also a dentist). My mother had heard them play at a hunt ball at Ludlow and they were perfect, running through all the old songs with wit and verve.

When it came time to leave, I had planned to wear the cape that came with the dress, but Theresa said it wasn't grand enough, so lent me a much more luxurious one in black velvet. As for confetti, it's every groundsman's nightmare, so Frances had filled enormous baskets of potpourri, which did the same job, people throwing handfuls of dried rose petals at us as we made our way through the gun hall to the waiting Rolls and set off for Stapleford House, just twenty minutes away.

Next morning, we should have gone straight to London for our flight to who-knew-where, as, in time-honoured fashion, our honeymoon destination remained a secret. It gave Frances an enormous shock, therefore, when the Rolls-Royce crunched to a halt in front of the castle. This was a complete change of plans and definitely not the done thing, but I desperately wanted to chew over the wedding with Mum and Dad: What did you think of this? What did you think of that? There were no mobile phones, so I couldn't even warn them we were coming. We just rocked up! After all, isn't half the fun of a party talking about it afterwards?

Then it was down the A1 to London and a night at the Turf Club. David's thinking was that, now we were married, we could stay there, so we should stay there. But, sadly, girls were still *personae non gratae* and not allowed to walk up the front stairs, so I had to go in the lift . . . I had never been to David's club before and I was truly shocked. Everything was in need of a facelift, more so in fact than the Farmers' Club. That night as we lay in our less-than-comfortable bed in our less-than-luxurious room, I was beginning to see the contrasts of my new life.

Everyone has a tale to tell about disastrous honeymoons, but if my parents are anything to go by, they are no indication of how a marriage will turn out. They were married in 1962 and had their honeymoon in Positano on the Amalfi Coast. While my mother's olive skin goes brown at the first hint of the sun, my father's Celtic complexion, pale and freckly, just burnt, so he spent most of the honeymoon in their hotel bedroom, red as a lobster, watching through binoculars as Mum was being chatted up by sun-bronzed Italians.

Our honeymoon was far from disastrous, because as long as I was with David, I was happy. Looked at dispassionately, however, it could have been better. Our first stop was Florida, where we hired a car and drove down through the Florida Keys to a hotel recommended by David's Uncle Brian, which turned out to be a golfing hotel. Not only did neither of us play golf, but the place was completely deserted. However, the sun shone and I was happy just lying by the pool working on my tan and feeling smug in that just-married way. Next stop, Washington, where David was keen to visit the National Air and Space Museum. I have to admit that looking at aircraft carriers is not top of my list of things of interest, but I let it wash over me and David was as happy as a flea. Things began to look up when we arrived in the Blue Ridge Mountains in Virginia, specifically the Red Fox Inn in Middleburg, a historic tavern that dated back to 1728, beautiful and romantic and good food. What more can a besotted pair of newlyweds ask for?

Lastly, we flew to Charleston, which proved the highlight of the trip. The origins of Charleston are even older than Middleburg, founded in 1670 when Charles II was on the throne and America still belonged to the British Crown. We stayed with a family friend in an old colonial house, which luckily was undamaged by the hurricane that had ripped through the city a few months earlier, though the destruction was evident everywhere we went. To round off our stay, David took me on a romantic drive in a horse and carriage into the historic centre, but there was a thunderous downpour and insane winds and my abiding memory is of the horse rearing up on its hind legs and my thinking, *That's it. We're going to die!*

As our plane began its descent into Heathrow and I looked out at the immaculate patchwork of fields that is so uniquely England, I wondered to myself what the future held in store. One thing was sure: a chapter was over, and another was about to begin. My life from now on would be very different from anything that had gone before.

Chapter Eight
Home From Home

THE LAST FEW months – even the last year – had been a heady time. Now, the euphoria over, it was time to get on with real life. The plan had always been to live in one of the houses on the estate once we were married, but before the wedding it hadn't seemed that pressing to make a choice. After all, we would have David's flat in the Old Saddlery. It had been decorated by one of his old girlfriends and was quite 'designery', with lovely Colefax and Fowler curtains. That would do until we'd made up our minds.

I had never given much thought to our future domestic arrangements, but I imagined that Mrs Pacey would go and that I would take over. In fact, I had been looking forward to the usual housewifely things, particularly breakfast chit-chat with no clattering of saucepans coming from the kitchen. But no. Mrs Pacey would appear in the morning – dropped off by Horton, one of whose jobs was to pick up staff who lived in Woolsthorpe and the other Belvoir villages – to make breakfast and would stay until Horton arrived to pick her up at around five. It wasn't really about Mrs P as such. I just missed having my own space.

As flats go, the old Saddlery was really quite big. It took up the whole of the top floor and had a wide hall, a drawing room large enough for a dining table as well as sofas, a study, a bathroom and a kitchen. The kitchen was functional but basic. Immediately inside the door was a small drop-leaf table where David and I would have breakfast which was separated from the business end – Mrs P's domain – by a peninsula.

The only time I ventured into the kitchen was to make supper, which I would spend hours planning, poring over cookery books, then wandering around Safeways in Grantham to get the ingredients and finally – once Mrs P had gone – cooking it, making sure I didn't leave any mess.

If there were guests for dinner, she would be the one in charge, and the pheasant casserole, or whatever it was, would be put on a marble-topped console table on a hostess tray to keep warm, while she'd be in the kitchen clearing up.

I knew that David liked everything just so, and it turned out that Mrs Pacey shared this obsession. If I put the mustard back in the wrong part of the fridge, I'd get admonishing looks from her and what amounted to a dressing down from David. Yes, it was his home, and we all have our little quirks, but I was his wife, so it was my home too. He had promised to endow me with all his worldly goods, but apparently not the right to decide where to put the butter.

It wasn't as if I didn't have an eye for detail – when you're re-designing somebody's house and they're spending a fortune on, say, a Cole & Co wallpaper at £100 a roll, you can't afford to make mistakes. But whether you place the pepper to the left or to the right of the salt surely shouldn't be a hanging offence.

I soon came to realize, however, that they had their own routine, almost like an old married couple, and saw no reason that that should change. After all, Mrs P had been looking after David for seven years, ever since he'd moved out of the castle, and to some degree she had been his surrogate mother. In fact, she didn't look dissimilar to Frances; she was quite as glamorous and had the same aura about her of command and the same confident way of holding herself. The first time I went to the Old Saddlery, I had assumed she *was* his mother.

It's not that I didn't like Mrs P, because I did. And I knew she liked me. Right from the start she'd thought I was 'the right girl' for David. And I think in some strange way she felt indebted to me for having stayed the course. And now here I was, a new bride who felt more like an awkward guest than a wife. In a way she was like David's guard dog, but she also wanted to look after me.

In those first months, largely through trial and error, I learnt what David liked to eat, from rollmop herrings to my own home-made pâté, and fish and chips from a van that parked up in Woolsthorpe every Thursday.

But, like a dog shut in all day when his master is at work, I fretted. How was I supposed to pass my time? We had no garden of our own, there were no dogs to walk. I'd sold my half of the business to Janet, so I no longer had a job – a job that I enjoyed, which involved meeting people, helping them make decisions, seeing something through from a pencil sketch on the back of an envelope to the finished project – and now I had literally nothing to do. Apart from making supper, brushing my teeth twice a day was the most energetic thing on my schedule. It got to the point where I'd wait for both David and Mrs P to go out before I'd surreptitiously get out the Silvo and the Marigolds and attack some of the silver we'd been given as wedding presents. Because if David saw me, he'd tell me that was a job for Mrs Pacey.

I found it increasingly difficult to sleep through the night. I'd nod off immediately only to wake up at midnight and spend the next three hours staring at the ceiling. When I did finally get back to sleep, I'd be woken by Mrs Pacey hoovering or wanting to make the bed.

Sleep deprivation doesn't make you a nice person, and I was pretty horrible to be around during this time. Mrs P worried about me as much as David and did her best to help me to relax. She'd get me to lie down and tried to teach me how to meditate, seeing it as a kind of medication in itself, but I never managed it.

Mrs P's background wasn't straightforward. She was born in 1934 and never knew her father. He had come over from Malta, started courting her mother, but then totally disappeared. The birth was kept secret, as being born out of wedlock brought shame on the family, so she was brought up by her grandparents. Her mother had stayed in her life for a few years, probably in the guise of an older sister, but then she too left. Mrs P had lived with the stigma all her life. They say that what doesn't kill you makes you stronger, and those difficult early years had given her enormous pride.

She held her head up high and allowed nobody to put her down. No one was going to make her feel like that ever again.

For David, of course, my insomnia was a mystery. Life hadn't changed for him and nor did he want it to. But he hated seeing me unhappy and hated even more having his nights disturbed by my pacing up and down or putting on the bedside light in the hope that reading something would help me nod off.

I don't think I was depressed as such, but I felt anxious all the time and my head would be spinning. I registered with a GP and he gave me some pills. And when I told him they weren't working, he told me to 'just take some more'. I felt I had lost my identity, lost my purpose. I mean, what was I for?

The one joy in my life was exercising Penny, the bay hunter David had given me as a wedding present. She had belonged to a Migs Greenall, a legend in the foxhunting world, who by then was in her eighties. Migs was as tough and leathery as they come, both physically and mentally. In fact, it was an ancestor of her former husband who turned the Belvoir foxhounds from a private pack, run originally for the benefit of the dukes of the day, into a public one, so that hunting with the Belvoir became open to all.

Penny was about 15.3 hands and full of character. I kept her at livery with Mick Toulson in Barkestone-le-Vale. Mick was a real personality with a strong Nottinghamshire accent, and both Theresa and Susannah Constantine kept their horses with him, as did Princess Margaret's son David Linley, who was then going out with Susannah. In fact, Mick seemed to have a monopoly on all the great and the good in the area.

I had ridden with the Teme Valley hunt ever since Gay Lady came into my life when I was about fifteen, but I hadn't realized just how different the Belvoir would be. In Radnorshire there weren't any fences or hedges to speak of. We'd just gallop the hills, from Offa's Dyke up onto Radnor Forest and open moorland. My most pressing problem was always to work out how to get Gay Lady back to Heartsease at the end of the day.

With the Belvoir it was more like the Charge of the Light Brigade. There might be twenty or thirty horses coming at a fence, and it was terrifying. I was a perfectly proficient horsewoman and could ride just about anything with four legs, but I hadn't done much jumping. Down in the Vale it was hedge after hedge, like a never-ending point to point, one jump following another in quick succession. Seasoned hunt riders take it all in their stride and just think, *Get on with it*. But that wasn't me.

Hunting isn't just something rich people do for fun. For stock farmers foxes are vermin and controlling them is essential if they are to protect their animals. Cubbing is the simplest way to keep numbers down as, although the cubs do run, they're easily caught. As the name suggests, it's about killing that summer's brood and is seen as a warm-up, a way of teaching young hounds how to stay in the pack and not run off. In fact, it helps everyone – horses and riders to get them saddle-fit, ready for the upcoming season. Cubbing can only start once the harvest is over because the last thing a farmer needs is a pack of hounds and galloping horses tearing through his wheat.

Over the previous five weeks I'd been out cubbing every Saturday on Penny, and so I'd had a certain amount of practice, but it was still with a mixture of excitement and trepidation that I set off early one November morning to the opening meet of the Belvoir Hunt at Croxton Park, about five miles from the castle, and Mick Toulson came with me. Just like at Knighton every Boxing Day when we'd meet up in the car park behind the Regency Hotel, sausages and port were handed around before the off.

It was a beautiful day, and we'd assembled at Croxton (pronounced Crowson) by the three-tiered lakes, put in originally by the canons of Croxton Abbey to keep carp, which they ate on Fridays when meat was forbidden. The abbey was dissolved in 1538 – just one of hundreds of religious houses that were shut down during the reign of Henry VIII. No visible signs of the abbey itself remain, because it and the land that went with it were acquired by the 2nd Earl who was then building the second (Tudor) castle at Belvoir, on top of the ruins of the first Norman one, and most of the abbey stone would have been used in the reconstruction.

It's also said that King John's heart is buried somewhere in the vicinity. The king died in 1216 in Newark and was given the last rites by Adam, Abbot of Croxton. He was to be buried at Worcester, two hours away now by car, so possibly several weeks back then. The viscera – heart, liver and other 'entrails' – would have been removed before this long journey as they would have putrefied quickly, particularly in a corpulent man, which John is reputed to have been. Abbot Adam would most likely have taken the most valued – the heart – to be kept at the Abbey, but where it is now is anybody's guess.

Then we were off, Mick tucked in behind me, and for a while all went well until we came to a tiger trap, a manmade wooden A-shaped jump over a ditch. Behind me I heard Mick call out, 'Go on, kick on.' I hate being at the front, but now was no time to worry about that. Just as I was going into the fence, kicking her on, another rider cut in from the right, Penny lost her stride and almost fell into the tiger trap. Somehow she got through, but I fell off while she galloped on. I curled up in a ball and scrambled to the side as the hunt continued to jump over me, and as landing hoofs thudded around me, I remember thinking, *I'm going to die*. They were going at such speed I don't think they even saw me.

Having seen what had happened, Mick had gone after Penny and brought her back, and he said 'Hop on' with such authority that I did. I jumped a few more hedges but I was in agony. Somehow I managed to ride to the horsebox, dismounted, handed her over to Mick, crawled into my car, then drove back to the flat, where I lay down on the sofa. I assumed whatever I'd done would get better on its own, but three weeks later I was still flat on my back when Anne Hill-Wood popped in to see me to talk about Knipton Lodge, a house on the estate where she lived with her elderly mother which she ran as a smallholding. As it was just the two of them, she'd offered to move to somewhere smaller so that David and I could have it.

Anne was a real animal person, a wonderful country woman who raised greyhounds and whippets and took in abandoned dogs. Anyway, she took one look at me and said, 'That leg's not right,' asked where the phone was, went into the kitchen, and then I heard her dialling. By that afternoon I was in the Park Hospital in Nottingham, and on the operating table that night. All three ligaments in my leg had snapped.

John Webb was a charming Welshman who after training in spinal surgery in Oswestry had gone on to set up the centre for spinal studies and surgery at the University Hospital in Nottingham. I could not have been in better hands. As for his bedside manner, we chatted about Welsh rugby.

Across the corridor was another casualty from the hunt and the next morning he screeched out, 'All right, old girl? See you out on Saturday!' And I thought, *Not me, you won't. I will never jump again.* And I never have. I'll go out with the Belvoir, trot along at the back with the ladies with cake and sloe gin in their saddle bags, I will go through gates, but I will never jump again.

I spent my first Christmas as the Marchioness of Granby in a plaster cast. But at least plans for a proper home were moving fast. Anne Hill-Wood and her mother had moved out of Knipton Lodge. Although incredibly run-down, underneath the peeling wallpaper and general grunge was a very pretty regency house, built as the farmhouse for the model farm designed by Elizabeth as part of her remodelling of Belvoir. It had five bedrooms, potentially a beautiful garden to the rear, and there was even a cottage for Mr and

Mrs Pacey at the bottom of the garden, which meant Mrs P wouldn't be under my feet the whole day, while Mr P would be our gardener. What clinched it for me was the cream-coloured Aga in the kitchen. Knipton would be my Heartsease, I decided. As if by magic, my anxiety disappeared. Like Elizabeth, I would start my marriage with a project, a remodelling of an earlier house, albeit on a smaller scale.

I had always wanted a large family. Although I was only one of three, Mum was one of five whereas Dad was an only child, and it had always saddened me that he didn't have the fun of cousins that we had through Mum's large family at Knill. Having so many cousins was one of the great pleasures of my childhood. So I was delighted when I discovered I was pregnant shortly after Christmas. This would be the first grandchild on both sides, so everyone was thrilled. Later, putting the dates together, I realized with horror that I'd actually been pregnant when I'd taken that tumble with Penny, yet somehow this new life forming inside me had clung on – even if I hadn't been able to.

The pregnancy made it even more urgent to get Knipton Lodge done sooner rather than later. The house was in a very tired state as for many years Anne and her mother had lived in only two rooms, and the decision was made that it had to be gutted. Each day I would go and take a look at what progress was being made. Walls were coming down; walls were going up. The whole place was being rewired, and a kitchen was being created at the back of the house because I wanted to be able to see out over the garden. The renovation of Knipton Lodge was also my introduction to the estate's enormous workforce, which, up until that point, I had no idea even existed. Getting to know the plumbers and carpenters and electricians, I felt reinvigorated, not least because it gave me a real understanding of the community that Belvoir supports and which itself supports Belvoir.

My mother-in-law was also very encouraging, particularly about getting the planting sorted out, as a garden can't be hurried, she explained. I knew nothing about gardens or gardening but, just like other Rutland duchesses before her, my mother-in-law did. Roses were a particular interest to Frances and she loved going on trips to nurseries and garden centres to find new ones. I always remember our first outing, which became the template for all those that followed. Dispensing with the services of Matthew, who usually drove her, we set off together in her Subaru, with a picnic in the back. Our destination was Attleborough in Norfolk, home to rose grower Peter Beales' famous nursery, then we went on to Mannington Hall, a glorious moated castle with stunning roses so I could see just what could be achieved. It also gave me an insight into the work involved in running a country house. Another of our jaunts was to Albrighton in Shropshire, to the nursery of that other great rosarian, David Austin.

As for furniture, there was plenty in the castle, Frances assured me, and she took me up staircase after staircase into various towers, with dedicated rooms filled with everything from chests of drawers, wardrobes and beds, to carpets, curtains, lamps, vases and even chamber pots, most of which dated from Elizabeth's time, when she'd been faced with furnishing the entire castle and had employed Mr Gillow, of Waring & Gillow, to oversee it. He had a brought with him a team of carpenters who stayed working at Belvoir for as long as it took.

Frances had a great eye for what would work where, and putting together Knipton Lodge as a family home felt like a real joint effort. David always teased me that my 'dowry' was the Welsh dresser, my grandmother's farmhouse kitchen table and the five chairs I brought with me from Heartsease, and they, as far as I was concerned, would take pride of place.

In a subtle way, Frances was beginning to teach me what it meant to be the Duchess of Rutland. For example, she took me clothes shopping in London and guided me through the kinds of outfits I might find useful. I had always been a bit off-beat in my dress sense, and we'd often go back to M&S in Oxford Street where I'd bought that unfortunate airhostess dress. But she could also splurge. She once bought me the most extraordinary beaded evening dress with a price tag of over £500. I nearly died.

The summer of our engagement year, I had watched Frances present prizes at the Bakewell show in Derbyshire. To my horror, shortly after we were married, it was the new Marchioness of Granby who was invited, and I was absolutely terrified. I had nothing remotely suitable to wear, so I had gone to a second-hand shop and found a dress that equated to my idea of what a Marchioness should look like, and borrowed one of Susanna Welby's more sober hats, so that at least I'd look the part. Once I'd written out what I was going to say, the fear subsided. I had the costume,

I had the script, and the rest was simply the performance. And I knew I could do that.

David came with me and we stayed the night at Haddon Hall as Bakewell was only a few miles down the road. Although it was August when the family were normally in residence, for some reason they weren't and while Mrs Whitaker was there to greet us, there was nobody else, and she clearly felt quite aggrieved at having to put us up.

There is always damp in the air at Haddon, and that night it felt even damper than usual, particularly the sheets, as I suspect the beds hadn't been aired. We were put in a fabulous room, the bedroom that Lord John and Lady Mary used. As the younger brother, Uncle Johnny, as he was known, had the right to live there during his lifetime. It all felt quite odd – David and I had dinner on our own, and I suspect the cook had been brought in just for the two of us.

Later, lying in bed, I had the strangest feeling that I was being watched, a real sense that someone was looking at me. I'd never had that at Belvoir and I didn't sleep a wink. But the following morning, looking out of the most exquisite Elizabethan window, mist rising over the River Wye as the dawn came up, it was incredibly romantic. I thought of all those women, down the centuries, who, like me, opened the window to air the room, and paused, like me, to breathe in the clean unpolluted air of the Peak District, and looked out at exactly the same scene, and with exactly the same emotions. I felt extraordinarily privileged just to be there.

As for my speech, David said it went down well and that

he felt very proud of me. It might not have been as flawless and elegant as Frances's the previous year, but I realized that didn't matter, because she and I were different people. I didn't have to copy anyone. I could be me.

A year on, I wasn't going to Bakewell or anywhere else, as by now I was the size of a bus. In terms of the nursery, I had Mrs P guiding me through all the steps, but, not wanting to tempt fate, I left the decorating as late as possible. As we didn't know if I was having a girl or a boy, I opted for a blue and yellow colour scheme and got everything in the way of equipment from Jessops in Nottingham.

As for names, we had settled on Montagu if it was a boy and Violet if it was a girl, after the 8th Duchess, David's great-grandmother, whose role in the design of the garden I had recently begun to appreciate. Mum was absolutely horrified when I told her. 'But that's the name of the cook at Brampton Bryan!'

As for Knipton Lodge, there was a concentrated push to get it finished before the baby arrived, and I became very aware of how much this must be costing. Whatever we needed, the next day someone would be there to sort it. Everyone working on the house was employed on the estate and not for the last time I wondered how much it cost to keep Belvoir afloat. And what were these people doing the rest of the time when they weren't at Knipton?

David and I moved into the house in July 1993, a month before our baby was due. I was flooded with relief and gratitude. To finally have somewhere we could call our own, where nobody was going to tell me what to put where, felt like a weight had been taken from my shoulders. Upstairs, the nursery was painted and ready for its little occupant, whoever he or she would turn out to be, and in the kitchen our puppy Pagan, daughter of my beloved Lottie, rushed around in her puppyish way and it felt like home. I decided the spirit of Heartsease was alive and well.

With all of my pregnancies, at the slightest twinge, I went straight to hospital. I was determined that my baby would be delivered by a professional, someone who knew what they were doing. Frances had wanted me to have it privately in London. But here I put my foot down. For all the obvious reasons, I wanted to be closer to home, and as Nottingham City Hospital was less than half an hour's drive away, that was good enough for me. At the sign of my first contraction, I climbed into the back of my Volkswagen Scirocco and Mr Pacey was summoned from his lawnmower and drove me while David followed behind with his mother in the Rolls. As planned, he called my parents before we left Knipton, so I had the comforting thought that just as we were in full dash across the Vale to Nottingham, they were doing exactly the same thing from Radnorshire.

Although I was determined to have the baby on the NHS, we had asked to have a private room. By the time I was in bed, having had the usual tests and examinations, Mum and Dad had arrived and were pacing up and down with David and Frances, the four of them wearing out the linoleum, as each contraction came and went. When the baby showed no signs of wanting to come out, Dad took matters into his own hands.

'Right,' he said. 'I'm taking everybody for a Chinese,' then, turning to me, added, 'If you were a cow, you'd go into the corner of the field and give birth when it's all quiet. It's not going to happen with all of us standing around.'

So when, less than two hours later, I pushed my baby into the world, it was just me, a midwife and the obstetrician Mr Tyack, who said: 'You've got a beautiful little girl.' I sensed a slight hesitation when he said it, as if this wasn't the news he thought I wanted to hear, that I would be upset that my first child wasn't a boy, but he needn't have worried. I had given birth to a healthy and utterly beautiful daughter who was perfect in every way.

People sometimes ask me whether I was disappointed that David wasn't there for the birth. Quite the contrary. I was extremely relieved.

When my parents, David and his mother eventually returned, their excitement was palpable. David was spellbound and couldn't stop gazing at her. She was as delicate as her namesake flower and even Mum, unsure whether to laugh or cry so ended up doing both, had to admit that Violet suited her perfectly. Dad, meanwhile, was simply relieved that all had gone well. As for Frances, she was clearly utterly besotted.

'Look, David! She's got Granny's hands.'

I stayed a further two nights in hospital, learning how to breastfeed and how to change a nappy. But being tucked away in my private room soon lost its appeal, so I took to eating my meals with fellow new mothers on the ward, hoping there might be someone I knew from my antenatal class who I could chat to, but there wasn't.

'So, is your husband coming in to see you this afternoon?' I asked one woman in an effort to get a conversation going.

'Oh, I have no idea who the father of this one is,' she replied.

So then I tried another tack. 'How are you finding breast-feeding?'

'They're making me try,' she said, 'but once I get out of this place, that's it. You get formula for free on the social, so I'm not going to bother.'

Three days later, David arrived to take us back to Knipton. I just loved being pregnant, loved having babies. I loved the whole process. But the magic was bringing the baby home, wrapping it up in a shawl exactly as Mum had done and looking after it myself. A complete and utter joy.

Like most new mothers, it took me a while to settle into a routine. Mum came to stay for a few weeks and filled the freezer with enough meals she'd cooked to last several months. David loved nothing more than to sit and stare at our little miracle for hours on end, though when she cried or needed her nappy changing he made a swift exit. Under duress he had agreed to attend antenatal classes with me, but only came once – and not one of the sessions involving hands-on help. Meanwhile, Mrs Pacey was there at the end of the garden. Having had five children herself, she was a reassuring presence. However, one day when Violet wouldn't stop crying and Mum and I tried all the usual remedies, Mrs Pacey put a dummy in her mouth and the crying stopped immediately. I was impressed. Mum, on the other hand, was horrified.

'None of my children had dummies,' she said. There was definitely an element of benign competition.

Inevitably the moment came when she had to leave. I

was pegging out nappies on my whirligig washing line, which, in spite of disapproving looks from Mrs P as not being quite the thing, I had been determined to have, as we had one at Heartsease. Throughout her stay Mum was always batch cooking and filling the freezer preparing for the moment when she would no longer be there. And now that moment had come.

'Right,' she said, giving me a bright smile. 'Better leave you now. I must be off.'

I watched her walk to the car, pulling her suitcase. She opened the boot, put her suitcase in, then turned and, giving a little wave, got in, started the engine and slowly pulled away.

It was just heartbreaking seeing her go like that. For all my life she had been there for me, and I knew that in many ways she still was. But I felt suddenly incredibly empty and thought, *That's it, then. I'm on my own now.*

After Mum left, Mrs Pacey would come over every evening to do the night shift to give me a few hours' uninterrupted sleep. During the day, I would have expressed enough milk for Violet's night feed. It was like having a monthly nurse and I couldn't have done it without her. A real team effort.

Over the years I had no problem getting pregnant. My problem was keeping them. I had five miscarriages and I really struggled carrying boys. I realize that for most women in that situation, it's devastating, but I felt it was nature's way of ensuring that only those babies with a good chance of surviving would last the full nine months, a matter-of-fact approach that owes more than a bit to being brought up on a farm, where sentimentality is as rare as hens' teeth.

At six weeks, Violet had her first jab and had a bad reaction to the extent that she was put on antibiotics. As she got over that, we pushed on with the other jabs, but then in November she had stopped putting on weight and couldn't keep anything down. When her breathing became laboured, that was it. We ended up in Queens Medical Centre, part of Nottingham University Hospital, with Violet on a little ventilator machine while I slept on the floor by her side.

Once again Violet was put on antibiotics and once again, Mum and Dad came up to help because I was shattered. We'd been given a little syringe and it took half an hour to get the requisite number of drops down. And she was still losing weight. She was still tiny, a scrap of humanity, only six months old, and I felt we couldn't continue to stuff her little body full of antibiotics, which in any case didn't seem to be doing any good. So I took her to see a herbalist in Mansfield who did a series of tests which suggested an allergic reaction to dairy, but also that she had candida in her gut which needed to be addressed.

Mum didn't believe a word of it because Violet hadn't been diagnosed by a doctor and she was horrified that I intended to follow the herbalist's advice and stop feeding her milk. Not surprisingly, having successfully brought all three of us up on milk fresh from our own cows milked by hand, first by Grandpa and then by Dad, they were firm believers that milk was the most natural and complete form of nutrition there was. But I stuck to my guns. Slowly but surely, I was learning to trust my own instincts.

It proved really difficult to wean Violet off SMA, which Mrs Pacey swore by. But, as I pointed out, SMA was still milk – albeit dried and with vitamins added – so I had no option but to get her onto solids as soon as possible. As for the candida, she was given revolting stuff which I mixed with fruit juice to camouflage the taste. It took time, but it worked.

It wasn't that I doubted modern medicine; it was rather a belief that we don't know everything and that my first responsibility as a mother was to protect my child, and if that meant exploring other, less conventional options, then I would, and to hell with what anyone else thought. David was behind me all the way, and that was all that mattered.

Chapter Nine
Another Wonderful Little Girl!

THE BIGGEST JOY I ever had was becoming a mum. But much as I loved being a hands-on mother, I knew I would never be happy as a traditional housewife, content to look after my husband, potter in the garden, join the WI, make jam and learn to play bridge. I had worked all my adult life and saw no reason to stop now. That left one outstanding question: what was I going to do? I had thoroughly enjoyed the interior design business with Janet, so the obvious thing was to build on that.

For as long as I could remember, I have loved fabric. There was a chest of drawers in the room I slept in whenever I went to Knill to stay with Granny, which was filled with leftover material, bits of lace, buttons, scraps of fur and feathers, and I would spend hours poking around in it. Granny made her own clothes and I think she kept these bits and pieces to trim her hats. She was of the generation who never threw anything away. Of course, there were also her 'finds' – chintz curtains from various stately homes, probably job lots that she'd bought at auction – which filled old leather suitcases up in the attic, and I could happily wile away a wet afternoon up there just rummaging through them. Then there were the trips that Mum and I would make to Hereford looking for dress material either for her or for me. Later on, one of the pleasures of advising clients after something with a bit more zing than John Lewis or Sanderson was exploring the world of expensive textiles which I would never have contemplated buying for myself as they were simply way outside my budget.

What if I could set up a no-frills warehouse selling these kinds of high-end fabrics at low-end prices? They might not be first quality, but I knew from experience that flaws in top-of-the-range brands – seconds – would be practically invisible to the non-professional eye. Also, as new ranges came on line every season, so older ranges would be phased out and remaining rolls discounted.

In the end I decided it just wasn't practical. If I was planning to spend most of the next ten or so years pregnant – and I was – lugging around rolls of heavy fabric wasn't to be recommended.

Exactly why I plumped for conservatory furniture I can't now remember, but I think it was Mum who said that Knipton would make the perfect showroom where people could come to look and then order. 'And when they're there, you can guide them on what colours would work, and once they trust you, they'll say, "Can you come and help me?"'

From a practical viewpoint it made perfect sense. Knipton Lodge had several outbuildings that could be used for storage, and the courtyard behind the house – the original farmyard of Duchess Elizabeth's model farm – was perfect for displaying them.

What I needed now was a partner, someone enthusiastic, someone who I could trust, and someone who would be able to hold the fort when I was otherwise engaged having a baby. Someone like Janet, who had a head for figures and could deal with accounts, which was still a disaster area for me.

Since the never-to-be-forgotten hen night, Nicola Smith and I had stayed in regular touch, and the more I thought about it, the more she filled all the criteria, including – crucially – that she was planning a move out of London back to Leicestershire, where she came from. The first thing, of course, was to sound her out. And bingo! It was three ducks in a row. Not only was she up for it, but her father Geoff said he wanted to invest. And he was an East Midlands businessman, both tough and astute, who had made his money in textiles.

I was absolutely convinced that we could work brilliantly together. Nicola had inherited her father's business sense, whereas my strengths were on the creative side. In Switzerland there had been a couple of glitches (e.g. the frozen cakes) but they had only demonstrated resourcefulness and imagination, exactly the qualities needed in an entrepreneur, and she knew by then that I was always going to push boundaries. Over the following months we spent many nights sitting round my granny's table in the kitchen at Knipton Lodge planning while I rocked Violet to sleep in my arms.

By the following year, our business plan was done. My

father-in-law had insisted on his lawyers going over our partnership contract and they had changed the 50/50 share to 51/49 in my favour. Spotting this, Nic's dad had wheeled in his own lawyers and, as I had always wanted, it was now an equal split. However, the Duke had been so impressed by the arguments put forward by Geoff's lawyers that he said he was thinking of changing, and how much had they cost? When Geoff cheerfully admitted that they'd done it for nothing, the Duke nearly had an apoplexy: 'Those bounders charged me £1,500!'

David agreed that the barns at the back of our garden would be perfect as a head office and showroom. Everyone accepted that I needed to be close to the house, but not actually in it.

So, without any hint of compromise, this had now been achieved. This was also a 50/50 operation, with Nic's parents as well as mine donning boiler suits to paint the barns, and we roped Frances in too. She had few opportunities to get stuck in, but the one area where she could was with horses. She was probably the best breeder of Arabs in the country. Like so many other women in her situation, she was actually very practical and she loved nothing better than going off in a lorry with the grooms, because it's a great leveller. She even learned Arabic.

The following year Nic and I went to all the appropriate trade shows and gradually built up a list of potential suppliers and manufacturers. Shortly after our wedding, Frances had taken me to the National Exhibition Centre where she would go to buy bits and pieces for the castle gift shop, and it had been a real eye-opener into how the commercial side of the castle worked.

Until then I had had no idea what running a shop in a stately home actually entailed. The sole trade fair I had been to before had been Decorex, the Interior Decoration Exhibition at Earls Court, which was very different. Going into the NEC Gift Fair was like walking into a chocolate factory. At every turn it would be, 'Ooh, what about that!'

Here Frances could indulge her unexpected taste for kitsch without any fear of censure by the good-taste brigade. For example, she was drawn towards anything that involved ostrich feathers. I remember a 'quill' ball-point pen for example – perfect for selling to children, which of course is exactly what you want in a gift shop. Fast turnover of small things that won't break the bank and yet add up.

There are stands selling the whole kit-and-kaboodle, from lavender sachets to pencil cases, tea caddies to lace nighties, novelty doorstops to miniature watering cans, quirky candles to Rubik's cubes. The NEC Gift Fair caters to every kind of shop owner, from garden centres to corner shops and everything in between, including stately homes.

Among the buyers there were always a considerable sprinkling of chatelaines of some of the country's most high-profile country houses, clearly visible from the way they dressed. I remember seeing the doughty Mollie Salisbury – the Marchioness of Salisbury – from Hatfield House, with her hair piled up and looking extraordinarily elegant and glamorous, although she must have been well into her eighties. She always looked as if she had stepped out of a Cecil Beaton photograph and had totally her own style.

Immediately outside of the main entrance – Hall 5 – a whole row of parking spaces was reserved for cars with chauffeurs, a phalanx of never less than a dozen: a mix of Rolls-Royces and Bentleys. That first time with Frances, we had gone in the Rolls with Matthew driving, and I hadn't realized what a privilege this was until Nic and I turned up in my Scirocco and were directed to a car park so far away that we had to get on the shuttle bus. The NEC is huge, and hugely exhausting; in the course of a morning you could easily walk ten miles.

It was the same for the garden furniture show which takes place there in early January. I always seemed to be in a state of advanced pregnancy at that time of year, and we were always parked miles from the entrance. I remember once being squashed on the shuttle bus and thinking, *Oh my God, my waters have broken and I'm going to have the baby right here!* One time we were in a hurry and forgot to note down where we'd parked and then spent hours traipsing around desperately trying to find where we left the car. I absolutely adore the NEC because, apart from anything else, it's completely classless. From duchesses to market traders, in that way it's a bit like hunting, and I have to thank Frances for introducing me to it.

Of course, no matter how good your product might be, the first thing a business needs is customers. Early on in the process I had a brainwave, or more prosaically a well-timed example of lateral thinking. Who needed conservatory furniture? People who had conservatories – preferably new ones that weren't already kitted out. And who would know who these people were? Local authorities. We managed to get lists from every council within a hundred-mile radius of Belvoir of people who had recently applied for planning permission. Then it was simply a question of hitting the phones, cold-calling these potential clients and persuading them that their lives wouldn't be complete without something from Parklands Conservatory and Garden Furniture.

Nic had always had the gift of the gab and I wasn't far behind.

We decided to launch the company on the back of a charity event Nic and I were hosting for the Church of England Children's Society to raise money for disadvantaged children. We did a ladies' lunch and a fair for them and we invited everyone we could, raiding the address books of both Charles and Frances and Nic's parents Geoff and Angie. One of the stands was the people who run Oka – I think it was the first one they had ever done. Another was the diet and exercise guru Rosemary Conley – a local Leicestershire girl-made-good who arrived in a Ferrari. Much to our excitement, she ended up ordering two colonial-style, lime-washed sofas with four matching chairs for her conservatory, which, from memory, we got covered in a beautiful blue-and-white fabric which looked fantastic – one of our very first sales.

At this point Mrs P came into her own. Now known as Nanna P, she would look after Violet while Nic and I worked, whereas David and Mr P were in charge of deliveries. Looking back now, those early days of setting up the business and juggling motherhood were probably some of the happiest times of our marriage. We both had a role to play and were creating something together, a successful formula I had witnessed with my own parents' marriage.

Having said that, I could never have done it without Nicola, because we were such mates. Every morning Nic would bounce in like a human dynamo. In the summer, after the last order had been chased and the last phone call made, we'd walk up to the castle and wind down with a swim in the pool, and have a cup of tea and a sandwich. We were young, we were full of energy and we were making money, all the while living in the perfect house in the middle of the most stunning countryside.

Nic was the sister I never had. We did everything together. Every summer at half term we would take the children to Jersey, to the St Brelade's Bay Hotel, and in one of those coincidences that you wouldn't believe if you read it in a novel, it turned out to be the same hotel where Nanny Webb would take David on holiday as a child. Even more improbably, the old-style Italian who acted as the maître d' and showed you to your table was the same guy who had welcomed my future husband all those years ago . . .

As for the castle, there was no sense of our living in its shadows – we couldn't even see it from the lodge. David and I were sitting having breakfast one morning when we saw a car heading down the drive with outriders, and when it came to a stop, I realized with a mixture of disbelief and horror that it was John Major, the then Prime Minister, and his wife Norma. Disbelief, as it seemed so unlikely, and horror because I wasn't yet dressed. I leapt into action, haring quickly upstairs to grab something to wear, seeing this as a serendipitous opportunity for a sale, realizing that the Majors were among the people I had mailshott as they'd recently applied for planning permission for a conservatory.

However, not everyone was impressed at our distinguished guests. David was in no great hurry to finish his toast. 'The prime minister can wait,' he said with suitable *hauteur*, taking another sip of his coffee. It became a family joke. Like one of those H. M. Bateman cartoons chronicling social gaffes: 'The Man Who Made the PM Wait.'

Inevitably, I was soon pregnant again, and again we were both delighted. The idea of another baby arriving just as the business was taking off didn't daunt me. After all, I had Nanna P to help and Nic to take over the reins while I went into hospital. This time, however, I decided to take the test, though why I cannot imagine as it made absolutely no difference except to silence those Eeyores who kept assuming that I was desperate for a boy. When anyone congratulated me on the pregnancy, I would announce proudly, 'Yes! And it's another wonderful little girl!'

I was very conscious of how Violet would react to the new baby, as I still remembered how much I had resented William's arrival when I was about three. As a mother of five, Mrs P had form in that department, and she recommended that I get a doll ready to give to Violet when she came to visit her new sister in hospital. And, when contractions began to become more than just twinges, Mr P put me in the back of the Scirocco before the waves became a tsunami. In my suitcase, along with my clothes and nightdress, I had packed a little doll, just as she had advised.

I had always longed to have a little sister when I was growing up, and had been so disappointed when Roger arrived that I dressed him up as a girl. Now Violet had Alice, and together we would go for walks up to the castle to see Granny and Grandpa Belvoir – me wheeling Alice in her 'baby carriage' and Violet wheeling her doll in a toy version I got at Jessops. For all the babies we were lent the sumptuous Rutland pram, which probably dated from the 1920s, perhaps even earlier and which Frances had given me on the arrival of Violet. Advertised as 'the Rolls-Royce of perambulators', it had amazing springs and huge wheels, with the family coat of arms painted on its side. It was so huge I could easily put them both in at the same time. The nursery bed linen had also been saved. Made of silk, it had been kept in acid-proof tissue paper and stored in trunks in the laundry room at Belvoir.

Alice was born on 27 April 1995, two days after Nic's birthday, when Violet was a little over eighteen months old, and I remember that time of year for all the blossom covering the trees. It was a wonderful spring, unseasonably hot, and I loved nothing more than putting the babies outside to sleep in their prams, just as my mother did with William and Roger. One afternoon, however, I went to pick Alice up and found she was covered in a red rash. I was terrified, convinced she must have meningitis.

'Nanna P!' I called out a state of total panic. Mrs Pacey came running down the garden path and took a good look.

'It's just prickly heat,' she said. 'She's probably too hot,' and calmly proceeded to take her little cardigan off.

I wasn't convinced. With the terrifying dash to hospital with Violet all too fresh in my memory, I called for an ambulance. The paramedics arrived, took one look and arrived at the same conclusion as Mrs P.

Just like Violet, Alice was a delicate child. The Hunt Kennels was always a favourite destination of ours for a walk – it was on the flat – and even better when the puppy show was on. Children have a natural affinity with young animals, and I knew Violet would love it. When David's Aunt Mary spotted us, she came over to inspect the brand-new addition and pulled back the blankets in the pram to take a closer look. Bending down, she pressed Alice's cheek very lightly.

'See this?' she said, pointing out a faint web of veins visible under her paper-thin skin. 'Blue blood.'

Mary was married to David's Uncle Johnny and they lived in a house on the estate that was within easy walking distance of Knipton. She would regularly drop into the lodge and take Pagan for a walk on Knipton Pasture, pushing the pram at the same time.

I had originally wanted to call Alice 'Lily' – the idea being that, like Violet, she should have a flower name. But Aunt Mary was appalled. 'You can't call a child "Lily", Emma, it's far too common.'

Frances and Charles were never going to be hands-on grandparents any more than they had been hands-on parents, but they had other qualities to offer. Charles was like the pied piper; these two little girls would follow him anywhere, while Frances had the knack of finding exactly what they wanted when it came to birthdays and Christmas, as well as a succession of frilled and furbelowed party dresses.

As for the hands-on stuff, I had the Paceys across the garden. However, as the girls got older, they learnt to take advantage, running down to Nanna P if I told them off, who would usually comfort them with sweets or an ice-lolly, which, of course, had me gritting my teeth.

Six months after Alice was born, I realized I was pregnant again. But one day, standing at the sink, with the girls playing round my feet, I felt a terrible, crippling pain that made me double up in agony. Something was wrong. Really wrong. I called the hospital and was told that Mr Tyack was seeing private patients that afternoon at the Park, so I could reach him there.

It turned out it was an ectopic pregnancy, which means that instead of adhering to the wall of the womb, the foetus was growing in one of my fallopian tubes. An ectopic pregnancy cannot survive, so there was no alternative, he told me, but to operate, and I was rushed into theatre for emergency surgery.

For someone desperate to get pregnant, an ectopic pregnancy is terrible. You feel pregnant – and you are pregnant – but there's no chance of the baby surviving. Worse, you lose one of your two fallopian tubes – the tubes that deliver an egg to the womb every month ready for fertilization – so your chances of conceiving are reduced by 50 per cent. After the operation Mr Tyack explained all this to me, but then added, 'So my advice, if you want to get pregnant, is don't waste time. You're at your most fertile immediately after an ectopic pregnancy.'

And this was exactly what happened.

It was during this fourth pregnancy that we went for a week's holiday to Norfolk. Although the business was doing well, money for extras was in short supply and so in exchange for lending our paddock out to a neighbour for her ponies, she let us use her holiday home on the Norfolk coast. By chance, Mum and Dad had some friends with a beach hut nearby, and they kindly said we could use it, which was an added bonus. So, off we went: a pregnant me, David and the two little girls, as well as Terry.

The one problem with the English summer is that you can't control the weather, and this particular week was a classic. But one day when the sun actually shone, I suggested we try out the beach hut, so we duly set off for Brancaster. When we arrived, however, it wasn't immediately obvious where the huts were. I had imagined a cheery row of paintbox-coloured doors looking out to sea, but these were rather more Farrow & Ball and faced inland on top of the line of dunes that separated golf links from the beach. To get there, we had to drive down the side of this very smart course and then trudge across the dunes to reach the huts, carrying buggies, carrier bags and the rest of the baby paraphernalia. So, nothing daunted, we staggered up and down, the wheels of the buggy getting stuck in the sand so that Terry and I ended up carrying it. But when we found the right hut, the key didn't work. I couldn't understand it.

'I must have got the number wrong,' I said. 'It must be one of the others.' There was nothing for it but to try every door. By now David was getting a bit tetchy, and even Terry had gone quiet. Finally I put the key in a lock that worked, and it was Open Sesame! To say it was worth the struggle doesn't begin to describe what we saw inside. In fact, it completely took my breath away: chandeliers, crystal glasses, even a bottle of wine chilling in the fridge! It was so luxurious that I felt slightly uncomfortable. David, however, was in his element and within minutes, while Terry went off to find some crab sandwiches, he and I were sitting out on the veranda watching the girls playing roly-poly down the dunes. It felt like a proper seaside holiday.

Suddenly we heard someone calling out David's name, and we turned round to see a woman of a certain age wearing a bathrobe emerge from between two huts where there were wooden steps leading down to the beach. She had obviously just been for her daily swim.

'It's Xenia,' David explained – a friend of Frances's.

'What a surprise!' she shouted out. 'I had no idea you knew the Kents!'

David and I looked at each other. The Kents? The Duke and Duchess of Kent? The Duke is first cousin to the Queen, and while it was quite possible that Frances knew them, we certainly didn't.

My mystified expression probably said more than words ever could.

'But, you're in their hut!' she exclaimed, as heads turned towards us from other verandas.

Terry arrived back with the sandwiches to find us hastily packing everything up, grabbing the girls' things, throwing everything into various beach bags, and I told him I'd explain later. It turned out that my parents' friends' beach hut was not in Brancaster but Old Hunstanton, four miles down the coast.

Eliza was born in July 1997. As always, I was taken to hospital by Mr Pacey, and Mum and David followed. This time Dad stayed on the farm. Although nothing appeared to be happening, it was decided to keep me in just in case. Then, without warning, just as David and Mum were leaving, my waters broke, and at the same time, I felt an incredible urge to push.

'Get a doctor!' I yelled

Moments later, Mr Liu – Mr Tyack having by now retired – came running into the room just in time to catch Eliza. 'Little Bright Eyes' he called her, and still does, a translation of the Chinese term for a baby that's born with its eyes open, seen as a sign of a gifted child.

This time I hadn't taken a test to determine the sex. I had been convinced I was having a boy because the pregnancy felt so different. No one within the family showed even the faintest hint of disappointment that I had delivered another girl, but not everyone was so tactful, however. Eliza must have been around two months old when I went to a hunt ball in Quenby Hall, a beautiful Jacobean house about halfway to Leicester. Although I wasn't dancing myself – far too tired – I still enjoyed watching and was sitting on the sidelines when a local dowager came over.

'So sorry to hear the news,' she said.

'What news?' I asked, feeling my heart start to race. Had somebody died? Had a car crash? Fallen off their hunter?

'That the new baby is another girl!'

I excused myself with as much dignity as I could muster and went upstairs to find somewhere I could be alone, managing to hold it together until I found a bed I could lie down on, and then I cried and cried. I think I must have cried myself to sleep, as I can remember nothing more about that night.

Since our Norfolk holiday, I had become used to seeing ponies on our paddock, and when they left, I missed their calm presence and decided to find some Welsh mountain ponies for my girls. Ponies have been roaming the Welsh moors and mountains since at least before the Romans arrived and are notably sturdy due to the harsh climate and minimal shelter available in winter. You can still come across wild herds roaming the moorland, but those that have been domesticated are divided into two categories, unromantically known as Section A and Section B. Section A are the smallest, very hardy and look like stocky mini Arabs. Betty, my first pony, was probably a Section A, whereas Tina, my second, was a Section B, which is bigger and with more athletic ability. In the past these ponies were used for everything from ploughing to carting as well as being ridden to market. I got my love of them from Uncle Ken, married to Mum's older sister Jean, who lived at Felin Fach, near Brecon.

Riding generally, and the Pony Club in particular, was so much part of my childhood that I really wanted my girls to have the same opportunity. So, one weekend back at Heartsease I scanned the *Hereford Times*, saw a classified ad for two ponies, and then, with the girls in tow, set off to take a look. We turned up in a scruffy field where a family emerged from their caravan and the son, who can't have been more than twelve, showed off by jumping from back to back between Casper, a Section 1, and a little Shetland called Lizzy. My girls were utterly mesmerized. We all fell in love in an instant and I bought them there and then, somehow convincing the owner to deliver them to Knipton Lodge. They arrived a week later along with all their tack, saddles and bridles.

I found it difficult to make friends during those first few years living on the Belvoir estate. The social circle I now found myself in – monied or titled or both – wasn't my natural habitat and I struggled to 'read' people, to work out who I could trust and who I would do better to keep at arm's-length. But, as so often happens, it's children who bring young mothers together, whatever their social class, and when Violet was just starting to walk I met Anna Wallace through Mick Toulson, as she kept her horse at livery with him.

Anna was a fantastic horsewoman, a three-day eventer and as fearless on the hunting field as I was fearful. She was known in the tabloid press as 'Whipper Wallace' and had hunted a lot with Prince Charles, achieving a certain notoriety as his last girlfriend before he married Lady Diana Spencer as she then was. By the time I met her, Anna was on her second marriage and had given birth to a daughter around the same time as I'd had Violet. So, I asked Anna and Ophelia to Violet's first birthday party.

She was entirely different from anyone else I had met in the Vale of Belvoir and instead of going home with the other mothers, we ended up drinking champagne, putting on some music and bopping around our hall with its lovely regency stairway, babies bouncing on our hips. Before long we would spend hours trotting them round on the backs of her ponies on a lead rein. To say that she and I were kindred spirits sounds like a cliché, but in Anna's and my case it was true. Like me, she wasn't afraid of bending the rules, and she revelled in the time she spent outdoors, but best of all, she loved having fun.

Although my childhood had been extraordinarily happy and my mother remained my touchstone for how to bring up children, I was determined that my girls would have more freedom to express themselves than was generally the case when I was growing up.

Even at three and five years old, my girls loved nothing better than being let loose in Woolworths where they would run wild picking out whatever clothes they wanted. We would regularly leave carrying bags of leopard-print leggings and miniature high-heeled shoes which surprisingly caused no stir at the castle when we would go there for Sunday lunch. Although this weekly ritual was not without its stresses, I was always grateful for the invitation, as it was the one meal I didn't have to cook each week.

Sunday lunch at Heartsease was rather different. Just as William, Roger and I had done when we were little, the girls would sit on Mum's kitchen floor banging pots and pans with wooden spoons. As they got older, they grew to cherish the differences between the two ways of life.

I had always made it clear that I would never abandon my Radnorshire roots, and by the time Eliza was a toddler I was organizing rides, staying at different friends' or relatives' houses along the way. I wanted my girls to feel a connection to the land, to be close to the earth.

We would start out at Heartsease, and Dad would have been mapping our route weeks in advance. The first night we'd all be camping in tents and the next morning we'd set off. Mums on foot lead-reining the smaller children and bigger ones running alongside. The following night we'd make camp at someone else's house where an advance party had already set up. Our trek would finish at Monaughty, a pile recently bought by Sophie Blain, who ran the Teme Valley Hunt, and whose children had joined the ride. The building had been a prison for many years and it had always felt spooky but now Sophie had breathed new life into it.

Back at the castle, Mrs Pacey wasn't getting any younger, and when Nic gave birth to a little girl herself, even Nanna P had to accept that we needed an extra pair of hands. So, while she continued to pitch in with things like the ironing, I got a live-in nanny to help. Lindsey Foster was only eighteen and I can still remember the day her father dropped her off with all her belongings. (He would later become our family chaplain.)

Nic's daughter Harriet was the same age as Alice, and from the moment the pair of them bounced in every morning, the three little girls would all play together under the watchful eye of Nanna P. Around this time I met another mother called Camilla Bowlby, who lived the other side of Grantham and when I heard how she was really struggling, juggling a job with two little boys, I said that she should drop them off with me, as by now I had a nanny and an au pair, not to mention Nanna P – so frankly the more the merrier. Next it was Nic's turn to add to our numbers, in the shape of Max.

It was such a joy to find that, without planning it, we had created this wonderful, happy childhood space, always ringing with laughter. In the back garden we had a little slide and a paddling pool for hot days, while inside we had the comfort of the Aga, and Pagan, our Labrador, played his doggy part. We would all join together to have bonfire and Halloween parties. Not only was it an idyllic childhood, but for Nic and me it was a lifesaver, as it allowed us to devote ourselves to the business without the guilt that so many working mums are saddled with, because we were only the other side of the garden.

The thorny issue of the importance of a male heir was never far from the minds of the older generation.

'Just douche with bicarbonate of soda,' one elderly busybody volunteered when she popped in for a cup of tea.

'Douche?' I said, puzzled.

She gesticulated between her legs, and I suddenly caught the drift.

In 1998, David, the girls and I were at Heartsease for Christmas, and on Boxing Day David got a call to say that his father had suffered a major stroke and was unlikely to make a full recovery. The duke was then seventy-nine, a few months short of his eightieth birthday, and over the last few years had been growing increasingly fragile, having been treated for cancer. The stroke had happened just before Christmas, and Charles had been taken into hospital but then pneumonia quickly set in and the decision had been made to bring him home as nothing more could be done. We packed up immediately, put the girls in the back of our people carrier, and headed back to Belvoir. On the way there, I clutched my stomach and thought I felt the hint of a kick. I was pregnant again and, as a rule, I never announced it to the world until the three-month danger point had passed. I knew that I had to tell my father-in-law, however, because it was clear that he wasn't going to live to see this baby born.

We dropped the girls off with Nanna P and then hurried

up to the castle where we found the Duke in bed, very weak, drifting in and out of consciousness. Frances was at her best when somebody was ill and she had now assumed the role of Charles's nurse, caring for him with such tenderness, sitting with him for hour after hour, moistening his mouth with a sponge dipped in water to keep him hydrated. I found it intensely moving. On our arrival, she set up a 24-hour rota so that he would never be alone, and during my turn to sit with him, I held his hand and told him about the baby. 'And this time,' I said, 'it's definitely a boy,' and was rewarded with a slight pressure of his fingers and the trace of a smile.

Charles Manners, 10th Duke of Rutland, CBE, JP, DL passed away on 4 January 1999. But during the previous ten days, it felt like a huge weight hung in the air at the castle.

David was well aware that upon his father's death he would become Duke, and though he loved our life at Knipton Lodge, I knew he had always hankered for the day he would return to his childhood home. And now it had come.

After an intimate service in the chapel conducted by the family chaplain, we followed the funeral cortège to Bottesford Church, where until the mausoleum was built on a hill overlooking the castle in 1826, previous generations of the Manners family had been laid to rest. Every stretch of the road or path was filled with villagers or tenant farmers who dipped their heads as we passed. When we reached Kennel Bridge, the huntsman, wearing a black armband, stood with his black-and-tan Belvoir hounds and played

'Gone Away' on his hunting horn. We continued driving, past silent crowds, past the residents of the Earl of Rutland Hospital Trust Building (the estate's equivalent of the Chelsea Pensioners), resplendent in their uniforms, medals polished and pinned proudly to their chests.

After the funeral, we returned to the castle for the wake, held in the Regent's Gallery, where we drank champagne and ate canapés and gave the Duke a fitting send-off. At one point his youngest brother, David's Uncle Roger, came over and we talked about the enormity of the task that lay ahead.

'You've got to remember,' he said, 'change is never easy in these families.'

Chapter Ten
The 11th Duchess

B ARBARA CARTLAND USED to say that my father-in-law was the most handsome man in Britain, and admitted that he was the prototype for many of the dashing heroes in her romantic novels. It was certainly true that he had a twinkle in his eye right to the end. But he was far more than that. He was clever and principled and believed in service. During the Second World War he served in the Grenadier Guards but from then on, the main focus of his life was protecting Belvoir and the countryside in general. He was a true countryman, an amazing shot and a wonderful fisherman. The East Midlands is essentially one vast coalfield, and in the 1970s, in the wake of the oil crisis, there had been a big push by the National Coal Board to sink 'super mines' in the Vale of Belvoir to offset the lack of capacity in old collieries. But the Duke was having none of it, and was tireless in his campaign to prevent both further exploration and exploitation. He famously said that he would lie down in front of any bulldozer that attempted to move in, and it became a slogan for the campaign. He was a magistrate and a powerful voice in Leicestershire and his views chimed with what local people wanted. Girls were soon wearing T-shirts saying, 'I will lie down with the Duke'.

My father, who was a pretty tough nut himself, said that Charles was one of the kindest, most humble men he had ever met. He would never buy a new pair of shoes if there was enough wear in the old ones. He never put on weight and continued to wear suits that he had had made as a young man. David has inherited his father's humility in terms of his possessions. He lives on fresh air and asks for very little.

After the funeral, I was approached by an unlikely couple; he was a stocky five-foot-six while she was well over 6 foot. They introduced themselves as Roy and Theresa, and they had come to pay their respects to the Duke, they said. I immediately knew who they were. Roy had been a cage fighter and leader of the local traveller community and one night, following a severe snowfall, their car had got stuck in one of the lanes around Belvoir. Charles had come across them and given them a lift back to their caravan in his Rolls-Royce. After that, the traveller community in the area would do anything for him. I remember when one of the keeper's dogs was stolen, Charles got in touch with Roy and the dog was returned immediately.

Foreigners in particular find the titles of the British aristocracy endlessly fascinating, and one of the first things Mr Liu asked after he successfully delivered Eliza was, 'What will you be when the Duke dies?'

'A duchess,' I said.

There's no big announcement, no ceremony. At the moment of my father-in-law, the 10th Duke's, death David automatically became the 11th Duke of Rutland, and I, as his wife, became the 11th Duchess.

Did anything change? Nothing and everything.

The reality of what it meant, of how it would impact our family, didn't hit me until it actually happened. Until then I think I genuinely didn't expect that anything would change in my lifetime.

Did Charles's death affect me? Yes, though more because of its effect on David than on me personally. I became anxious and sleepless, and with small children who want to jump on your bed when you've only just dropped off to sleep, that's hard. Frances recommended I go to see the acupuncturist in Grantham who had brought relief to the Duke during the last months of his life, and she certainly helped to calm my nerves.

It was as if I wanted to turn back the clock, to be once again Emma Watkins – a bit wacky, a bit left-field, a bit of a rebel. Most of all, I wanted to stay in Knipton Lodge, with our paddock and our girls and the Paceys at the end of the garden. For David, though, this was the moment he had been born for, and he couldn't wait to move into the castle.

My main concern in those first few weeks, however, was Frances. It was heart-breaking to see how she just seemed to collapse. And it was hardly surprising. She had lost her husband of forty years, the man who had supported her since she was twenty-one. Although she was expert at controlling her emotions, she was clearly shocked to the core. As for the castle, it was a huge place for her to ramble about on her own. Deep down she knew that she would have to move out, but it would be a process. She would need to come to terms with it in her own good time.

In an attempt to make things feel less cataclysmic, I told her that David and I loved being at Knipton Lodge and had no desire to move: 'So we're very happy for you to stay here as long as you want,' I said.

She gave me a withering look as if to say, 'You don't understand, do you . . .'

And I didn't.

Yes, the ultimate goal was that at some point in the not-too-distant future, David would claim his heritage and move into the castle. But first there would be a period of transition.

The following week, grey-suited advisers arrived from London with bad news tucked inside their briefcases. Yes, David had inherited Belvoir Castle, but he'd also inherited £11 million worth of inheritance tax.

As far as we were aware, there had been no preparation, no planning, no discussion whatsoever about what would happen when it would be our turn to take over. No mention of what we needed to know, how things worked, or who it would be sensible to speak to. We were utterly at sea and only had each other to rely on, which wasn't saying much. We already had a business of our own to run, three children at home and, of course, I was now expecting a fourth.

Frances's view was that we should leave it all to the experts, but they were not the ones who would have to make this work – we were. As is always the case when you have a body of people, some of these experts and some of the trustees were forward looking and helpful while others were a little stuck in their ways and seeking to maintain the status quo – but it seemed to me that the status quo would no longer work.

At the heart of the upheaval was the sudden drop in income occasioned by losing Haddon Hall, which had provided half, if not more, of the overall revenue. Haddon had been gifted to David's younger brother Edward in 1986. In the past, the tradition had been that the younger brother would have the use of Haddon in his lifetime, but it would remain the property of the duke. However, among owners of stately homes at that time, there was a general fear of what a Labour government could do in terms of raising inheritance tax, so Charles had decided to split the estate between his two sons, therefore giving Haddon to Eddie outright as a way of securing the property.

Eddie was the youngest of the siblings and, like many younger sons, he bore less of the weight of responsibility and was always great fun, his eyes firmly set on the next adventure.

Compared with the Leviathan that was Belvoir, Haddon cost very little to run. For a start, it was unlived in, whereas its income was far higher than Belvoir's because it lay at the heart of the Peak District, one of the most beautiful areas of England, visited by hundreds of thousands of tourists every year. Charles had also made over to Eddie three very profitable hotels, one of which was the Izaak Walton in Ashbourne and another was Monk Fryston Hall in the Vale of York, a glorious building dating back to the thirteenth century.

I might have run a small business, but Nicola always handled the accounts side of things, and I was utterly out of my depth with anything more complicated than a petty-cash box. Yet here I was having to understand the complex finances of a stately home. Firstly, everything was controlled by the trustees of the Belvoir Trust. A trust is like a locked money box and the keys are held by the trustees for somebody else's benefit – in this case the Belvoir estate – and only the trustees can decide what to do with whatever's in there.

To mitigate death duties, deals are done with the government. In exchange for paying a lower rate, you are obliged to open for a minimum of thirty days. Even the private apartments had to open from time to time to provide public access to the artworks. Like so much else in life, it's a trade-off.

It was only a few weeks after Charles's death that David and I attended our first trustees meeting. At that stage I didn't even know what a trust was. I remember sitting there in disbelief, thinking, *How am I ever going to get my head around this?*

When I was handed the accounts, the figures bounced up and down, just as they had done at school. It was quite literally a jumble. These London lawyers and accountants were no doubt rolling their eyes at this numbskull they were having to deal with. I didn't care what they thought of me. The only way I was going to find out was to ask.

'So what does all this mean?'

'Just leave it to them,' Frances said. 'They know what they're doing.'

'How much do we need to spend on the castle in the coming year?'

'Say a hundred thousand?' the agent suggested.

'I may be numerically challenged,' I said to David, 'but surely you can't just conjure numbers out of the air like that?' We left the meeting none the wiser about the castle's position financially than when we'd gone in. Nobody, it seemed, could fully explain the position to us.

From the little information we had been able to glean, it appeared that the castle's running costs amounted to roughly half a million pounds a year, and following the loss of Haddon Hall, the income was now limited to the profits from the home farm, the tenant farm and rents from houses on the estate that were let out.

What we hadn't yet realized was that visitor numbers had been steadily dwindling for years, after the sudden death of Jimmy Durrants who died tragically young some years before I came on the scene. He had been the beating heart of the castle's tourist operation, a huge character in every sense, tirelessly drumming up coach companies both here and abroad. So a decision had been made to rein it right back, open for far fewer days and concentrate efforts on that. But that decision led in turn to the closure of the Museum of the 17th-21st Lancers, which, as the regiment associated with the Marquis of Granby, had been housed at Belvoir for some time and which was legally required to be open 200 days a year. That in turn led to a further downturn in visitors.

In 1994 visitor numbers had suffered another blow when the Sunday trading laws were changed and people who might have enjoyed a family day out at Belvoir now went to B&Q and Homebase. Previously the castle hadn't really had to sing for its supper, because it was subsidized by Haddon Hall. Suddenly everything had changed.

David and I would lie awake at night worrying. It felt that our life had suddenly taken a huge handbrake turn. Up until then, we'd been able to push the castle into the background – it had felt as if it was nothing to do with us – but suddenly it was demanding to be front and centre.

I'd created this wonderful safe world at Knipton Lodge. Now it was as if a hand grenade had been tossed into our gentle, happy life and we were being forced to upend it all for something neither of us had chosen. What was clear was that, for better or for worse, David and I were in this together. Yet although we attended each meeting of the trustees, we remained as confused as ever, even down to the role of some of the trustees themselves.

The upside of being numerically illiterate was that I had a sixth sense of the broader picture and have always been able to do mental arithmetic, for example, dating back to the days in the school holidays when I'd go with Dad to Knighton market and he'd get me to work out prices in my head. It was only when I was faced with written numbers that my brain went into freefall.

One of the first things I suggested was that my father be seconded onto the board. He was one person whom both David and I trusted implicitly. Thank God, he immediately agreed. I clearly remember the first few times he came over to Belvoir to get a purchase on how everything worked and immediately felt that the farm required some significant updating to improve efficiency.

He proved to be a hugely important ally. He wrote an entire paper for the trustees on how they could support us better because we were, after all, the future. He felt pushed to do this because one of the trustees had the gall to say, 'The Duchess would be advised to return to the nursery to look after the children.'

During the early days of our marriage, I had tried to persuade the land agent to give David a department to run himself – farm, forestry, anything really – so that he could get first-hand experience of how the business worked. But my pleas had fallen on deaf ears. I now started to realize that the last thing some wanted was for someone from the family to start stirring things up and asking uncomfortable questions. Whether this was a deliberate attempt at obfuscation or simply Charles not wanting to burden David sooner than was absolutely necessary, we will never know.

Meanwhile, Frances was still in the estate office running things as she always had. I can't say I blame her. She was only sixty-two, still full of energy and in the prime of life, and in no rush to relinquish her authority. When everything around her was in turmoil, she was a point of continuity – a much-needed steady pair of hands. I had no idea of what 'belonged' to us, and what 'belonged' to Frances, or Eddie or Theresa come to that. What I should have done was arrange to see the lawyers privately and get them to explain it all in terms that David and I could understand, but the only time we ever met was around a board table, and that wasn't the forum to challenge things.

Nonetheless, it was now our responsibility – debts and all. The central dilemma was how to increase the income when the expenses were galloping away like a runaway horse. Perhaps Charles had been perfectly aware that the financial situation was untenable and couldn't be resolved in any straightforward, Micawber-like manner. ('Annual income twenty pounds, annual expenditure nineteen, nineteen and six, result happiness. Annual income twenty pounds, annual expenditure twenty pounds ought and six, result misery.')

One day, years before, when the Duke and I were in the picture gallery, he had pointed at some paintings and said, 'Most probably you'll have to sell some of these one day.' In fact, that was the only time I ever remember him refer-ring to us taking over. But my feeling that afternoon was, *So what? The walls are groaning with paintings. What difference would it make having one or two fewer?*

As for our own little business, I didn't see how we could continue running both it and the castle. In its small way it had proved a great success and we had already been approached by someone interested in buying us out. So Nic and I had a chat and we agreed that was the best option. But I didn't want to lose Nic herself as I knew that I hadn't a hope of doing what I wanted to do at the castle without people at my side who I could trust.

Six months after the death of my father-in-law, Mr Pacey was again called upon to take me to the hospital. However, this birth wasn't going to be as straightforward as the previous three.

'The position of the baby is not good,' Mr Liu announced

when he examined me. The contractions were coming thick and fast and the baby's heart was showing signs of distress. This was not the time to take chances, he said, and I was whipped straight into theatre for an emergency Caesarean. I had a vague sensation of a cut and some tugging, and seconds later, Mr Liu lifted up a beautiful baby boy, yelling at the top of his lungs.

Mum and Dad were all too aware what this meant to David, and Dad wasted no time in congratulating him, saying, 'Well done. You got there in the end!' The birth of an heir to a dukedom is no less momentous to a country estate such as Belvoir than the birth of an heir to the throne. To mark the occasion, seven cannons were fired from the castle (from the cannonade where the wedding speeches were delivered) and the flag bearing the Rutland coat of arms was run up the pole.

As usual, Dad was his usual pragmatic self. My near-permanent state of pregnancy had always been a concern, so now that I'd done my duty, he said, it was time to call a halt. 'So get yourself sterilized, Em.' Nice try, Dad, but no.

We named our beautiful new baby Charles, after his late grandfather. Like David before him, as heir apparent, he was now the Marquis of Granby. It always struck me that Charles looked a little shocked when he was born, as if he had been distressed by being torn from my womb rather more quickly than he would have liked, as if he wasn't ready to enter this world where so much was unsettled.

I spent a lot of those early weeks in tears, more so than I normally did after giving birth. Perhaps I was grieving that

Charles would not grow up at Knipton Lodge and enjoy the same childhood his sisters had. What was undeniable was that I would spend less time with him than I had with the girls.

While I certainly didn't feel ready to move into the castle, I think the safe arrival of her grandson had shifted something for Frances. 'You only grow to love these buildings if you grow up in them,' she told us. She had begun to accept that it was now time for her to leave, though it would be a good year before that happened.

But where were we actually going to live? In Charles and Frances's time, David and his siblings had been housed in the nursery wing presided over by Nanny Webb, miles from their parents. I wasn't about to have my children anywhere other than a few yards away, and certainly not on another floor. Suitably adapted, however, the old nursery wing – a suite of six rooms – could form the basis of a home, I decided. To say it was dilapidated is putting it mildly. It turned out that it hadn't been lived in since David and the other little Manners were there more than thirty years before, so everything needed to be done. But when I suggested that Nanny Webb's old bedroom could be our kitchen, David was horrified. It would be tantamount to desecration.

We were allocated a budget by the trustees and a team from the works' department started converting the wing ready for our arrival. Inevitably there were hiccups. A fragile wallpaper by the Crace family – interior decorators since 1691 – had to be painstakingly soaked and then detached before joining the archive of Crace wallpapers held in the V&A.

We were still living at Knipton when late one night I got a phone call from a friend telling me that David was not where I had been led to believe he was . . . It was as brutal as that, and it hit me for six.

Perhaps another woman would have turned a blind eye – in aristocratic circles this was the norm, I was informed – but it wasn't the norm in the circles I came from. Over the next few months the future of our marriage was up in the air, and the renovation of the nursery wing was put on hold as we tried to work out a way to mend things.

But it was so, so hard. I remember breastfeeding Charles and just sobbing, tears streaming down my face onto his dear little cheeks. I felt utterly helpless and lost, with no sense of what direction to go in. My emotions were all over the place; I'd go from hurt at his betrayal to guilt about my own responsibility, the constant self-questioning, the 'where-did-I-go-wrong?' I castigated myself for having been too involved with other things – the business, now the castle. And then I'd veer back the other way and turn self-recrimination into pure anger at what he had put me through. The word that sums it all up is heartbreak. I felt utterly heartbroken. I loved him and I knew that deep down he loved me.

I think I had underestimated the strain that David had been under. The pressure of the last year had been huge. The death of a parent is always a difficult moment, not only for all the obvious reasons – the memories, the love, the lost opportunities – but it brings into focus the reality of your own mortality, and Charles was not an old man. Yes, he was nearly eighty, but he was such a vibrant presence in our lives, and indeed in the life of the castle, and his death had been shocking.

I also knew that if my husband's 'indiscretion', as Frances called it, became public knowledge, it would be much more difficult to mend the marriage. And in any case, my instinct was just to shut down and heal on my own. So I told only those people who needed to know: my mum, Frances, Mrs P and Nic – and that was it. To everyone else, nothing had changed. I would put on my brightest smile along with my make-up in the morning and do my best not to let it crack before I went to bed. Somehow, I had to swallow my pride for the sake of our four little innocents.

Over the next few months David and I had weekly marriage counselling sessions to try to find a way through. But when trust is shattered, it takes a long time to put back the pieces and learn to trust again. And perhaps the cracks never quite disappear.

Eventually, the renovation of the nursery wing resumed, and we moved on. But the budget granted by the trustees was simply not sufficient, so I had no option but to pull in as many favours as I could. I contacted the kitchen design company Mark Wilkinson, who agreed to do the kitchen in exchange for the publicity it would get being photographed in glossy magazines, and I spent every hour of the day sourcing materials and supplies to refurbish the rest of the rooms.

I spoke to Bob Peyton, the hotelier who had transformed Stapleford Park where we had spent the first night after the wedding. Each room had been done up by a different interior designer – ours had been the Nina Campbell suite. I asked him how much I should budget for a bathroom and was appalled when he said £20,000. 'But if I were you,' he said, 'don't bother. Just do them over time.' His wife Wendy put me on their list of people prepared to take their hand-me-downs when they refurbished, which apparently they did on a regular basis. The idea that I would go back and re-do a room again in my lifetime filled me with horror.

Every window alone required forty metres of fabric. One of my favourite places to look was the Designer Fabric Warehouse in Grantham. I became such a regular that I got to know the husband-and-wife team who ran the café franchise there. The food was good and the service was efficient – very different from the tearoom at the castle, which was as welcoming and as stylish as a hospital canteen, so I asked Geoff and Pam, as the owners were called, if they'd be interested in renting our tea room and running it as a franchise in a similar way. They agreed, and on the back of this I got the Fabric Warehouse to provide new curtains. However, this shake-up didn't go down well with everybody, especially the staff, as they weren't prepared to accept what was now being asked of them. Like so many other people on the estate, they liked things the way they used to be . . . I was getting a creeping sense that even the most simple of changes would make me deeply unpopular.

The castle was such an overwhelming project that it was difficult to know where to start. The gardens were an area that I felt could be improved reasonably simply and without too much expenditure. I found a nursery near Peterborough and spoke to them about taking over the walled kitchen garden and paying us a rent in return for running it as a commercial garden centre. It transpired, however, that the Duke had left it to Frances in his will, and she couldn't see the point of letting the public in, and so, for neither the first nor the last time, I found myself eating humble pie. In retrospect, she was absolutely right.

After my initial introduction via Frances, I had visited Peter Beales' rose nursery many times over the years, so they were another potential partner, I decided. The rose garden was looking distinctly tired and they agreed to re-plant it. When Peter told me that the soil needed changing, I set the gardeners to work, digging out all the existing bushes and replacing the topsoil with earth from the home farm. When Peter duly arrived with dozens of bushes ready to plant, he was horrified to see that the new soil was mainly clay, which would make it almost impossible for them to thrive.

David had inherited a huge workforce of about 130 people: 30–40 guides; 15–20 men in the works' department; five in the forestry; six or seven cleaners; twenty office staff; four butlers; ten people on the shoot – five of whom were keepers – and ten kitchen staff. They were all well thought of by my in-laws, and there were never any complaints, but even a cursory look under the bonnet showed there were departments that were overstaffed, and there was some spending that could not be accounted for. In the forty or so years since the late Duke had himself moved in, the economic climate had radically changed.

It was clear that we were going to have to make some unpopular decisions. Yet the people who lived and worked on the estate depended on its financial viability. I remember going to see Frances when I'd decided we needed to make several members of the garden staff redundant. Her eyes widened with horror.

I understand how hard it must have been to watch David and me make decisions that she and the late Duke would never themselves have made. I suppose each one was perceived as a criticism that they had been doing it all wrong.

After all, Frances knew most of these people personally, many of whom had been working at Belvoir for years, in jobs that usually came with a 'tied cottage', so if they lost their job, they lost their home too. It was no wonder we were so unpopular, but it was like pruning a rose. For the health of the plant and to ensure new growth, you have to cut deep.

It seemed to me that the opening of the castle was the thing to concentrate on, as it was potentially the most profitable area of the business. In its heyday, when Jimmy was still working his magic, it was attracting over 100,000 visitors a year. And I saw no reason why we couldn't reach those numbers again. We also had 500–1,000 acres of flat parkland that would be brilliant for concerts and game fairs, while the castle itself was tailor-made for weddings. These were the areas I hoped Nic would work on. Over the years, both she and I had become masters of cold calls, which was what this would entail.

'This is the PA to the Duchess of Rutland,' I lied. 'Her Grace would be very interested to meet you.'

I remember one man whom I had convinced had to come and see for himself what the grounds had to offer, and when he arrived I showed him around, holding forth on our future plans and ideas.

'It's really strange,' he said, 'but your voice is remarkably similar to your PA's!'

'Actually,' I confessed, 'that was me.'

In May 2000, Nic and I went to the Chelsea Flower Show. We'd always had a stand there selling our conservatory furniture, but now I went wearing the hat of the Belvoir estate. Wandering around, I came across a stand full of azaleas and rhododendrons, some of which I recognized from Belvoir and which had always reminded me of the woodlands around Stanage. The owner, Charles Williams, told me how his ancestor had brought cuttings of these acid-loving plants back from the Himalayas in the nineteenth century and that the Coltman-Rogerses had allowed them to be planted at Stanage. Ever alert to the opportunity of a deal, I told him how Belvoir was much better situated geographically than Cornwall.

'You supply your plants to us,' I suggested, 'we open up the gardens to the public, and they can see them in situ!'

Mr Williams didn't quite see it like that, however.

'I've met f***ing duchesses like you before,' he said, 'and you can go to hell.'

It was perhaps an inauspicious start, but I chose not to take his answer at face value. As a result, we became firm friends, and to this day he advises me and supplies plants for the gardens. But his 'language' is as bad as it ever was.

In June 2000, we gathered in the castle chapel for Charles's christening. More than a year had passed since David's 'indiscretion', and I had decided it would be the perfect occasion to renew our vows. David agreed because he knew how much I needed that reassurance.

Afterwards, Frances hosted a champagne reception in the private drawing room with a happy assortment of family and godparents.

I remember clearly standing at the bottom of the stairs as Aunt Isabel swept past.

'Oh, darling girl,' she said, almost singing, 'now you've had your heir, you'd better get on and have your spare!'

Chapter Eleven
Chatelaine

I T WAS JULY 2000 when we finally moved in to the castle. Although we would not be moving far in terms of geography, in terms of our lives, it was a seismic change, and we'd waited till the school holidays so that the whole process wouldn't be too traumatic for the children.

The night before David and I were due to move in, Frances invited us to dinner in the castle. It was a poignant moment. After hosting so many glittering evenings, this would be her last – albeit very low-key. She had a bottle of champagne on ice and we toasted our new futures, the now Dowager Duchess in Belvoir Lodge, near the entrance to the castle, the new Duke and Duchess up on the hill.

'And this, Emma, is for you,' Frances said, handing me a big, rusty tin.

Inside were hundreds of keys, one for every door, every cupboard in the castle, she explained, all of them beautifully labelled.

In order that the children would arrive in their new home to bedrooms that felt like their own rooms, complete with toys and teddies, Mum had offered to look after them for the week we were doing the move and had rented a caravan in Borth, the glorious beach on the Welsh coast where I had spent so many summer holidays as a child.

Meanwhile, back at Belvoir, I now had access to every room in the castle, and I determined to try to understand how it worked, and what needed to be done to make it work better.

I had never strayed this far from the main corridors and staircases before, and the overall impression was that it was at best tired and desperately in need of modernization. While Frances had been meticulous, sending cleaners up every tower and into every storeroom every spring, it was no longer enough, but it had probably needed new eyes to recognize it.

Charles had started on a scheme to overhaul the entire plumbing system, but once he became ill the plans had been shelved, and so that was the end of that. This meant that when anything went wrong, whatever it was – no water coming out of the tap, a leak or a blocked drain etc. – we had to send for Mr Higgins, who worked for the firm in Nottingham that had looked after the castle for years. No overall plan had ever been drawn up, so we relied entirely on his memory of what pipes ran where and which drains they connected to. As for the water itself, the tanks in the towers turned out be open to the elements, namely passing pigeons, so were completely unsanitary. As a minimum they needed to be enclosed to prevent bird droppings polluting the water.

The antiquated heating system also meant that we couldn't

heat the nursery wing without heating the entire castle. No wonder the bills were astronomical. The previous year they had been an eye-watering £80,000. Then we had a stroke of luck.

We had met Charlie Stopford Sackville through the Historic Houses Association and he and his wife invited us to dinner. Drayton House in Northamptonshire dates back to the thirteenth century, and stately homes of this age and size are always notoriously expensive to heat, so you go prepared to freeze and at least carry a substantial shawl or take other preventative measures.

When we got there, however, I couldn't believe how warm it was! It turned out that they had just installed a Biomass system, which used wood chippings – a by-product of their forestry business. Apart from the additional labour involved – minimal – it was cost-free, Charlie explained. So we looked into it and decided it was clearly the answer for Belvoir. However, it took literally years to persuade the trustees that the installation costs of £250,000 would be money well spent.

As for our electricity, it was not only inadequate to twenty-first-century requirements; in places it was positively dangerous. The entire place needed re-wiring. Although the castle had well over 200 rooms, the number of bathrooms could be counted on two hands.

Upgrading the interiors seemed more manageable, as at least each room could be done individually and would provide an instant psychological lift, which, certainly from my perspective, was sorely needed.

After our new family kitchen and the children's bedrooms,

which had been my first priority, I decided to attack the private drawing room, not least because Frances had removed some of her favourite furniture – including the two red velvet sofas – to Belvoir Lodge. This had revealed carpets stained with decades of dog pee. Further inspection showed that the walls were similarly sullied.

I had absolutely loved the curtains I'd had made for the drawing room at Knipton Lodge and thought that if I could find a way of re-using them here then I would, though of course they'd need many more yards of fabric added to them. As this was going to be our room for entertaining, I asked Ray Bradshaw, the decorator I had used back in Herefordshire all those years ago, and who had helped me with Knipton Lodge, to come on board as I needed someone I trusted implicitly. During that first visit, he also painted the new baby's bedroom, decorating his cupboards with red and navy soldiers standing to attention. Along with Nic, he was soon one of my most trusted stalwarts.

Originally from Australia, Ray's first job was in the West End making stage sets. So, he is a genius at themed parties. In terms of painting the castle, a bit like the Forth Bridge, it's never ending. One day, he says, we'll find him in a long-forgotten room 'with a beard down to here hanging off a ladder'.

Slowly, things were beginning to work out. The curtains were re-made with the fabric from Knipton, and Ray matched the paint colour perfectly, so I finally felt that we had at least one room in the castle that had my stamp on it.

And then came the night of the storm, when the girls

came running in to say that the castle was flooding, and we nearly lost the private drawing room to water damage. Far worse, the water cascading down the walls of the library had been disastrous, soaking a huge number of irreplaceable books, worth tens of thousands of pounds.

While Ray had been able to minimize the water damage in the private drawing room, the damage to the library was much more serious. Many of the books were completely drenched, but through the Historic Houses Association, I had met Viscountess Campden from Exton Hall in neighbouring Rutland, and she told me about NADFAS, the National Association of Decorative and Fine Arts Societies, who, among other things, send volunteers into libraries to help restore damaged books. Happily, through this means, most of ours were saved and NADFAS have been working with us ever since.

Lady Campden was an invaluable source of information, and had a lovely, gentle way about her which made me unembarrassed to ask for help. But the challenges I was faced with were on a far larger scale. Exton Hall wasn't open to the public, for example.

Everywhere you looked in the castle there were portraits of family members going back generation after generation to the seventeenth century, not only every Duke and Duchess, but their various siblings and children. What I always found hilarious was that there were many more paintings of dogs in the castle than there were of women. A case in point is one of the stars of the Belvoir collection: a painting by George Stubbs of 'Turk', a particularly fluffy dog. It was commissioned by the 4th Duke, who married the beautiful Lady Mary Isabella Somerset, daughter of the 4th Duke of Beaufort, and was a serious collector – his adviser was Sir Joshua Reynolds.

Like his father before him, when it came to his ancestors, David was a walking encyclopaedia, and he knew exactly who they all were. Whenever guests came to Belvoir for the first time, he would give little guided tours including thumbnail sketches of the paintings, such as:

'Here she is, the 5th Duchess: Elizabeth, otherwise known as "that dreadful woman who almost bankrupted the family", as Papa used to say.'

This was my muse Elizabeth that he was talking about, the young duchess whose glowing portrait had inspired my wedding dress. It was she who remodelled Belvoir into the 'Gothick' castle that we still see today. By any criteria, this was a phenomenal endeavour and would have taxed the imagination of a professional, but she started to rough out designs even before she married, when she was only nineteen. In 1801, she engaged the fashionable architect James Wyatt, leading exponent of the neo-Gothic and then working on Windsor Castle, to turn those ideas into reality.

Elizabeth had been distinctly unimpressed when she arrived at Belvoir in 1799 for her wedding with the 5th Duke. Few illustrations of the seventeenth-century castle exist, but a contemporary scale model, probably made by architects before it was completely rebuilt, shows a squat two-storey building enclosing a rhomboid-shaped courtyard. This ground plan was about the only element of the third castle that was retained, the shape dictated by the hill it sat on, the site of the original Norman stronghold built on a natural rocky outcrop, surrounded by running clay, and whose foundations are still visible.

Elizabeth was the daughter of the 5th Earl of Carlisle, whose ancestral seat was Castle Howard in Yorkshire – a stunning baroque building that had only recently been completed. It is perhaps no wonder that Elizabeth had wanted to create something equally magical for the home where she would spend the rest of her life. Or, to quote her great-great-granddaughter Diana Cooper: 'Neo Norman, Neo Gothic, Neo Everything.'

And that was what I had to do now. Not quite such a radical transformation perhaps, but somehow I had to make this new home my own.

Shortly after David and I had moved into Knipton Lodge, Frances had told me about one of the guides, an odd man, she said, who was in the habit of sending her notes insisting that they were from Elizabeth herself. He was called Mr Jenkins, and there was nothing he didn't know about the castle. So I decided to meet him and asked him to accompany me to the picture storerooms, where Christie's were busy cataloguing everything for the audit of assets following the Duke's death. Mr Jenkins was a small man, no more than five-foot-five, but he looked shorter as he was always bent over. However, I thought he had a very wise face and a kind smile.

Just as I'd hoped, as I was now holder of the keys, Mr Jenkins began to pass me notes that he had channelled from the 5th Duchess.

'Elizabeth wants you to know,' he wrote, 'that one of the portraits in the Regent's Gallery is incorrectly labelled.'

Either he was totally batty or he had a genuine gift. Either way, we had nothing to lose, so David got in touch with a friend of his – Sir John Guinness – whose party trick was to reveal the lineage of a portrait without knowing the provenance, so we asked him to come and take a look.

Sure enough, he confirmed that the portrait was indeed incorrectly attributed. I could barely contain my excitement waiting for Mr Jenkins' next note . . .

Not only had Frances left me the box of keys, she'd also prepared a file of the annual calendar, a month-by-month guide to the castle's operation. For example, I'd had no idea that the moment Christmas was over, spring cleaning started. She left instructions on how to clean each and every Waterford crystal chandelier with her own recipe for a spray that removed the grease, though in practice I preferred to get up there with a sponge and a bowl of Fairy Liquid suds. She'd impressed on me early on that it was good for the staff to see me cleaning, as it reminded them that this was our home, not a museum.

Most of the furniture that we had in Knipton Lodge had come from the castle originally, and the week that the children were away bucket-and-spading in west Wales, the men from the works department were bringing it all back again. So, while their new home would obviously feel strange, at least they would be surrounded by their familiar old furniture.

Young children often have imaginary friends, so when one of the girls started telling me about the children who were coming out of her wardrobe every night, I didn't think too much about it. When I talked to her teacher, however, she said she'd been told the same thing, and – worse – that the 'children' had told my girls how we weren't going to be in the castle much longer. I had heard stories about ghosts in the castle but had never given them any credence, but now I was taking no chances. I wasn't going to have my children frightened out of their wits. If they had an axe to grind, then they could haunt me. I had had enough.

I raced back to the castle, ran up the same spiral staircase I'd followed Horton up that first momentous Friday afternoon, and opened every wardrobe and cupboard door in our wing, shouting at the ghosts to leave my children alone.

Nor was it just this one time. Another of my daughters told me there was a man who was 'horrid' to her and when I asked what he looked like she described someone who could only have been a cavalier. 'Sometimes he makes me walk through him to get to the kitchen,' she said.

I decided to invite the Bishop of Leicester for dinner and explained the nature of the problem we were having, so after our meal he said a few prayers and went around sprinkling holy water in the children's rooms. Sad to say, it made not a scrap of difference.

I decided we needed to 'occupy' the castle a bit more in order to change the energy, so I encouraged the children to play 'runner' – their version of hide and seek – up and down the corridors. This proved a great success with their friends, as it would keep them entertained for hours. It didn't suit the guides, however, who would tell them off for making too much noise and for touching things. But I wanted the children to feel that this was their home, so of course they could touch things!

As a result, I went into resistance mode and equipped them with water pistols. 'Hide under the beds,' I said, 'and if the guides are horrid to you, shoot!'

Inevitably it soon got out of hand. Not only did they squirt the guides, they'd hide in the balconies each side of the chapel and launch paper aeroplanes at them. Although I didn't get any direct complaints, I sensed their frustration at this boisterous young family who were now taking over the castle. They weren't used to tripping over the odd football, or a bike left in a corridor, or even a dog poo – and as for those water pistols . . .

Once the private dining room had been redecorated, I decided to invite all the guides to lunch, introducing them to a part of the castle they had never seen before. They were fascinated to go backstage, as it were, and hear how I was planning to do re-enactments in the castle, dressing the guides up in costumes. To my complete surprise one of the guides, who I'd already warmed to because she had a lovely Welsh lilt to her voice, absolutely loved the idea. And Ree's enthusiasm had a ripple effect among the others, who immediately started volunteering for roles.

It was at about this time that I decided to set up a male voice choir because I'd noticed that the men all had such beautiful voices and Rhi offered to be the choirmaster. Every week we'd find a piano and they'd practise on what's called the forty-acre landing. (Why, I don't know; it's certainly large, but not that large.) They worked towards a Christmas event – Belvoir by Candlelight, where we had bell ringers, candles, mince pies and, the highlight of the evening, our very own male choir who performed an array of Christmas songs. It was a triumph and they still come and perform to this day.

This marked the beginning of a change of heart in terms of the children, and I subsequently would overhear them telling members of the public that they might see them running and generally playing, but that, after all, the castle was their home.

I began to realize that what I needed above all was a mentor, someone who could teach me the ropes – like Jeremy Hope had done before Janet and I opened the branch of his interior design agency in Ross-on-Wye, when we had spent six weeks with him in London.

So I decided to contact the Duchess of Devonshire.

The strange thing was that, although I'd been a marchioness for eight years, and was now a duchess myself, I had never met another duchess apart from my mother-in-law.

Debo, doyenne of duchesses, was a legend. She had published a dozen or so books and was a regular on TV. The youngest of the Mitford sisters, she broke the mould of how a country house was run.

When death duties were introduced in the last years of the nineteenth century, they had a huge impact on large country estates. On the death of her father-in-law, they were faced with a bill for inheritance tax of £222 million at today's value. During the war, Chatsworth had been used by a girls' school and so required a huge amount of work done before the new Duke and his family could move in in 1959. As the cost of running the house and the estate was around £4 million a year, she decided it would have to pay its way. In the face of considerable tut-tutting among the chattering classes, she brought in all kinds of commercial activities which previously had been viewed as very 'infra dig'. She had opened a shop, a garden centre, an adventure playground and goodness knows what else. But if there was anyone who could advise me, I decided, it was the Duchess of Devonshire. I discussed this with Frances and asked if she knew her. She did but suggested I contact her myself, her advice being, 'Just drop her a line. She can only say no.'

Debo, as she was known by friends and family alike, had married Andrew Cavendish, the younger son of the 10th Duke, in 1941 when she was twenty-one. Andrew's elder brother William, was killed in action in 1944, so Andrew effectively became the heir to the dukedom, which he acceded to in 1950 upon the death of his father. It was these two deaths within six years that had proved financially ruinous to the estate.

Although I had never met her, I had read her books and knew just how much she had done to restore the house and turn the estate into a commercially viable enterprise. So I wrote to her, along the lines of, 'Dear Duchess, I am new to the castle and am in dire need of someone to guide me and I would be immensely grateful if you could help.' She wrote back: 'Dear Emma, I would love to meet you and David. Do please come and have lunch.'

We stayed the night before at Haddon Hall, which is only a ten-minute drive away, and around midday we set off, David complaining at how embarrassing it all was that I had written to her completely cold. I pointed out that had she been affronted by my admittedly rather direct approach, she wouldn't have invited me to lunch. She was the icon of how to run heritage. Why not go to the top?

I hadn't been to Chatsworth before and it is both gorgeous and immense, set above a shimmering lake. We entered via a wide marble entrance hall and were welcomed by the butler, a really personable man. He accompanied us upstairs to the Duchess's sitting room on the first floor that looked over the side of the house to the Emperor Fountain, built by Joseph Paxton. It was a room of immense charm – a kaleidoscope of colour and everything in a wonderful muddle, chintz chair covers, photographs everywhere, very much in her own idiosyncratic style. How had she made it feel so lived in? On every available surface there were china chickens and, more surprisingly, Elvis memorabilia.

And then Debo herself breezed in. She was in her seventies and the epitome of what a duchess should look like: no make-up, tweed skirt, pearls, 'done' hair and a large lobster brooch. She had her own artsy-meets-outdoorsy style. After coffee she took us to meet the Duke, leading us down long corridors lined with glass cabinets full of Cavendish-crested china and porcelain. I remember thinking that we could do the same at Belvoir, where we had storerooms full of massive tureens, sauce boats and other dining paraphernalia – largely useless objects these days – that just languished in cupboards gathering dust. Used in this way, they brightened up those interminably long corridors.

Lunch was in a small room with just the four of us – very simple but perfect, with lovely fresh flowers. While Debo had a focused intensity, Andrew had a real twinkle in his eye and always lightened the conversation. What was wonderful was how encouraging they both were. Andrew said we should get in touch with the GNER, the rail company that then ran the East Coast line, as he thought they had a carriage on the *Northern Belle*, a UK equivalent of the *Orient Express*, called Belvoir Castle. 'You could get it to take passengers from London straight to Grantham,' he said. It dated from the early 1900s, and was decorated with panels of inlaid wood. Debo, meanwhile, was very keen on TV-related projects, and later put me in touch with a documentary director that led directly to a six-part documentary called *Diary of a Duchess* for BBC's *Midlands Today*.

Towards the end of the meal, Andrew turned to David, who was obviously getting bored with listening to various ways of maximizing income potential, and said, 'In my opinion, old boy, the women make the money and we spend it.' What was fascinating was that although we were left in little doubt that it was Debo who was rolling up her sleeves, there wasn't one moment when she disparaged her man. He was definitely always the Duke. Throughout the visit I'd had the sense that the Duchess was weighing me up, and as we left, she said, 'I think you're going to be absolutely fine, Emma. Trust your gut instinct.'

Of course, she had her own reasons for wanting to meet us. As my brother-in-law Eddie had now inherited Haddon Hall, she was desperate to find out all there was to know about her new neighbour Lord Edward Manners.

I never saw her again, but she did write to me asking for any information I might have about the great friendship between Georgiana, 5th Duchess of Devonshire, and Mary Isabella, 4th Duchess of Rutland, who were direct

contemporaries, having been born in 1757 and 1756 respect-
ively. Mary Isabella was a great, great beauty. The daughter
of the Duke of Beaufort, she had been brought up at
Badminton and her wedding train was near enough the length
of the ballroom, while her shoes were a size 2. How can I be
so exact? Because when Frances was showing me around, she
took me into the laundry room, where hundreds of pairs of
sheets and so forth are stored. There we came across a card-
board box, opened it and found this extraordinary wedding
train wrapped up in tissue paper, along with the size 2 wedding
shoes . . . Before this exciting discovery, she showed me a
trunk filled with literally dozens of babies' nightdresses. The
5th Duchess's, she told me by way of explanation.

'Good heavens,' I said, 'I know she had eleven children
over the years, but this seems excessive.'

Frances shook her head and suggested I feel them. They
weren't fine cotton or linen, but somewhat rough to the
touch. They would be given to every villager who had a
baby, she explained. Once the baby had grown out of them,
they'd be laundered and returned to this trunk ready for the
next arrival.

My last contact with Debo concerned a bed similar to
one we had at Belvoir, which John, the 9th Duke, had had
restored with the help of the Royal School of Needlework
and that was now displayed in a protective glass box in the
picture gallery. It had originally come from Haddon Hall,
and there was a near identical one at Chatsworth, Debo
said, so she thought they might have been made by the
same person, probably a Huguenot – Protestants who fled
France in the sixteenth and seventeenth centuries to escape

religious persecution – and so I sent her all the information we had.

That visit opened the doors to other stately homes, although the results were not always as useful. I wrote to the Duchess of Northumberland, known for her stunning gardens at Alnwick Castle, to ask if she had any advice for getting started on the gardens at Belvoir. 'It's wonderful that you are considering creating a garden,' she wrote back, 'but it's very hard work so you need to think very carefully before taking it on.'

Annette 'Scruff' Howard was another friend who proved to be a valuable source of advice. She had been the chatelaine of Castle Howard, but when her marriage collapsed, she'd had to leave. We all loved Scruff, particularly the children. She had no children of her own though she had tried for years – including eleven attempts at IVF – and that had undoubtedly contributed to the breakdown of the marriage.

For her, spending time with us at Belvoir filled a gaping hole in her life. For us it was brilliant as she knew everything there was to know about running a huge stately home. Her great passion was shooting and on shoot days she'd come racing up the drive in her huge Audi and emerge wearing cowboy boots, skirts with tassels, topped by a mane of unruly blonde hair, like a scaled-up version of Dolly Parton. Piling all the kids in the back, alongside her red setters, we'd roar off to meet the guns with the boot open and me squealing that the children might tumble out, though thankfully they never did. It was really Scruff who got the children out shooting.

Happy families on the private terrace for Alice's christening. My father-in-law is on the arm of the bench beside the Duchess. Mum and Dad are on the other side, and standing at the back (*left to right*) are Roger (godfather), Lottie, Eddie (who I always thought looked like David Essex) and Theresa. In the front, Violet is being hugged by Anoushka D'Abo, Aunt Ursie's granddaughter.

(*above left*) In the kitchen at Knipton Lodge with new baby Alice.
(*above right*) Our wonderful nanny Lindsey with her last little Manners baby, Hugo, at his christening in the library.

On a caravan holiday at a farm above Aberdovey. On my lap is Katy, my niece, then Violet. David is standing behind Mum with Alice, while Eliza keeps a bit aloof on the right.

My beloved Knipton Lodge, where I did my best to recreate my childhood home at Heartsease.

Belvoir Castle in all its glory

In the Elizabeth Saloon, with Hugo on my lap, Charles to David's right and Eliza.

At the CLA Game Fair, beneath the castle. Charles, Violet and Aunt Ursie with her arm around Alice. Aunt Ursie was a very special person and brought sunshine into their young lives whenever she was around.

David cutting his fiftieth birthday cake, made by Mrs Pacey.

David with Hugh Grant and Elizabeth Hurley. Elizabeth turned out to be a fantastic singer. Hugh was terrified of ghosts.

One of my favourite images of Aunt Ursie. It hangs in our private dining room.

Violet and Alice hunting. I've just been handing out sausage rolls which is why I'm not on horseback. On top of my jodhpurs, I'm wearing my favourite go-to vintage mink, which I bought second hand at Burghley horse trials.

Hugo and Charles at Hugo's eighteenth birthday party.
My two boys will be mates forever.

Hugo off to school.
A very emotional day for me.

Three generations: Alice, Mum, me
and Eliza at Palm Beach, Florida,
launching the American Friends of
Belvoir Castle Foundation.

Phil and me at Frog Hollow.

An al fresco supper party with my friend Susannah Constantine.

The rose garden – an unfailing
source of peace, joy and solace.

Ella Bella, my Gypsy horse.
She loved to keep me on my toes,
though sadly now she's lame.

She was also immensely practical. She showed me how to squeeze a bathroom into the tiniest of cupboards, and gave me recipes that would work for huge numbers of people. She was a true character and we all just loved her.

One thing that still desperately needed attention, of course, was the roof. To nobody's surprise a surveyor's report recommended urgent attention, so I got two quotes. One was for £150,000 and the other for just £6,000. Why such a dramatic difference? I needed to find out because faced with that size of fee, you look not twice but three times.

I must have been about sixteen when I first met Ben Sinclair. He lived in Norgrove Court outside Redditch and I was introduced to him by a boy I was going out with at Malvern. I have a very clear memory of sitting beside this enormous fireplace and just chatting. He struck me even then as a bit of a maverick and I don't think he's changed that much. He went into the army and then returned to Worcestershire to work with his mother making stained-glass windows for churches and cathedrals across the British Isles, which he still does to this day. He's a proper craftsman, but incredibly forthright and outspoken, and he got on very well with David. Anyway, Ben knows everyone and everybody in the world of heritage, so I rang him and asked if he knew anyone who could advise me regarding these two quotes for the roof.

He suggested I get in touch with Peter MacFarlane, who was then working on Grimsthorpe Castle, an old house with a baroque façade by Vanbrugh, not far from us in Lincolnshire, and who had also helped in the restoration of Lincoln Cathedral. So, Peter came out and I took him up on the roof. He was brilliant and explained everything to me clearly and succinctly. The slates on our roof were Welsh, he said, – very thick and very heavy. New slates would be considerably thinner and that to re-do the roof in its entirety was unnecessary. We only needed to replace those slates which were actually broken. So, he said, I should go with the cheaper quote, as that's what they were suggesting. I learnt a lot about roofs that afternoon but, just as importantly, that Lincoln Cathedral kept birds of prey to keep the pigeons away.

'We need to have our own birds of prey here at Belvoir,' I told David that evening. So we got Purcell the barn owl and Scooby the Harris hawk, who David absolutely adored.

All too often, I've discovered that, no sooner do I find a solution to one problem, another one appears as a consequence of that solution. A little late in the day perhaps, I realized that our birds of prey needed looking after, and asked Danny, our maintenance man, if he could keep an eye on them. But keeping an eye on them wasn't enough. It transpired that looking after birds of prey was a full-time job and not something he could do once a day like feeding the dogs. This was a time when I was having to make huge redundancies, so I had to be very careful about taking on any new staff and increasing our wage bill. However, following the success of the books that had been restored by volunteers, I thought I'd see if there were any potential volunteers to look after Purcell and Scooby. This didn't strike me as NADFAS territory, so I put an ad in the *Grantham Journal* and to my amazement got twenty-five replies! We now have a rota of nine or ten, and it works perfectly. And running the hawk volunteers is the wonderful Rhi. Later, inside one of the towers, we would find thousands of birds eggs that David's grandfather, the 9th Duke, had collected, and in the same way managed to find a group of volunteers who would care for the collection.

Through a succession of unrelated events, I was discovering that heritage meant as much to the community as it did to us, and that our volunteers' sense of pride in the castle was (and still is) no less than ours.

I also began to realize that there was an army of retired people out there with a whole range of skills who were only too willing to get stuck in, not only with helping to restore the books in the library, but also the gardens. When you finish your working life, or when your children leave home, it leaves a void, and volunteering gives people an identity, a sense of belonging. It's as if it's a tribe, and I have to find ways of leading it. Because you still have to earn their respect in order to take them with you. And they truly have so much to offer. I felt I was replacing the negativity of the past with the wisdom of the past. I could be wilful and impetuous, and they had a lot to teach me.

There were also younger people, studying landscaping or land management, longing to learn on the job through work experience on the estate. The University of Lincoln had a Restoration and Fine Art department and students would take broken china and gilded objects to restore. For example, the torchères in the Elizabeth Saloon were re-gilded by students at Lincoln.

Places like Belvoir Castle have survived into the twenty-first century thanks to community support. For the annual spring clean, it was all hands on deck. Mr Baxter would come up from the village and clean the guns in the guard-room, while I polished the brass peacocks either side of the mantelpiece.

I had taken up Debo's idea about display cabinets in the corridors, and once a year Terry would open them up to do the dusting, refusing any help as he just loved them. I also invested in a huge waxing machine to polish the stone floors, whereas in Frances's day, there had been a whole army of women scrubbing them. I have always enjoyed scrubbing floors, and if I had been born 100 years earlier and found myself at Belvoir, more than likely I'd have been a scullery maid . . .

It worked the other way too, when people contacted me to ask for help. One of the first to knock at the front door was Laury Dizengremel, a sculptor from Montana in the United States who wanted to be our first artist in residence. In exchange for somewhere to live and somewhere to work, she proposed creating a sculpture trail in the gardens. I also asked her to make busts of the girls, and they sit in my bedroom to this day. Laury's presence felt like a natural progression in the castle's history, particularly as Violet, the 8th Duchess, had been such a talented sculptor herself.

Another more local artist who contacted me was Tim Grayson, a poet who lived in Leicester, and again, in exchange for coming to stay on the estate for creative inspir-ation, he became our poet in residence. He continues to organize retreats and writers' festivals and education programmes. I was learning all the time just how useful these connections to the castle were to the local community, to artists, to poets, just as they had been throughout history.

David's Aunt Ursie was a great supporter of ours and, having grown up in Belvoir, she knew more about the castle's history than anyone. She was the first of the children born to the 9th Duke and his wife Kathleen. Born in 1917, she was two years older than Charles, and quite a stickler for how things should be done in a quite old-fashioned sense. I'm sure that although she must have watched me make dreadful mistakes, she never even raised an eyebrow. She'd dip into everyone's lives but never comment, simply embrace whatever it was we were doing in a marvellous, uplifting way.

Soon after David and I moved into the castle she told me that she disliked how the furniture had been rearranged after the war in the Elizabeth Saloon and convinced me to put it back to how it had been when she was a girl.

She could still remember Winston Churchill sitting there, she said, with tears streaming down his face as he listened on the wireless as Edward VIII announced to the world that he was abdicating, as he couldn't do his job as king 'as I would have wished . . . without the support of the woman I love'.

She could remember the days when guests would come and stay for months, and how if one guest took a shine to another, there was a hiding place where notes could be left with instructions as to where to find them.

She remembered how, in the dining room, exquisite pastries would be laid out for the shoot teas, filled with cream and vanilla custard, and she would run down the table, dipping her fingers into them and licking them clean.

In the last years of her life, Aunt Ursie would write to me regularly, saying, 'Darling girl, where are you? What happened to you?' And I would send a driver to London to pick her up and bring her to stay at the castle. She might have been a frail old woman in her late eighties, but within seconds of my putting her on a train back to London, after insisting she needed no help, I would find her charming some smart young man to lift her suitcase onto the rack.

Ursie's mother had been Kathleen Tennant, known by the family as Kakoo. The Tennants were Scottish and had been tenant farmers outside Glasgow. One of Kakoo's ancestors had made a fortune by inventing bleach and the family was reputed to have the tallest tower in Glasgow. The bleach money helped to ease their way into society, which was how Kakoo met and married David's grandfather, the 9th Duke, and subsequently produced Charles, Ursula, Isabel, John and Roger.

The history of the castle was revealing itself to me all the time, and I loved hearing stories that brought it to life. However, some stories I would rather have done without.

One weekend, David and I were away from the castle on a shooting weekend, and we left the children in the charge of Lindsey and one of her friends. In the middle of the night Lindsey had woken in a state of total terror, convinced that she had been possessed. Whoever it was had bodily lifted her off the bed, to the degree that she could see the floor underneath her. The man had a name that she remembered, and when we checked the archives, we discovered someone of that name had indeed worked in the castle in the nineteenth century.

I couldn't have young women being terrified in this way, and was determined to rid the castle of ghosts once and for all, but as to how, I had no idea.

Then I went to stay with Antony and Jane Braithwaite at Haughton Castle, a few miles north of Hexham, Northumberland, whose origins dated back to the thirteenth century.

'Have you installed heating?' I remember asking Jane, as it was a good deal warmer there than at Belvoir.

'No,' she said, 'I just got rid of the ghosts.'

She told me about a woman called Doris who lived in Newcastle and used 'radionics' to 'move ghosts on'. By this time, I was desperate and ready to try anything. When I phoned to arrange for Doris to come to Belvoir, she said it wouldn't be necessary.

'You've got two little boys trapped in this world near the bathroom that your children use,' she said. 'You've also got a medieval man. Don't worry. I'll sort it out for you.'

I'd heard stories of horses that had been treated of certain ailments at a distance, but ghosts?

Believe it or not, it worked – at least until the next time we started doing any major work – then there would be rumblings, because ghosts really hate change and someone would pick up on it. So I'd call Doris and then things would calm down.

Nic and I were then working in the estate office, which was separate from the castle, so we had no option but to leave the children 'at home', i.e. the nursery wing, looked after by a succession of nannies and au pairs. Needless to say, the best game of all was trying to outwit them. Old castles were not designed with small children in mind, and the spiral staircases in particular – most without handrails – were lethal even for grown-ups, and I was always terrified that something dreadful could happen. When it came to the really little ones, Charles, and Nic's daughter Mathilda, we kept them with us in the office, as they were now crawling.

The line between public and private was difficult to police. Often doors had to be left unlocked because of short-cuts and access, but signs saying 'Private' were not necessarily respected. We had large screens made to try to protect our privacy, but it wasn't that simple. The entrance to our laundry was overlooked by the ballroom, for example, and one day I made a dash to turn off the washing machine wearing only a nightie and was stopped in my tracks by a loud American voice saying, 'Isn't that the Duchess?' I looked up and was greeted by a sea of faces wearing baseball caps plus a couple of Stetsons – a party of Texans who'd got more than they bargained for.

One day the girls and I were riding through the estate and came across a group of local boys fishing in one of the lakes. Quick as a flash I trotted over to them. 'That looks fun,' I said. 'Do you need a permit?'

'You don't need to bother with that,' said one. 'Just come in through the back gate. It's always open.'

'But what happens if the Duchess catches you?' I asked.

'Oh, you don't want to meet her,' he said, 'she'll have your head on a plate.'

Chapter Twelve

Living Above the Shop

WAS I A monster?

We'd been installed in the castle for no more than a few months when I pushed open a swing door on one of the spiral staircases and overheard a conversation between two of the staff.

'So, have we broken her yet?'

I was devastated. They were clearly talking about me.

I knew there was a power struggle going on around the issue of staff redundancies, but I had no idea that it was directed towards me personally.

'Have we broken her. Yet . . .' The words went round and round in my head. It sounded like a line from a play, a psychodrama where a woman is slowly pushed to the edge. *Have we broken her yet?* I hadn't misheard. In those dark stairwells, although you can't be seen around the infinite spirals, voices are clear, bouncing off the bare stone walls, with no carpets, no curtains to deaden the sound. They were actually trying to 'break' me.

I didn't tell David, but I remember asking him if we couldn't simply run away from it all.

'Why don't we just move to Australia?' I said, plucking the furthest place I could think of out of the air. I just wanted to get as far away from the castle as possible, because everything felt so hard. Every door, whether it was real or metaphorical, had to be pushed open, and it felt like behind each one there was a trustee or a member of staff asking me to justify why we needed to open it.

The sale of a Van Dyck sketch of Hampton Court Palace had covered the inheritance tax, but the castle was still running at a loss and we had estimated that it cost around a million pounds a year just to stand still. I had no shame in telling returning guests, like those that big wealth management companies brought to us, that their last visit had paid for a pair of curtains in the Elizabeth Saloon, or the renovation of some more of the guest bedrooms. They didn't seem to object, and on the contrary seemed to positively enjoy the feeling that they were contributing to a piece of history.

Living above the shop, there was no switching off at five o'clock. But two school runs a day meant time was always tight. It wasn't unusual to see me at the school gate in a mink coat I'd rescued from an attic, over a slinky evening dress and a pair of glittery Jimmy Choos. To the other waiting mums, I probably looked more high-class hooker than duchess, but I was absolutely insistent that whatever happened in the day, I would be there to drop the kids off in the morning and pick them up at the school gate at going-home time; it was a vow that I had made to myself, my small way of keeping life ordinary for them in this extraordinary world.

Once safely tucked up in bed, stories read, lights switched off, back on would go my corporate head, ready to pick the brains of these various asset managers, asking them what they would do to get the castle up and running again. We'd stay up until the early hours, playing the game, drinking in the library, and often the party would continue long after David and I had gone to bed. I remember finding Horton one morning in the butlers' pantry looking exhausted and telling me he had found the host of one of these groups asleep on the billiard table.

The mornings after these kinds of events were the hardest, but with four children I had no choice but to struggle on, hangover or no hangover. By 6 a.m., whatever time I'd gone to bed the night before, I was up. By 7 a.m., their lunch-boxes and uniforms would be packed and their individual breakfasts would be waiting for them – I knew who had Cheerios, who had sliced apple, who had toast – and not a moment could be wasted, because by 8 a.m. on the dot we had to be heading for the back door where the people carrier would be backed up and waiting.

The wedding season proved particularly disruptive. The children would rush into our bedroom at gone midnight screaming that the castle was under attack, when it was the wedding fireworks. The disco that traditionally ended the day was held in the cavernous old kitchen and the *boom-boom-boom* went on until gone midnight. The central courtyard that separated the old kitchen from the girls' bedrooms acted as an echo chamber and, if that wasn't enough, at around 5.30 a.m. we'd get woken by empty bottles being collected and thrown into the bins.

The summer is a wonderful time to be at Belvoir. Canada geese and wild duck take to basking in the sun beside the lake, utterly unconcerned, knowing there's no nasty man around the corner waiting to take a pop. If it's hot, the swimming pool is perfect. And yet this was the time of year we were busiest, so Mum rented a caravan at Borth and we would all go there for a classic summer holiday. As our numbers swelled – and usually included an au pair to help my parents take the strain – it simply wasn't big enough, so they bought a commanding house right on the seafront at Aberdovey across the bay, which had once been owned by a famous sea captain. It proved completely perfect. There was room not only for all of us lot, but the attic could take any number of small people, so when my brothers and their families arrived, somehow, we all squeezed in.

The garden behind was very steep, but the soil had been improved by this captain who had done the Irish run and had brought back peat to revitalize the soil. Mum took it upon herself to plant it up, helped by her chief under-gardener Charles – and the other under-gardeners when she could persuade them.

From then on, we would spend a whole month there every summer. We'd take a picnic and make camps in the sand dunes, and the kids would pull on their surf suits and spend all day in the water bodyboarding while David and the older ones would go off and explore nearby castles. We'd spend the evenings crabbing in the harbour after which the children would have crab races, and when the tide was high, they'd terrify their grandfather by jumping off the end of the pier. I opened an account at the ice-cream shop and the children were allowed one ice cream a day. After a day of surfing, you'd see them wandering along the quay, bodyboard in one hand and cone in the other.

Sometimes even Frances would join us, staying at the Trefeddian Hotel, whose owners, the Cave-Brownes, allowed us to use their indoor pool in wet weather. They became real friends, and in later years they would come up and visit – I remember they came to David's fiftieth.

Aberdovey turned out to be a melting pot of interesting people. It was there I first met the writer Simon Jenkins, then head of the National Trust, and we talked for hours about heritage and how he was trying to get the original families back in their historic houses. Then there was the mayor, David Richardson. He became a really great friend. He was a passionate gardener and would happily come up to Belvoir and spend hours weeding the borders of the private terrace.

At Belvoir there were no local shops where the children could inspect the sweet counter or choose a comic. Here, however, they could wander down to the local Londis and buy a packet of midget gems, and no one was judging them. No one knew who they were or where they were from. They could wear what they liked. They were free to be themselves. All too soon, though, these summer idylls would come to an end, and it would be back to school or work.

My father-in-law had banned balls in the castle due to people 'misbehaving' on the bed made for Catherine, Countess of Rutland, wife of the 9th Earl, in 1696, which was one of the few items known to have come from the third castle. But in our mission to bring the castle back to life, we decided to revive them. The reception would be held in the castle, while a marquee would be set up on the north terrace for dancing.

Susannah Constantine – known then for her TV fashion show with Trinny Woodall – was a regular guest. She had grown up across the road from Knipton Lodge, in a house called the Priory, and knew the castle backwards. She remembered the nursery wing as it had been when David, Edward and Theresa were growing up. She particularly remembered the ballet classes in Nanny Webb's bedroom, now doing duty as our kitchen.

Susannah was one of the people who really helped me in the early days and was my guide to the dynamics of the Manners family – she could have been my sister-in-law – and was fully aware of everything David had been through, for example. She had a way of relaxing him whenever she came over.

At the time we moved into Knipton Lodge she wasn't around that much, as she was then working for a newspaper in Fleet Street, but her mother, Mary-Rose, became a darling friend of mine. She was devoted to Mick Toulson, which was how I first met him. And we'd go across to the Priory for Sunday lunch if we didn't go up to the castle.

By the time I met her, Susannah was part of a glamorous London-based set, and she persuaded them to come to our hunt balls – people like Elizabeth Hurley and Hugh Grant and David Furnish and the shoe designer Patrick Cox. Just like anyone else, the best part for them was getting out into the country and going on long walks. But in the evenings, we'd get out the karaoke machine in the private drawing room. Elizabeth Hurley turned out to have a surprisingly good voice, and she and David Furnish would always do a duet to Elton John's 'Don't Go Breaking My Heart'.

After one charity do, David Furnish asked if he could bring a few friends up for the weekend along with Elton's chef. Of course, we said yes. Among these friends were David and Victoria Beckham and their kids. I thought Victoria was the most amazing mum. Her children were small and the eldest, Brooklyn, had a little trike, and when he started pedalling across the private drawing room, she yanked him off.

The girls were thrilled, as they were all huge fans of the Spice Girls and had dressed up and rehearsed an entire routine. So that Charles wouldn't be left out, David kicked a football about with him on the north terrace.

'How many nannies do you have?' David asked me.

'Just one,' I said. 'How about you?'

'Oh, we don't have a nanny, but our parents help us out.'

Later on, Victoria asked me how many cleaners I had.

'One and a half,' I said.

'Oh, I've got three,' she told me, apparently surprised to hear she had more than me.

Hugh Grant also came up once for a shooting weekend. He was absolutely terrified of ghosts and the children delighted in playing tricks on him. When you live in a castle in the countryside, you're never very far from a rat;

they're in hedges, in ditches, in cellars. They run along corridors, chew through wires, so we have a rat man to get rid of them. One day Bill happened to mention that he played the bagpipes, and so I had a light-bulb moment. For our shoot weekends, I would get him to play the bagpipes to wake the guests up. Belvoir might not be in Scotland, but I felt that having someone play the bagpipes added to the overall castle experience, especially if you were American.

On that particular weekend that Hugh was staying with us, he was frightened to go to bed because he hated ghosts so much and the children had been entertaining him with their experiences, so he was well primed. Then, after he'd gone to his room, the girls began making scratching noises with their nails on his bedroom door, scuttling away before he could catch them at it. We were still in the drawing room when Hugh rushed in as white as a sheet, and I went looking for the girls, expecting to find them giggling, but instead they looked as terrified as he did.

'What happened?' I asked.

They told me that they had heard the bagpipes playing.

'But you can't have done,' I said. 'Bill only comes in the morning. He'll have gone home by now.'

I followed the girls down to where they said they could hear them, and it was true. I could hear the unmistakable sound of bagpipes inside the castle . . .

Another of Susannah's famous friends who she brought up was Lulu, who was adorable. When Charles was about three, she bought him a Spider-Man outfit, and he lived in it. He wore it to play, he wore it to bed, he wore it everywhere. When I asked him what made it so special, he said, 'Well, if I was Spider-Man I could go up the walls of the castle and fix them in a jiffy.' Funny yes, obviously, but for me, so, so sad that he was already feeling the weight of responsibility at only three . . .

While Mr Jenkins continued to send me occasional messages from Elizabeth, he also had less appetizing stories to tell, such as the curse put on the Manners family by the 'Belvoir witches'.

In the early seventeenth century, a mother and her two daughters, Joan, Margaret and Philippa Flower, from Bottesford, were employed at the castle to prepare for the visit of King James I. They were then denounced as 'healers' and were dismissed. Shortly afterwards the 6th Earl and Countess fell ill with a vomiting bug, and the two sons, Henry and then Francis, died, along with their sisters, leaving the earldom without an heir. Two years after the death of the second son, the Earl accused the women of putting a curse on the family and had them arrested. They were taken to Lincoln to stand trial, found guilty of witchcraft and hanged. On the Earl's tomb at Bottesford, an inscription reads:

IN 1608 HE MARRIED YE LADY CECILA
HUNGERFORD, DAUGHTER TO YE HONORABLE
KNIGHT SIR JOHN TUFTON, BY WHOM HE HAD
TWO SONS, BOTH OF WHICH DIED IN THEIR
INFANCY BY WICKED PRACTISES AND SORCERYE

I have always had a tendency to be superstitious and this story sent shivers down my spine. I thought of David's birth, of his younger brother's early death . . . Even my father-in-law had been a sickly child, his mother Kakoo so convinced he wouldn't make it to adulthood that she took it for granted that his younger brother would inherit. David's grandfather, John, the 9th Duke, had been an early visitor to Tutankhamun's tomb, which his friend Lord Carnarvon famously opened, and he died from pneumonia at the age of only fifty-three. John's father, the 8th Duke, had also suffered great loss when his mother had died in childbirth.

Was I just letting my febrile imagination take over? Or could there be any truth in the curse? Charles was at that age when exploring was everything, and he was always going off and getting lost. I thought of all the dangers – the staircases, the sheer drops, the heavy doors that closed without warning and were hard enough for an adult to open, let alone a little person.

I was then experiencing regular panic attacks. I would put the children to bed at the end of the day, lie down to read them a story and my heart would be racing. I couldn't relax, and at night there was nothing I could do to get to sleep and so I just paced the corridors. In the end, I went to see a local healer called Ralph Ticehurst. David couldn't take alternative medicine seriously, not to mention my spiritual beliefs. He would dismiss them, saying, 'Oh, she's gone all witchy on us.'

After hearing the story of the Belvoir witches, I asked Ralph if he could help me lift this curse on the family. Perhaps just to humour me, however, David agreed to take part.

So, the three of us gathered in David's study, the same room that had once been his father's, and he sat down in his old oak-tree chair that had been at Waterloo as Ralph started speaking, asking over and over again for the curse to be lifted. And when I looked back at David, I swear that the chair was swaying beneath him. I had always sensed that power was buried within the walls of the castle, and this episode confirmed it to me. After an hour it was over, and everything was as it had been. I could only trust that the chains of the curse were severed.

Even now I reflect on the part I have played in the Manners' line of heritage. Was it ordained? As a farmer's daughter who understands the need to broaden the genetic inheritance, is it too much of a stretch to imagine a need for new blood in this ancient family? The battles now being faced might no longer be matters of life and death, but foes still exist in the form of dry rot, the taxman, and health and safety officers.

Charles was three when I found I was pregnant again. I'd miscarried two years earlier, but had been quite fatalistic about it, convinced that the right life would stick. However, I was approaching forty and had had four children in ten years and was so enormous this time round that I felt like a landlocked crab. I was desperate to get it over and done with. But this baby was in no hurry. I drove myself back and forwards to Nottingham City Hospital at least five times around the time of my due date, thinking I was about to pop, but nothing. In the end, Mr Liu performed an elective Caesarean and Hugo arrived on 24 July 2003. The birth certificate says Hugh because my father said that Hugo sounded too foreign, but he's still Hugo to us.

Just a few days later, the seven of us piled into the people carrier and headed west for our month in Aberdovey, where the plan was that I would take it easy and recuperate. With this tiny newborn in his carrying cot – completely oblivious to the raucous singing of 'There's a Hole in My Bucket', 'She'll Be Coming Round the Mountain' and the rest of the Roma Watkins repertoire, which was our traditional entertainment on long car journeys – I remember waddling down to the local Londis where Adele behind the counter looked at me with concern and asked, 'So when did you say the baby was due?'

Although we had stripped the staff right back, we still had the Hortons. Mr Horton, who had been deputy butler – and stoker of all kinds of fires – was now the only butler. Mrs Horton had been my parents-in-law's cook and now we inherited her too. Her kitchen was on the ground floor and there was a convoluted system of getting hot food upstairs to the private dining room. First, she deposited it in the dumbwaiter, a miniature lift that took it up to the corridor directly above, then pulled a bell and a butler would haul it up via a pulley, rumbling and rattling as it went. It was then put into what was known as the hot cupboard. The next stage of the journey was to the butler's pantry. Finally a butler would transport it to the dining room, where it would be transferred to a hotplate on a marble-topped console table. Not surprisingly, by the time it arrived on your plate, it was at best tepid if not actually cold.

So Mrs Horton made all our meals. In contrast to her very tall husband, she stood at a little over five feet. However, perhaps to mitigate this, she always wore heels and took great pride in her appearance, though her fingers looked like they had suffered on the end of a chopping knife more than once.

I had been determined that when we were finally installed at the castle I'd have a proper kitchen, a room that was at the heart of things, like at Heartsease. Everything about life there revolved around the kitchen – preparing food, serving, eating, washing up, chat. To me the kitchen has always been the hub of the home, and I'd done my best to replicate that at Knipton Lodge. So when we moved to the nursery wing, as our kitchen I chose the nicest, sunniest room, which (to David's great dismay) had been Nanny Webb's bedroom. It was airy and it had big windows where we would put the table as well as a wonderful view looking east, so perfect for the morning sun.

The old kitchen, Mrs Horton's domain on the ground floor since she first came to Belvoir, would become the accounts office. When I explained the new arrangement, she was simply horrified. She didn't want to move. But although I understood how attached she was to how things had always been, I was determined. The children needed to see how food is prepared, I explained. 'I can't have them thinking it just appears by magic. How else are they going to learn to cook?' And it would be so much nicer – new oven, new fridge, new everything, drawers that didn't stick, you name it. Still she stood her ground. Her kitchen was bright and airy and most importantly hers. She began to yield when I promised to build vast cupboards that she wanted to house her 'pots'. Once I agreed to that, she relented, though I hid them behind a large folding screen. At least the Hortons got somewhere nicer to live: the castle's 'superior' staff flat, which previously had been Nailor's.

Unfortunately, the problems didn't end there. The Hortons were old-school, used to working to a strict timetable that simply wasn't practical for a young family. We weren't always available to sit down on the stroke of one, and much of the time the children wanted different things.

Sunday lunches became the weekly battleground because I never knew how many people there would be. I wanted things to be spontaneous, so each Sunday I would organize pony rides and encourage the children to invite everyone back for a roast, parents included. And each week Mrs Horton would ask me in the morning: 'How many for lunch?' When I suggested, 'Perhaps fifteen?' I feared she might have a heart attack.

As for me saying, 'It really doesn't matter – just do some more roast potatoes, mash and gravy and it'll be fine,' it drove her mad. Worse still was when I offered to help, saying, 'I'll do the potatoes,' or 'I'll make the gravy.'

We'd usually end up in the private dining room, queuing up while Horton attacked the roast with a lethal-looking knife, while the veg was basically help-yourself on the side. Pudding was nearly always apple crumble with lashings of Bird's custard. Then, just like when I was a child, everyone would sing a song or recite a poem to round off the day.

Charles didn't like riding, so while I was out with the girls and their Pony Club friends, he would go ferreting with Clive the rabbit man and as soon as he was old enough, Hugo would go too. Clive was a real Nottinghamshire lad from a mining village. He didn't drive, so his brother Sean would drop him off at the castle about 9 a.m., then he and the boys would set off for the area known as Hill and Holly, where rabbits abounded, probably the old medieval warren serving the estate. He would put a ferret down a hole to bolt the rabbits, knocking them on the head as they emerged. Over the years he taught the boys how to skin them and basically get them ready for the 'pot', then all three would come back to the castle for lunch. Clive reminded me a bit of Michael Sockett, and, just like Michael, Clive was my litmus test whenever I brought new people back to lunch. If they couldn't get on with Clive, I couldn't get on with them.

David of course loved being fed by Mrs Horton, as her repertoire included all his favourite 'nursery' food, from toad in the hole to spotted dick and back again. By the time the children went away to school, Mrs Horton took to polishing the silver to fill the time as well as doing the ironing, and my clothes have never looked so beautiful. Fortunately, just like her predecessor Mrs P, in time Mrs Horton learnt not only to accept the children but to spoil them rotten. As for Horton himself, he fell for them too, and as Charles grew up, Horton took to carrying him on his shoulders down to the north terrace for a game of football.

I now realize that my run-ins with Mrs Horton were evidence of a more fundamental problem. David had grown up surrounded by staff, whereas I hadn't, and I found it disconcerting when Mrs Horton bustled into the bathroom asking what I wanted for dinner when I was taking a shower. Belatedly I came to realize that I was deeply shy, as are many people who end up as performers. Taking on the identity of someone else, even for a couple of hours, means you don't have to be you. Performance was always a mask for me and finding myself living out my life in public has been the hardest part of my journey.

I was never on my own. Whether it was nannies or volunteers or other members of staff, there was always somebody there. Most days I would climb up on the roof just to be alone, to find a bit of space for me, somewhere I couldn't be discovered. I've never found it easy being part of a group, which is probably why I ran away from school, and why my ponies were such a solace. The truth is that deep down I am a loner, however much I might pretend not to be.

Considering my own experience at boarding school, it's perhaps surprising that I chose the same route for my own children. They had all gone to the local primary but, as children from the castle, there had been problems. So, in 2004, when Violet turned eleven, she started at a lovely school I'd found in Yorkshire, where she could be comparatively anonymous. Then, in September 2007, when he had just turned eight, Charles went off to board at prep school. In turn, Alice and Eliza followed Violet to Yorkshire, so by 2008 there was only Hugo left at home.

Once he started at primary school, I decided we no longer needed a nanny, so reluctantly, after twelve years, we said goodbye to Lindsey, as I was convinced that Mrs Horton could manage a few hours of Hugo on her own. Unlike Mrs P, however, Mrs H had never had children, so her ability to control him was limited. Guests would sometimes get up from the table to find that their shoelaces had been tied together . . . I wasn't too bothered, though. The fact that Belvoir was clearly a family home, with dogs and children and mess and toys left lying around, was all part of its charm, I felt.

And that charm was finally starting to pay off. With the large-scale events that we were holding, we were able to renovate more and more of the castle. We installed a state-of-the-art kitchen next to the state dining room, where chefs were able to cater for hundreds when we had big conferences or dinners, and most importantly the food was no longer cold because it didn't need to be walked miles from the kitchen.

We started re-enactments at the castle. The guides, headed by Rhi, acted out the story of the witches in the former butler's bedroom (which for years had been full of rubbish) where we recreated a Regency school room and groups of children would come and have classes complete with slates and chalk. There they would hear about the tweenies, the children used as chimney sweeps back when the castle was built. We had costumes made and I got my own children to dress up and allowed Rhi to tell them off and make them stand in the corner.

By 2008, it was becoming clear to me that the shoots weren't working. They were haemorrhaging money to the tune of £100,000 a year, and in spite of having five keepers headed by the aptly named Mr Partridge, it was all beginning to unravel.

One day I was chatting to Sarah Skelton, mother of one of the girls' Pony Club friends, who said she knew someone who might be able to help. 'He's had the most awful time recently and I think it would be good for him to have a new focus,' she said. 'And if there's any funny business going on he will smoke it out. He knows what he's doing.'

Phil Burtt turned out to be a true countryman. Farming was in his blood. By the age of eleven he was on a combine harvester and as a young man he had turned 300 acres into 6,000. However, a hideous divorce led to him having to sell the whole lot. And if I still needed convincing, he was one of the top grouse shots in the country. Incredibly, he said he didn't want paying. So obviously I said yes.

He took it very seriously and would meet all the guns in the guard room on the morning of the shoot so they could draw their peg numbers, then lead them to their first drives. Our keepers always looked really smart, as I'd had a Belvoir tweed created in the same colour as the ironstone of the castle, with peacock buttons to match the family emblem. Phil had all the knowledge required to run the shoot successfully; he would pour their drinks at elevenses and decide on the best drives, reading the wind to gauge which direction was best to make the birds fly over the guns. Within a matter of weeks, the shoot started to run perfectly.

Slowly but surely, we were breathing new life into the castle, but it was still laden with debt. We now had two sons, and while Charles would one day inherit the castle, just as David had done, we would also have to provide for Hugo, just as Dad had had to do for Roger when William took over Heartsease. And then there were the girls . . .

When I finally realized Hugo needed someone more experienced with children than Mrs Horton, I decided to advertise for a nanny/housekeeper in the *Grantham Journal*. Caroline Rayson arrived for her interview on the dot, scrubbed up and looking smart. Unlike other potential staff I had seen over the years, she managed to find the right door. It turned out that not only was she a Pacey, but her grandmother had been a housekeeper at the castle for fifty years.

'So, tell me about your experience with children,' I said.

'I don't really know much about them.'

'Then what are you doing here?'

'My mum says I can do it.'

I asked about her current employment.

'For the last twelve years I've been working in the circus,' she said.

I sat up.

'What did you do in the circus?'

'I trained horses and lions.'

We have all experienced light-bulb moments in our life – times when you suddenly know where you are going. Hugo might run rings around Mrs Horton, but if this girl could tame lions, she'd know exactly what to do with him. I offered her the job on the spot.

Chapter Thirteen

Islands in the Stream

U P UNTIL THE early years of the twentieth century, once an heir and a spare had safely arrived, you were free to do what you pleased. But even then, some arrangements were more unconventional than others.

In 1717, John Manners, the 3rd Duke, married Bridget Sutton, a seventeen-year-old heiress. The couple's first three children – all girls – died in infancy, but then she gave birth to three healthy boys in quick succession: an heir and two spares. A further four children also died young. Bridget herself died when she was only thirty-four and in fairly short order the Duke took up with Elizabeth Drake, a fifteen-year-old village girl who had been Bridget's maidservant, and the first child of this new union was born within the year. Although, as a widower, the Duke was free to marry, for some reason he never did, although he did have three further children with Elizabeth. Both sets of offspring were brought up alongside one another, and meals were had with his legitimate children down one side of the table and the illegitimate along the other. Even stranger was that Elizabeth's brothers were also present in the dining room, as they had jobs as butlers . . .

It was May 2009 and David was turning fifty, by any measure a huge milestone, so I decided to throw him a huge party – a sit-down dinner for 320 guests with tables that stretched the length of both the State Drawing Room and the Regent's Gallery.

Growing up at Heartsease, we had always had amazing parties, and they usually had a theme. For David's fiftieth I chose the 1920s. I just loved the look, and the '20s was probably the last hurrah for country house life, when money was no object and excess and glamour were the order of the day – a kind of celebration at the end of the Great War.

I had such fun just organizing it. I designed what the girls and I were going to wear, bought the material from my favourite fabric shop in north London, then got the outfits made up by somebody in the village. The boys dressed up as New York gangsters, complete with fedoras that I had made at Lock & Co.

We had singing waiters who burst into operatic arias as they were serving, and when they launched into *La Bohème*, I couldn't stop myself. I got up on my chair and sang Musetta's aria, 'Quando me'n vo", and as the top notes rang out, the whole of the State Dining Room erupted!

In the Regent's Gallery, where David was host, he sliced his birthday cake with a random sword we'd found languishing in the silver room and which Mr Baxter had got all spruced up. The cake itself was the size of a wedding cake consisting of tier upon tier. It was made by Mrs Pacey, who was a brilliant baker, and over the years she had done all the children's birthday cakes. She had iced it with the family's coats of arms around the sides and the whole thing topped with a multi-coloured peacock, the Rutland emblem. All of us from the State Dining Room had moved across and I remember watching David as he sliced through the cake while everyone sang 'Happy Birthday', thinking just how far we had come, marvelling at all we had achieved. And when the band struck up, I looked around the room at our friends – some of them glamorous, some of them people who just happened to live on the estate – and I felt truly alive, as if the energy and excitement in the room were contagious.

I went up to David and said, 'Let's dance.'

'I'm busy,' he said. 'I'll see you later.' And I watched as he walked away without a backward glance.

I felt as if I'd been punched, as if I was fighting for breath, and I looked wildly around the floor for someone, anyone – silently pleading, *Please, please, somebody ask me to dance. Please take me out of this hell and rescue me.* And then somebody did. As we circled around the floor, this stranger and me, someone to the best of my knowledge I had never met before, I smiled at the guests, and they smiled back. Everyone was so happy, and yet the music seemed far, far away, and my ears were ringing.

Of course, David and I had had our differences and moments of irritation. What married couple doesn't? But to snub me so publicly? Perhaps no one had witnessed it, but at that moment, it felt as if the whole world was watching. As my good Samaritan prattled away about what a great evening it was and how he had never been to anything like it before and probably never would again, I knew that something life-changing had just happened.

Over the previous few months, David had seemed rather remote but he was deeply involved in researching for a book he was writing, a dual biography of the two Manners brothers, Charles and Robert, sons of the Marquis of Granby, the hero after whom so many pubs are named. And what did it matter if someone else had taken his eye? A lingering look here, a backward glance there. Flirting was harmless fun, wasn't it?

As my partner and I sashayed around the floor, I scanned the dancers to see where he was. Spotting someone among hundreds of moving people isn't easy, but when it's someone you have shared a bed with for twenty years, someone you have watched over in sickness and in health, you can single them out in a matter of seconds. And suddenly there he was, dancing with a woman who rented a cottage on the estate who I barely knew but whose son I had regularly given a lift to school. Though not particularly striking first thing in the morning, that night she looked a million dollars, and she and David were laughing. And then I knew.

Did I face him with it? Of course. Did he try to wriggle out of it? No. On the contrary. He said he was lonely. That I hadn't paid him enough attention. I countered his accusations with all the force I could muster – the pressures of bringing up five children, overseeing the transformation of the castle, and all the rest of it. It made not an iota of difference. This wasn't a flirtation gone a bit far like last time, he said. This was real.

It had been nine years since David's 'indiscretion', and I

thought we had got over it. I had been confident enough in our future to bring another Rutland baby into the world. I have always believed that, just as it takes two people to make a marriage, it takes two to break one. And I had stayed true.

And so we limped on, both desperately unhappy. I would disappear into the private dining room, where I would shut the door, smoke cigarettes, drink wine and dance on my own to 'I Will Survive', and 'Islands in the Stream'.

My parents were devastated. They would drive past her house and there would be his car. Dad wouldn't say a thing, Mum was more vocal.

They both adored David, and couldn't understand how such a kind, gentle man could find himself in this situation, difficult not only for me, but for the children. Because, whatever the eventual outcome, one way or another it was going to affect them.

By then I was a governor of the school in Yorkshire where the girls were, and the head of the governors was a well-known divorce lawyer. She recommended a law firm where I could go to for advice.

Financially, they told me, I had nothing to worry about. I had turned a failing enterprise around. I had also had five children. They said I could leave the estate and ask for £30 million. I laughed. I knew better than anyone that the estate couldn't afford a fraction of that. I had seen other stately homes fall into disrepair or bankruptcy due to the breakdown of marriages and expensive divorces. It was the reason so many fell out of family hands and into corporate ownership to become soulless conference centres instead of being passed on and cared for by future generations. No amount of money could compensate for the family being destabilized. All I wanted were the clothes on my back and my granny's kitchen table.

David never mentioned the word divorce, but over the next eighteen months, I decided I didn't want one. If we divorced, I'd have to leave the castle. I'd seen what had happened to Scruff, how, without Castle Howard to run and look after, she had become completely unanchored. Was this what I wanted? I knew Belvoir inside out and back to front – each tower, each storeroom, each chair that needed new upholstery, which tap needed fixing, which flagstone needed re-grouting. Nobody else had that breadth of knowledge.

But, more than that, if we divorced, it would create a vacancy. As Duchess, I was also the guard dog, safeguarding the land and estate. Would this woman hailing from who knows where be as determined and work as hard to keep it safe if her bloodline wouldn't benefit? Maybe she would but I had no way of knowing, of course, so I just hardened myself and got on with the job. As a farmer's daughter, I believed that heritage was more important than hurt feelings – a belief that both farmers and aristocrats have in common.

What I wanted was a legal separation, which would leave David free to continue his relationships unhindered and me free to protect the legacy of the castle that was my son's inheritance and the Manners' family legacy, as it had been for generations. Staying a Duchess was bottom of my pile.

David and I were legally separated in 2012, and slowly our relationship evolved into one of acceptance and pragmatism and yes, friendship. All I asked in return was to continue to run the castle and the estate until I retired at sixty-five. David agreed and I was officially appointed CEO. But we carried on living in the castle together.

I stayed in the nursery wing with the children while David moved into the Shepherd's Tower that I had been in the midst of renovating, ready for us to move into. (In fact, I had already moved half my wardrobe up there before this whole thing happened.) This arrangement meant he had his privacy, and the new woman in his life could come and go as she pleased.

From then on, I never used the front entrance – the door Horton had answered all those years ago – and instead I would come in through the estate office, because, however grown-up I tried to be, the smallest things could make me dissolve into tears and I didn't want to see her car in case it tipped me over the edge.

On a day-to-day level, life remained much the same. I was still mother to our children, we still had holidays together as a family. And I was still running David's business. Part of that role was to remind him of the painful fact that we were losing around half a million pounds a year, having spent a fortune getting the castle up to scratch.

Following the loss of Haddon Hall, the estate's biggest asset was its property portfolio of some 300 cottages and houses, but they had required £4 million to get them in sufficiently good order to ensure good rents.

'We're going to have to sell something if we want to get rid of this debt,' I told him.

There was no other choice, and so, with great reluctance, as it had been in the family since the eighteenth century, we settled on a Nicolas Poussin painting from a series called *The Seven Sacraments*, bought by the 4th Duke in 1784. One of the set had been lost, while a second was sold in 1939 to the National Art Gallery of Washington. In 2010, a third went to the Kimbell Art Museum near Dallas. This latest, *Extreme Unction*, was given to the Fitzwilliam Museum in Cambridge as part of a deal with the government in lieu of taxes that hadn't been paid by the 9th Duke in respect of the Poussin that went to Texas. The remaining three Poussins in the series went on loan to the Dulwich Picture Gallery.

What this meant was that we could finally rid the estate of debt, buy a farm for Hugo and a London house for the girls to be held in trust for them. I felt satisfied that now all our children would be taken care of.

One of the few houses in Knipton not owned by the estate had recently changed hands and had been bought by a man named Phil O'Brien, who approached me about setting up a charitable trust centred at the cricket ground. He had an eight-year-old son and a year or so back had formed a club for the Under-11s called the Belvoir Bees. Through cricketing contacts he'd heard about a scheme at Arundel Castle that had been going since 1985 that brought children out of the cities into the countryside. He thought it could work here.

I was immediately taken with the idea. There was so much we could do to introduce these kids not only to cricket but to country life and the countryside in general, and it was a great way to connect with the wider community. So, game on.

It proved a phenomenal success, and within the first three years we welcomed over two thousand children from primary schools to the ground, both rural and urban, as well as some from special needs schools. Marylebone Cricket Club was one of the sponsors, and I became the foundation's patron, my job being largely to front the fundraising element. I remember Tim Rice, a well-known cricketing enthusiast, attending one of our dinners. He was enjoying visiting Belvoir, he said, 'But it's all very confusing as to why we're here.'

Given that Sir Tim featured prominently in the *Sunday Times* Rich List thanks to his extraordinary catalogue of musical successes across the world, I thought it must be obvious. Or perhaps it was just an example of his dry sense of humour . . .

On those fundraising nights, the shoot dining room was turned into a nightclub, with glitterballs revolving from the ceiling. Top names in the cricket world like Ian Botham, Graeme Swann and Darren Bicknell could be seen dancing the night away, and the following day – hungover or not – they'd be playing for the Duchess's XI against a local team, all proceeds going to the foundation.

The presence of these glamorous names from the cricketing pantheon did not go unnoticed and provided plenty of grist to the local gossip mill. Though unknown to the press, David's new relationship was an open secret on the estate. The only outstanding question now was: 'And what about the Duchess?' I only had to meet Phil O'Brien for lunch at the Manners Arms and all Belvoir would be buzzing.

'Apparently we're having an affair,' he'd say, indicating with a quick flash of his eyes someone watching us.

'Your wife doesn't think that, does she?'

He laughed. Nothing could have been further from the truth.

Mrs Pacey was also a great source of gossip, and she'd often ring and tell me about the latest person I was supposedly infatuated with. None of it was true.

I first came across Heather McGregor when I featured in her Mrs Moneypenny column in the *Financial Times*. I finally met her in person when she came shooting with the UBS wealth management group, and subsequently became a great friend. Her husband was Australian and involved with the Bradman Foundation, which was set up to 'inspire youth to develop these character traits that lead to a better society among the cricketing nations of the world'. She wanted me to twin our trust with theirs. So, to this end, she arranged for me to go out on a whirlwind three-day trip to Australia, where I was chaperoned by Sarah Ferguson's sister Jane. Jane was horrified when she saw that I'd brought three large suitcases with me. 'For a weekend!' she exclaimed. But, naturally, I wasn't just promoting the cricket trust; I was banging the drum for Belvoir, too, and I must have done ten or twelve different events and so needed ten or twelve different outfits.

As a coda to this story, many years later, in 2019, I had the pleasure of welcoming the Bradman Foundation XI to Belvoir, where they played the Duchess's XI. The home team was captained by Darren Bicknell and it proved to be the one match that the tourists lost. One last footnote, I discovered many years later that the

Arundel Trust that had kick-started this whole thing was actually set up by another duchess: Lavinia Duchess of Norfolk.

Of the 17,000 acres that make up the estate, most of it is worked and lived in by tenant farmers who pay rent to Belvoir. To some degree it is irrelevant who owned the land, because the farms are passed down from father to son, just as they have been for centuries. Only 1,200 acres – the home farm – is run by us. Paradoxically, farming was the one area that I had failed to get to grips with and when, around 2010, I discovered that the home farm was losing around £350,000 a year I asked one of the tenant farmers to take it over. But even that failed to stop the rot. It was still losing money: the crops weren't growing, the sheep were worm-infested, and so I decided to get rid of everything, sold all the farming equipment, simply to try to recoup something from this disaster.

Belvoir is a close-knit community, and there's little that goes on that isn't public knowledge by sunset, and I knew word had got out that the home farm was in trouble when I had a call from Phil Burtt, who had been running our shoots so successfully for the past eighteen months.

He thought I might be interested to meet a friend of his, he said – a leading agricultural scientist specialising in soil management called Christopher Green. So the three of us met up a few days later.

Chris Green's assessment of our situation was blunt and to the point. 'What you're doing on this estate farming-wise is disastrous,' he said. Far from taking umbrage, I sat up and listened as he talked me through everything that was wrong. He explained that the home farm is the heartbeat of any estate; it maintains the ditch dykes, mends the fences, covers the crops for the shoot, creates roads to access the woods to harvest timber, holds the birds before they fly over the guns on shoot days. But it wasn't too late, he said. In the right hands, it could be turned round.

'But I've sold all the farming equipment to recover some of the losses! So what can I do?'

'The answer is right here in front of you,' he said, looking at Phil. 'You know his background, I take it?'

I nodded. He had taken 300 acres of farmland north of Belvoir and made it 6,000. After a hideous divorce he had sold the farm – Court Leys – to James Dyson as none of his four daughters were interested in taking it on.

'Hand it over to Phil,' Chris Green said, 'and he'll turn it around for you. He knows what he's doing.'

They were precisely the same words Sarah Skelton had used when she had suggested Phil for the shoot. And she had been right. Everything Dr Green said had rung bells. God knows I had to trust someone. He trusted Phil, so why shouldn't I?

'Okay,' I said. 'Let's do it. But on one condition: this time I pay you.'

Phil shook his head. 'I'd just like to prove to you that I can get it right.'

He didn't need Christopher Green to tell me all this stuff; he could have done it perfectly well himself. But I think he was a bit in awe of me, in the sense that I was independent and not always prepared to listen and he didn't want to get his head bitten off. In reality, I was just protecting myself.

You know when you've made the correct decision when your body relaxes, and you feel light-headed with relief. The next morning, during my daily run to Frog Hollow, at the far end of the gardens first laid out in the time of the 5th Duchess, I no longer felt tears well up as I passed Moss House, the folly where David had proposed to me. It would all be all right, a voice seemed to say. I liked to think it was Elizabeth herself, talking to me down the centuries.

Right from the start I had identified with her, and Mr Jenkins's notes only reinforced the sense that I had somebody looking after both me and the estate.

As I ran that morning through the dew-heavy grass, I felt newly energized. At Frog Hollow, with its two rather sad, neglected lakes, overgrown and unloved, instead of comparing them with my own feelings of abandonment, I saw it as somewhere that needed sorting out – and sooner rather than later. I determined then to get it cleared, to bring some light and air back into it.

A couple of days later, I was walking past my favourite portrait of Elizabeth in the ballroom and my mobile rang. I stopped to answer it and, while listening to whoever it was, found myself staring closely at the painting. I had never given much thought to where it had been done, but with the light now fully on it I saw exactly where it was. She was in the Spring Garden, standing next to a statue that was still there, engraved with a poem about how much she loved the gardens. But then I looked beyond in the near distance and saw water. *How had I never registered that before?*

There was no pool there now; it was just a boggy, marshy area. So, I called Mark, our man with the digger, and asked him to go down, take a look, and see what he thought. That afternoon he came and found me. Yes, he said, there were clearly remnants of a pool there, but from a long time ago. It was now completely overwhelmed and overgrown.

'So, what do you say we try to bring it back to life?' I asked.

Unlike so many of the changes I'd attempted to make at the castle, this one went off without a hitch. It now shimmers in the sun, watched over by a classical statue that I decided had the look of Elizabeth herself.

As for the home farm, it was turning out to be a major job. First, we needed to get out of the contract with the tenant farmer, and that was a very awkward conversation. Next, we needed to rebuild, mend or buy every single piece of equipment I had been foolish enough to get rid of. Meanwhile, the costs continued to soar.

While I might have felt daunted by the extent of it all, Phil Burtt was taking it all in his stride and his optimism was infectious. This was someone who clearly loved the land and it was not about what it could give to him, but the very opposite; it was about what he could give back.

During my early morning runs I'd catch him talking to farmers and estate workers. I'd hear bursts of laughter, and see smiles and waves. I could tell people liked him and respected him, because he was efficient, didn't waste words, didn't ask the impossible, and was always the first in line to pick up a shovel and do it himself, if that was what it took. And I began to think: If Phil could turn the farm around, what about other areas of the estate? The forestry section, for example. Even the gardens . . . And so, less than three years after he took over the shoot, Phil became our new estate manager.

Meanwhile, Elizabeth was still coming to me via Mr Jenkins, and in one of these notes she said that I needed to look in the archive for some 'garden plans'. I remember quizzing him, asking, 'What can she mean?' But he just shrugged.

The clearing of Frog Hollow wasn't proving as straightforward as the pool. It wasn't just restoration it needed, the two lakes needed serious repair; the dams were about to burst, water was spewing over the top, and if we didn't act fast, we were going to lose them altogether. Rather than sink into despair, however, I would think: *Phil will know what to do.* And he did. I talked him through what I thought the problem was and asked him to oversee Mark. Under Phil's supervision, the undergrowth was cut back to reveal the original contours of the lakes. He discovered an old boathouse that had been completely hidden by rhododendrons that had gone native. In all, Mark spent three months on the job, but it was worth it. Once Frog Hollow had been returned to how it had been originally, we took Aunt Ursie there for a picnic. By chance, we had chosen a perfect summer's day, and while Charles and Hugo paddled canoes, the rest of us swam. As for Aunt Ursie, she clapped her hands with excitement when she saw it.

'Oh, darling girl,' she said, 'it's exactly as I remember it as a child!'

Later, she found a photograph of her father out in a boat

on the lake with his two dogs, and she was absolutely right; it looked now exactly as it had been. It was as if we had given it the kiss of life, air where it had been suffocating – light where there had been only darkness.

In October 2011, I was offered a stand at Hudson's Farm, a prestigious shoot show near Andover, New Jersey. I'd heard of it from Gwyn Evans, who ran an incredibly successful family-owned shoot in Welshpool, north Wales, called the Bettws Hall Shooting Estate, and I knew that he never missed this event as a way of promoting his business to the US market. So, when I was given the opportunity to take a stand myself, I didn't think twice.

By then, I was used to my role as a travelling sales girl. Back in 2008/9, I wrote my first book on the history of Belvoir. It was produced in conjunction with Christie's, with whom Belvoir has had a relationship for literally centuries, and they arranged for me to promote it in New York. It was then I discovered that Americans have a weakness for anything to do with the English aristocracy, whether fictional (*Downton Abbey*) or real (Belvoir), and were very happy to reach deep into their wallets to preserve heritage this side of the Atlantic. As a result, I set up the American Friends of Belvoir Castle Foundation, inspired by Henrietta Spencer Churchill whose father, the late Duke of Marlborough, had done the same at Blenheim Palace. I met Henrietta in Palm Beach. She became one of my inspirational women. In a way she was archetypal, so obviously a duke's daughter yet so practical and down to earth.

Over the years since then I must have given dozens of talks all over the States, which not only helped raise funds to restore the fabric of the building and secure its future, but also put Belvoir on the map and encouraged shooting parties or conference and wealth management groups to come and stay at the castle.

It's fair to say that I also enjoyed being able to take a few days away from the estate, just to breathe and do something entirely different, as I find a change of scenery can do wonders for the morale. I wasn't going to turn down the chance of both a break and expanding our reach at the same time.

However, this would not just be me standing up and giving my standard talk, which I'd done a hundred times before and could recite in my sleep. And perhaps Phil sensed my unease as I packed up my stand along with the brochures and other literature, wondering just how I was going to manage.

'I don't think you should go on your own,' he said, as if reading my thoughts. 'It's a hard sell. Wouldn't you be better with some support there?'

I looked at him. 'Why don't you come?'

Hudson's Farm is an up-scale (as the Americans put it) private members club situated in the most glorious grounds outside Andover, New Jersey.

We flew into Newark and were met by Matthew Hall, a dedicated anglophile, and on our way to the club he talked us through the difference between the shooting culture in England and in the States. In England, you are invited to a shoot – farmer or millionaire, you don't pay. In America, however, everyone pays their way. Over the years, Matthew became a sort of ambassador for Belvoir, gathering groups of Americans together who would then come and shoot.

On arrival at the clubhouse, I was given the presidential suite while Phil was put downstairs.

The following morning we were given a trestle table and set up our stand. I wandered around and spotted the Bettws Hall agent there looking mildly horrified that there was competition from another British shoot. While I wafted around in my glad rags being a duchess, Phil was chatting knowledgeably to potential clients. This was his world, after all, and he was in his element. If that wasn't enough, when they found out he was Phil Burtt, the master of the grouse moor, they called him the Grouse God . . . He had been completely right, of course – something like this was so much easier when there were two of you. It proved the perfect arrangement.

Potential clients weren't always easy to categorize. At one point a huge Rolls-Royce with black windows arrived, and a short man who looked like an American mafioso got out. He approached our stand and started talking to me in a way, shall we say, that he wouldn't have been talking to Phil. Phil saw him off pretty quickly, and I remember thinking, *That's really odd . . .*

As we sat in the departure lounge about to board our flight for home, we had a glass of wine and talked about how well everything had gone. I was so overwhelmed by his support, at how thoughtful he had been, that I reached out and touched his cheek. 'Thank you for everything, Phil. I couldn't have done it without you.'

And that was the moment I felt it – like a bolt of electricity had run through me. There was no kiss, no acknowledgement, no words spoken between us. But in my head, it was a very big thing, because I realized I was falling in love.

We took it very slowly, but because of my farming background, in many ways we already spoke the same language and little by little our feelings for each other deepened.

In 2013, we began an extensive restoration project on 500 acres of woodland within the estate. We were working with John Phibbs, a surveyor and expert on historic landscapes, particularly those created by Capability Brown, and had shown him the plans that David had found in the archives dated 1766 when we had first moved into the castle, back when we were still trying to get to grips with the place.

We were out in the Land Rover, when John put his hand up and got me to stop as he compared the plan with the existing landscape that was laid out in front of us. Then he looked at me in amazement. What we had here, he said, was pure Brown.

Lancelot 'Capability' Brown was perhaps the greatest landscape architect England has ever produced. Unlike William Kent, he was a hands-on gardener and, in addition to the sweeping vistas of serpentine lakes and valleys that he is best known for – created by flooding valleys and removing villages that didn't fit in with his grand schemes – he also planted 'pleasure gardens' with flowering plants and shrubs. In his later years, he also designed houses to go with the gardens, rather than the other way round.

We knew that such a scheme had been commissioned by the 4th Duke – including a house – but he had died very young, at the age of thirty-three, and so it had come to nothing.

It had always been assumed that although Belvoir bore many of the hallmarks of a Brown landscape, it must just have been simply a copy, because the work was carried out long after the great man's death. However, delving deeper into the archive, we found that Elizabeth had paid a surveyor called Jonathan Spires to execute Brown's plan, and now, with these plans in front of us bearing his name, there was no doubt, John Phibbs said.

I felt a shiver run through me. This must have been what Elizabeth was referring to in the note I got from Mr Jenkins about the 'garden plans'. I know that many people find it hard to believe in a psychic connection between the 5th Duchess and me, but what cannot be denied is that this was the most extraordinary discovery, and it was soon confirmed by other experts in the field. What made it even more exciting from my point of view was that, on studying the plans, not only could we see where and how we could restore the landscape, but we also found areas where Brown's designs had yet to be implemented.

It would take years to achieve, I realized, but I knew it would be all right – that I could do it. It wasn't simply the adrenaline that comes from making such a momentous discovery. It was knowing that I wouldn't be doing it on my own.

Chapter Fourteen

Running on Empty

ONE THING I really admired about Phil was how direct he was, though sometimes that could come across as naive. My parents knew him as the saviour of the home farm – I had sung his praises long before our trip to New Jersey. And they had also met him of course at this event or the other on the estate. Then one evening, after a family barbecue at Frog Hollow, when I had gone back to the castle with the children, Phil had stayed on chatting with them as the sun sank lower in the sky, and out it came . . .

After David and I had agreed to separate, Mum and Dad had been really concerned. Like any parents in this kind of situation, they had been worried that from now on I'd have to deal with everything on my own, so in a strange way this completely unexpected revelation came as a relief. Given the unhappy circumstances, they couldn't have been more delighted.

'I'm sure this won't be easy for you, Em,' Dad said, 'but you only have one life.'

My parents knowing about Phil and me was one thing, but the children . . . that was something else. Dealing with this crisis in their parents' marriage had been hard enough without an additional layer to confuse matters.

Needing to keep our relationship quiet meant that when Phil and I did spend time alone it was usually away from the estate. Although he'd sold Court Leys farm, which was a few miles north of Belvoir, he still had a house in Stamford, a market town down the A1 – close enough to get to easily, but far enough away not to run into people we knew.

I had written my first book, a history of Belvoir Castle, when things between David and me were tense. I had needed somewhere to put my energies, to focus on something other than what was happening at home. And it had helped get me through. So this time I did the same, and began research for another book. I wanted to understand what shooting was really about. I'd seen how different the culture was in the States, but what about closer to home? It also gave Phil and me the chance to spend proper time together, even if it was still behind closed doors.

In all we travelled 4,700 miles across the British Isles, and it was truly fascinating. We started at Sutherland, the very tip of Scotland, where we lay in a ditch at five in the morning to try to shoot Pink Foot geese. They never arrived. We went to the Isle of Muck to shoot snipe, and to Ireland for woodcock, where I learnt how they are nocturnal and fly all the way from Russia and land in Ireland at the full moon, only to be woken up by guns blasting at them. Sometimes I do wonder what I really feel about shooting.

For me the high point was going to Stanage, one of the

most prestigious shoots in the country. As a child I would look at the castle longingly, fascinated by what it might be like inside. And all these years later, here I was! It was like a childhood dream come true. But the biggest thrill was when the gun bus dropped us off for lunch in the classroom where Dad had gone to school . . .

The strangest of all was in Norfolk, a shoot run by John Alexander, a great friend of Phil's who had been an early member of Genesis, which is how I ended up talking to Roger Daltrey, Eric Clapton and Peter Gabriel. Sadly I missed another regular attendee: Dame Kiri Te Kanawa . . .

The Belvoir estate proved surprisingly leakproof, and it was a good ten months after Hudson's Farm that word started to get out that the Duke and Duchess of Rutland's living arrangements were 'unconventional' and the tabloids sent in their hounds.

Belvoir has six villages on the estate, some of them, like Knipton itself, no more than hamlets. There are very few public footpaths, and until the twenties, even the roads were private until the cost of keeping them up became exorbitant and they were handed over to the government. As a consequence, the population is small and the presence of strangers very noticeable. My chief of intelligence (Mrs Pacey) had her own team of watchers who were reporting back that people with no idea of how to dress for the country were nosing around asking questions . . .

When Mr and Mrs P retired, they had moved to the Rutland Hospital Trust in Bottesford. Although now housed in an eighteenth-century building, it was founded in 1590 to look after estate workers in their old age, and, over 400 years later, it does exactly the same. Whenever we went to church as a family, the children would always run in to see their Nanna P.

And then came the knock on the door.

It was Hugo who answered, as he was the only one living at home. Had I warned him to be careful? No. The most important thing to me was that my children should lead as ordinary a life as possible – to be open, not afraid. The last thing I wanted was to sow the seeds of paranoia. But the rewards to the newspaper who broke the 'story' were great, because it had the two key ingredients the great British public require in their scandals: sex and the aristocracy.

'Can I come in?' I heard a male voice say, in an accent that wasn't local. 'I'm from the *Daily Mail*.'

'No, you can't,' I countered, putting my arms around Hugo. 'And if you don't leave immediately, I will call the police, because this is private property and you are trespassing.'

Having failed at the front door, he then tried the office door where Nick Pacey, one of Mrs P's sons, now shoot manager, showed him off the premises.

I immediately contacted the Leveson Inquiry into press standards, set up following the News International phone hacking scandal, and the harassment stopped but we knew it wouldn't be for long. In the meantime, I'd been put in touch with a 'reputation manager' – a former reporter and editor at both the *Telegraph* and the *Mail* called George Thwaites. George's advice was to give the *Mail* the story they wanted, or as he put it, 'to present the facts in a way that the media can understand'. It's why on the first day of a skiing holiday the royals let photographers take photos, the deal being that they're then left in peace. It's a trade-off. To retain some degree of control, and to protect the children as much as possible, you are forced to sup with the devil.

In order to draw a line under it, George said, I should write an article. It should be as straightforward and as open as possible. It should be honest and, above all, dignified. There should be nothing salacious, nothing that pandered to the voyeuristic elements of the *Mail* readership.

He then brokered the deal with the *Mail*. Now all I had to do was write it.

That August, 2012, we all went off to Aberdovey as usual, but perhaps for the first time ever I didn't join in the family singalong on the journey down. And while everybody else was enjoying the familiar pleasures that the dunes and the quayside and the castles had to offer, I was on edge the entire time, my anxiety levels going through the roof. I knew I had to do it, but at the same time part of me feared I would be opening Pandora's box.

In the end it was all there. The happy childhood in the Welsh Marches, my meeting with David, the early years at Knipton, the struggles we faced after Charles's death, and above all my concern for the children. What this admittedly unusual solution offered, I suggested, was the ultimate in joint parenting. There would be no disputes over pick-up times, and all the rest of the triggers that can act as emotional flashpoints. I stressed above all that my husband and I were still friends. Had I made myself a hostage to fortune? Only time would tell.

I hadn't wanted to mention David's original 'indiscretion', but George advised me to leave nothing out except for names. He helped me tidy it up, and it appeared on 12 September 2012 under the headline: 'The Duchess's remarkable response to her husband's infidelity'.

In fact, the withholding of names was a mistake. The 'other woman' was described as 'a lady who had been living on the estate for a number of years', while Phil was 'a man who works on the estate', and it wasn't long before the hounds were out, looking for their quarry. While the other woman would be comparatively easy to unearth, I thought, Phil would prove more difficult. As the estate manager, he was a familiar figure in the castle, with every reason to meet up with me, and he hadn't changed his comings and goings in any way.

On 27 December that same year, we were just setting off for a skiing holiday, with our two cars all packed, when I had a call from Nick Pacey. His mother had died that night, he said. She was seventy-eight. The entire family went into meltdown. When the girls were growing up Nanna P had been a presence in their lives and she and Mr P had been like in-house grandparents. Mr P was always ready to take a small passenger on the lawnmower, readily accepting offers of help when digging the flowerbeds, and he would do the school run when I couldn't. We discussed cancelling the holiday but, in the end, decided it would serve little purpose. But Mrs P spent the night before the funeral laid in the chapel and the wake was held in the castle, postponed until after we returned. For years afterwards, whenever I felt down, I'd remember her voice telling me, 'Just go and put your face on and then we'll get you into the hairdressers and you'll feel fine.'

In fact, it wasn't until three years later, in the autumn of 2015, that Fleet Street's finest finally sniffed Phil out and, even then, it was only by chance at the launch party of my book on Capability Brown. Again, the launch was at Christie's, but this time I had made my entrance on my trusty Bonny, kitted out in what appeared to be hunting gear but in reality was a velvet cape that had once belonged to Sharon Osbourne and which I'd bought at a charity auction on the advice of Susannah Constantine. In fact, it wasn't just me being theatrical; it was a reference to a portrait of the 5th Duchess, who had led me to Capability Brown. During the party Phil was chatting with an old friend who asked how things were going up at Belvoir. Phil had said fine, that David had actually asked him to become a trustee and that, although it was a strange scenario, against the odds, it was all working so basically he was delighted.

He only became aware of the girl hovering behind him about halfway through this conversation, and then she moved off and he didn't think anything more about it until the next day when I called him. 'Well,' I said, 'you've really done it now.'

He had no idea what I was talking about. Only when he read the article did he realize that this girl behind him must have been a reporter, who had noted down what he said more or less word for word. He swore that he hadn't talked to her, that he hadn't even known she was there. 'If I had I would have stopped her.'

Like a pickpocket relieving an unwary tourist of his wallet, it had been done in seconds. And Phil, bless him, is a man of the country, not of gossip columns and so didn't stand a chance against a tabloid journalist whose stock-in-trade is winkling information out of innocents.

The *Mail*'s big reveal was that the Duchess of Rutland was consorting with her gamekeeper, claiming that there were 'uncanny parallels' with D. H. Lawrence's infamous novel, casting me as Lady Chatterley and Phil as Mellors. I was mortified but I suspect that for Phil it was a relief that it was now out there. When George Thwaites said I should just describe him as 'a man who works on the estate', he must have felt utterly humiliated. It was degrading. Both I and the estate owed everything to Phil, and I felt dreadful. The last thing I wanted was for our relationship to be 'hole-in-the-corner'. I wanted to shout it from the rooftops. Here was this remarkable man who over a scant few years had transformed an agricultural basket case into a thriving business. We now had five chicken sheds and used the muck to fertilize the land; we had put in root crops and fifty acres of potatoes; we had a contract to grow peas; we were putting in wheat, barley, oil seed rape, oats. For the first time, perhaps in decades, we were able to invest the money back into the home farm, and this was all down to Phil. Yet, for the sake of a titillating headline, he was 'the gamekeeper'.

As for David, he never referred to my new relationship, probably because he was very preoccupied with his own. And while we still had meals together when the children were at home, he was deep into writing *Resolution*, his dual biography of the eighteenth-century Manners brothers and spent half his time immersed in the archives, the other half in the library in front of a pile of books.

In April 2016, Phil and I took Mum and Dad to the Canaries. Seven years earlier, my father had been diagnosed with Parkinson's. It's a progressive disease and incredibly cruel as one faculty after another shuts down.

When I think of that gentle giant who had carried me on his shoulders up on the moor, who trudged out through the snow to rescue lost sheep, sitting up all night with lambs keeping them alive, it breaks my heart. Now he was no more than a bunch of skin and bones. I remember watching him being winched into the plane in his wheelchair and it was unbearable. As for my mother, she somehow kept herself together. A few years earlier they had moved out of Heartsease, handing it over – as was always planned – to William and Jane and their growing family.

They didn't go far – just a few hundred yards up the lane, having bought what had been Stanage's old laundry that Mum had made into the most lovely, welcoming house. Being considerably higher up, the view was much better than at Heartsease. Not that my parents had ever had time to look at the view when they were younger, as they were too busy working.

It was just one month after the despicable *Daily Mail* article, while Phil and I were in Philadelphia to do a talk on the estate's Capability Brown landscape, that I got the call to say that Dad was being airlifted to Hereford Hospital. He had suffered a massive stoke and it was unlikely he would survive. I was about to do a talk to 300 people, but in that moment nothing was more important than being beside my father. I was determined to get to his bedside and say goodbye, so I did the talk and immediately boarded a flight home.

Sitting beside Dad's bed, I thought back to how moved I had been when I saw how Frances – whose emotions had always been kept firmly under lock and key – cared for the Duke in his dying days, and I decided to do the same, putting a wet sponge to Dad's lips to keep him hydrated, feeding him vanilla ice cream – the one thing he loved. I refused to move from his bedside and, no doubt much to the displeasure of the nursing staff, I slept on the floor beside him.

One by one his senses were closing down, and they say that hearing is the last to go, so I played him music and talked. I talked about the past, about the gratitude I felt every day of my life for having had such a happy childhood. He had never balked at putting down an animal that was in pain – it's what animal husbandry is all about – but when it comes to humans, it seems, that kind of compassion is out of the question. All I could do was plead for him to be given more painkillers. And still he clung on.

Hereford might have been a better-equipped hospital, but it had one major flaw: it was in England, and I decided he needed to go back to the land of his fathers. So we arranged to have him transferred to Knighton Hospital, where his own mother had spent her last days.

I had one commitment I couldn't miss. Hugo had just turned twelve and was finishing his prep school and the mums and dads had been asked to go with their kids on a final challenge, climbing Scafell Pike in the Lake District.

Ever since doing my Duke of Edinburgh (I'd done my gold medal and with my mates from Ellerslie had gone to Buckingham Palace to collect it), I'd always loved mountaineering. So Hugo and I climbed up, but there came a point where you needed ropes, and I didn't have any. Looking around this beautiful wilderness, I was reminded of Radnor Forest, and knew I couldn't stay and had to be with Dad. The headmaster was fine about it, and I said goodbye to Hugo, set off down the mountain, got into my car and four hours later arrived at Knighton Hospital still in my walking boots. Dad was still clinging on to life. Everyone was there, and I told Uncle Bev that I was going home to get Zach, Dad's old Labrador with the little short legs that refused to grow.

'You know dogs aren't allowed,' he said.

Once a rule-breaker, always a rule-breaker.

I'd noticed there was a fire exit near Dad's room, so I propped open the door half an inch with an apple core and then went to fetch Zach from the house. Back in his room, I lifted this old yellow dog, Dad's trusty companion since a puppy, onto the bed and within a couple of hours he was gone. It was 13 June 2016.

That night Mum and I went back to her house on the hill. As she made us a bite to eat, I went outside and looked down at Heartsease, just visible through the trees but now dwarfed by huge warehousing and bottling plants. That old farmhouse, my childhood home with all its memories, was now the centre of a vast global empire. And I knew how proud Dad had been. He was always someone who found it difficult to get a pound out of his purse, but it had served him well. He had achieved so much with grit and determination and not much more, and now this extraordinary human being was no longer.

By now it was dark, and as I did the washing up, Mum went out. It was a warm, starry night and she just stood on the terrace they had made together, looking out across the Teme valley to the hills beyond, just wailing, 'Where are you? Where have you gone?' Even now, writing these words, my eyes fill with tears.

Dad hadn't wanted to be buried, so close friends and family went to Hereford Crematorium. Then we drove to Brampton Bryan, where he'd been churchwarden for so many years, for a thanksgiving service. By the time we arrived, people were already overflowing into the churchyard. All fourteen grandchildren were there and either sang, recited poetry or read lessons. Among the mourners were the contingent from Belvoir who had come by coach, including Phil.

Dad's father, Grandpa Jack, used to say that, after getting married, the best party is a funeral. Unlike his son, Grandpa Jack was a showman, while Dad was genuine to his core, which was why he had been held in such respect. Yet, in this, the showman was absolutely right. For the Welsh, just like the Irish, the wake is a very important thing.

John Watkins had touched so many lives. He never gave advice as such; he was simply genuinely interested in people, and he had more than his fair share of wisdom. You felt it. Mum had stipulated no black, and so she and I both wore bright pink. In the end Dad had a proper send-off, copious amounts of champagne and happy memories circling around like butterflies. Jackie Cox was there, as was Nicola. And, of course, Michael and Ivy Sockett. Michael had been the physical side of their partnership, while Dad had been the thinker, and Michael was inconsolable, totally broken at having lost his lifetime workmate.

The next morning, I drove up to the Pales Meeting House where Dad had taken me so many times over the years. Although he was churchwarden of Brampton Bryan, at heart he was still a Quaker. He believed in hard work, in generosity, in compassion. It was exactly 300 years since the meeting house had been built, and apart from a new coat of thatch, nothing had changed. Bare boards, simple wooden benches – nothing else. Quakers have no priests, no hymns, no services, nothing to take away from communion with God. If you feel moved to speak, then you speak, but otherwise it's just shared silence. I went inside, sat on a bench and wept. What were we going to do without him?

After the funeral I had drowned myself in champagne and cigarettes to numb the pain, but as I drove back to Belvoir a few days later, I thought I heard Dad's voice. It seemed so vivid he could have been in the car sitting beside me.

'You've got to stop all this smoking and drinking, Em,' his voice said. 'It's killing you.' I have never smoked another cigarette since.

To mark the tercentenary of Capability Brown's birth, we had decided to install the last part of woodland that he had intended for the estate, and work had started in 2010. The entrance to the castle had been planned to come through the village of Harston, and the 4th Duke had tried to buy the necessary land from the Welby family. They had refused to sell though and because of this dispute the last part of Brown's plan had never been carried out, the main approach coming instead from the village of Denton.

Our first step had been to dredge the fish ponds next to the cricket ground in Knipton. Fed by natural streams, they were originally dug out in 1826, and stocked with trout but had been no more than a marshy bog for at least a hundred years. In fact, during the Second World War, they had been used as a general rubbish tip. I renamed them the Memorial Lakes, not just in memory of Elizabeth, who had been such a guiding presence, but also to mark the sacrifice of the young men from the estate who had been killed during the First World War. Beside the lake, we also planted trees in their honour to compensate for accidentally felling a memorial tree when 15,000 saplings had been planted as part of our programme of rejuvenation.

In late 2015, the last stages of the scheme were filmed as part of Channel 4's programme to mark Brown's tercentenary, a three-part series presented by Alan Titchmarsh. He had been completely blown away when he saw the plans that John Phibbs had unearthed, but he also rapped my knuckles about woodland we had cleared. I'd done it on the advice of Charles Williams, I explained, the man I had met all those years ago at the Chelsea Flower Show and whose ancestral home in Cornwall I had visited for the shooting book. In order for historic woodland to survive another thousand years, he said, you had to be ruthless. My reputation for over-zealous tree-clearing gave me the soubriquet 'Duchess with a Digger', but there was a positive side in that we uncovered blue clay, which has high water-holding capacity and so was perfect for lining the lake bed. In keeping with how things would have been done in the eighteenth century, sheep were used to paddle the base to flatten it.

So much of myself had been given to the estate, and I had been aware for some time that I was running on empty. Over the past few years, there had been so much to deal with: the fallout following the separation from David; guilt over a new relationship; losing Dad. I was no longer solid bedrock; I was a single stone, standing alone with nothing to support it, all too susceptible to breaking, so it was no surprise that I eventually did.

It was a few weeks before Charles's sixteenth birthday in 2017 that I suffered a nervous breakdown and hid myself away in the bedroom on the south side of the castle known as 'the Duchess bedroom' where my mother-in-law had slept, the room that my father went into by mistake a lifetime ago. The rooms in the nursery wing, where twenty years before I had made our 'home', had originally been 'the other side of the green baize door' – where servants and children lived. The doors linking the two sides were literally padded with noise-absorbing green baize, so each side was out of earshot of the other. Perhaps that's why I chose it, simply to distance myself from the hurly-burly of family life, the other side of that green baize door. Perhaps it was because, although my mother-in-law was the last duchess to sleep there, I imagined that Elizabeth might have been the first and that she would help me find peace.

I took nothing with me other than the dress I was wearing – a green and blue cotton with buttons down the front –

that I washed in the basin. There was no lock on the door so nothing to prevent people coming in – but I never went out. Mum couldn't understand why I couldn't just 'pull myself together', but it was as if I had no strength left. Just to get out of that bed, or brush my teeth, felt like a momentous task. Phil would sometimes come and sit with me, and I could see he was distraught, mainly I think because he felt helpless. He's a doer, someone who believes every problem has a solution. And with me he had none. When I was on my own – which was most of the time – I cried, cried till my eyes were so swollen I could hardly open them.

For the best part of three months, I lay in that vast room, with its dated 1970s blue wallpaper and hideous carpet, and it seemed that I was determined to make myself suffer, that I was punishing myself. But what for? For not being like my father? For not trying hard enough with David?

Eventually the tears dried up and I found I couldn't cry. I was empty, numb. It was as if my emotions had been cauterized or filled with novocaine so I could feel nothing. Although I never went through the green baize door, sometimes I'd go downstairs to the private drawing room where I'd sit, hunched up on a sofa clasping my knees, staring into space.

Robin, whom I had met and had fallen for all those years ago the Guildhall, had since retrained as a psychologist. Some years before, at David's and my invitation, he had come to live at Belvoir at weekends. During that terrible summer he would arrive late on Thursday night from London and not leave till Monday. When he felt I wanted to talk, he listened. When he sensed I needed distraction, we would discuss other things. When he thought I might be receptive, he would persuade me to walk in the garden. Nature, he believed, was a great healer. He reassured me that I would recover but he also thought that I could benefit from a very low dose of medication, perhaps for three or four months. It wouldn't be a long-term solution, he said, but it would help get me through the dark time and allow me to re-calibrate. I refused. I was determined that when I was ready, I would get myself out of this without recourse to pills. But just knowing he was there for me made a huge difference.

Then, little by little, things began to move. I began to brush my hair, to venture out for short walks once the public had gone home, in those summer evenings when the sky turns peach and the sun seems to balance on the horizon while the world stands still.

During the day, Belvoir is all bustle. Kitchen staff start arriving about seven, the cleaners around eight. The back-office girls get in an hour later, about nine. At half-past ten the guides and tearoom staff arrive ready for eleven, when the castle opens to visitors. Deliveries arrive, men in white vans, here to fix a sash cord on a window, a squeaking floorboard, to sort out a fridge that's packed up. And always noise. The banging of doors, the clatter of shoes on the stone staircases, the crunch of tyres coming up the drive, the ringing of bells . . .

So many people on the estate relied on me, not least my own family, yet all I wanted to do was to escape.

'When anyone else feels like this, Mum, they go away,' Hugo said, holding my hand.

'I know,' I said, 'but I can't.'

One day I was persuaded to go riding in the Peak District, and I had a massive panic attack, my heart feeling as if it would explode out of my chest. The groom who was with me saw I was struggling to breathe and, after helping me dismount, she lay me down on the turf and placed her hands on me. I felt heat radiate into my body and, lying there, looking up at that wide empty sky, the anxiety drained away as quickly as it had arrived. My heartrate stilled. She told me that this was reiki, a Japanese technique of healing, where energy is transferred from the palms of the practitioner to the person suffering to encourage the body or the mind to heal itself. You don't have to believe in it, she said – horses and pigs benefit from it as much as humans, and in fact she did it with her horses. She had trained with a man who had healed his pigs through reiki.

'I've got to get in touch with him,' I said.

Over the next few years, I did all three levels of reiki with Owen Wheatley. I have never practised on anyone else, I simply learnt how to heal myself.

Chapter Fifteen

The Rose Garden

Lunching in Claridge's with my future mother-in-law in the spring of 1991, she made it clear that her preference was for a long engagement. 'Next year would be better,' she said. 'June is such a lovely month for a wedding; the rose garden at Belvoir will be in full bloom.'

That had been my first indication that I wouldn't be married from Heartsease . . . But in terms of the rose garden, she was absolutely right.

From the moment we moved into the castle, it had always been a place of solace for me, as it had been for so many of my predecessors, and it became doubly so during that difficult summer of 2017. It was close to the castle, so I could just slip out and sit and do nothing, my absence not even registering. Although my brain felt numb and no longer capable of rational thought, my senses were on high alert, and in the rose garden I had it all: the hum of the bees and the splashing of the fountain; the scent of the roses and lavender that lined the paths and which I would pull off and rub between my fingers; the intensity of the colours:

magenta clematis, lime green lady's mantle, cobalt agapanthus, purple globe dahlias, carmine roses, and fluttering in the sunshine, going from flower to gaudy flower, dancing butterflies.

I would find a hidden corner and just sit there, trying to make sense of everything that had happened. Perhaps after nearly twenty years of marriage I should have been on my guard. But it had genuinely never occurred to me. Someone appears in our lives as a neighbour, I befriend her – to the degree that I take her child to school – and then suddenly, without warning – she's a cuckoo in my nest and is trying to push me out.

Should I have seen it coming? I was flat out running this place, which was not only our home but our livelihood, and most of all there were our five children – the centre of my world – and perhaps foolishly I thought that David would see it like that too. Although not his fault, his physical difficulties inevitably meant that I often had to bear the brunt of the day-to-day childcare. Life doesn't always play out as the fairy tale we think it will be when we're thirteen, however hard we try. And David and I did try, but he seemed to be completely infatuated. It was like a drug and the situation became unmanageable.

It's a story as old as time itself.

It happened with Violet, the 8th Duchess. However, unlike David and me, her marriage looked ill-fated from the start. Apart from their age, she and the Duke had little in common. While he was a dyed-in-the-wool Conservative, she was a card-carrying Bohemian, already a prominent member of the Souls, a society of intellectuals forming an amorphous social elite. At the time she married Henry – Marquis of Granby as he then was – she was already a sought-after artist who exhibited regularly in prestigious London galleries.

There are literally hundreds of drawings in the castle of the prominent figures that peopled her life, and each one shows she had a real gift for capturing the person behind the portrait. The symbolist painter G. F. Watts ('I paint ideas, not things') became her mentor, persuading her not to forsake her art when family life became complicated. He described her portraits as 'A great series of artistic records of the men and women influencing the age'. Though for me it's her drawings of children that cut straight through to my soul; they feel as real and as contemporary as if they had been done yesterday.

She gave birth to four children, including the requisite heir and a spare, but when Robert, the heir and her second child, died at the age of nine, she became utterly distraught. The life-sized sculpture she made of her dead son – still in the chapel at Belvoir with a copy in the Tate – is both extraordinarily accomplished but also utterly heartbreaking. Meanwhile, Henry, who appears to have been fairly boorish, sought comfort in the arms of a succession of actresses, including one who gave birth to a daughter. Later, Violet took up with Henry Cust of Belton House, the other side of Grantham, also a 'Soul', who fathered her last child, Diana, aka Lady Diana Cooper.

When Violet's husband acceded to the title on the death of his father, the family moved from their house in London to Belvoir and, like other duchesses before her, she proceeded to make changes. She brought in electricity, the telephone and bathrooms. She removed the balustrading from the Regent's Gallery and installed those glorious mirrors at the far end. But equally importantly, she re-thought the rose garden. Just as Elizabeth had brought in James Wyatt, the celebrity architect of the day, Violet brought in Harold Peto, the *sine qua non* of early twentieth-century garden designers who introduced Italianate gardens to those who could afford them. After several years of travelling around Europe, Peto had bought Iford Manor in Wiltshire and used the garden there to try out his ideas, incorporating statues and other artefacts that he'd collected during his travels, and in doing so turned it into 'the most romantic garden in England'.

There had been a rose garden at Belvoir since Elizabeth's day, when she brought in huge quantities of earth as topsoil for a series of terraces cut out of the steep hillside that led down from the castle in the direction of Knipton and the model farm. Her initial focus was to reposition seven seventeenth-century statues that had been commissioned by the 1st Duke from the sculptor Caius Gabriel Cibber. They had been designed to embellish the otherwise austere pathway that encircled the mound on which the third castle sat – the castle that Elizabeth so disliked that she persuaded her husband, the 5th Duke, to let her knock it down and start again. Originally Danish, Cibber emigrated to England as a young man and had worked with Christopher Wren among others, and by chance was then living in nearby Grantham. (His son was the prolific eighteenth-century playwright Colley Cibber.)

Very little of that earlier castle or anything connected with it remains, these statues being a notable exception – perhaps because they fitted easily into the romantic mould. They included the Four Seasons, as well as the senses of Smell and Taste, and finally Juno, the Roman goddess of fecundity and childbirth, whose sacred symbol was a peacock, the Manners' family emblem. Presided over by Winter, the only male in the group, they then descend level by level, two on the next terrace and four at the bottom.

One day, during this dark period, I was in the rose garden, sitting with my back against a huge evergreen oak that must be several hundred years old and would certainly have been there when Elizbeth was creating her garden, when I spotted a piece of dark grey stone wedged between the roots, which, when I picked it up, felt surprisingly smooth. As I turned it over and over in my hand, I realized that the shape reminded me of something: a finger. I got up and went to look at the figure of Winter a few feet away and, yes, he was missing a finger. How long had it lain there? The break wasn't recent . . . Is it too fanciful to imagine it could have happened when it was last moved, some two hundred years ago?

The discovery of the signed plans which proved categorically that Belvoir was a Capability Brown landscape, even though the work was carried out after his death, led to my decision to write an account of the evolution of Belvoir's gardens, something I hadn't touched in the first book, which was limited to the history of the castle as well as the Manners family itself.

Elizabeth's legacy survives in the pleasure gardens that lead the walker along serpentine paths, via a sequence of follies, one enchanting vista giving way to another, a succession of pools and streams spanned by ornamental bridges, everything designed to surprise and delight. These gardens, each with their separate identity, remain largely unchanged, or at least we have been able to identify the bones and restore them; my mother-in-law, a wonderful plants woman herself, played a huge part in uncovering them after a century of neglect. Planted with acid-loving azaleas, magnolias and rhododendrons, Elizabeth's pleasure gardens stand apart from those areas of the estate that earn their living, including woods, park and farmland.

While Harold Peto left the Cibber statues and Elizabeth's terraces as they were, he completely re-thought the rose garden itself. It takes the form of the prow of a ship, making the most of the difficult site. The decorative elements that convey its Italianate feel – stone figures of children for example, as well as decorative urns, copies of classical busts and stone seats – were found scattered around the grounds and in dusty corners of the castle. One of the most surprising was a centuries-old Chinese horse presented to the 5th Duke, Elizabeth's husband, by the celebrated naval commander Admiral Sir Thomas Cochrane. It had lain invisible for years, smothered by rampant rhododendrons gone wild. Against the advice of Peto, Violet positioned it in the 'prow' of the ship – in my view to great effect. Appropriately enough, one of the few things she did import to the garden was a Corinthian marble column, probably Roman, bought on a trip to Italy with her then fifteen-year-old daughter Diana.

On 7 November 2017, we heard some very sad but not wholly unexpected news. Great Aunt Ursula had died, six days short of her 101st birthday. The last time she came to

Belvoir she'd been in a wheelchair and I wheeled her into the cavernous old kitchen, now the venue for our wedding discos. She was born in 1916 and, having grown up in the castle, could still remember when it had been a working kitchen, where the cooks would be whirling around in a flurry of activity, she said, her hands gesticulating as she spoke. Everything about Belvoir triggered her youthful memory and looking around she pointed out various things that, inevitably, had been put in the wrong place.

We couldn't go far, but I took her down to the rose garden and positioned her chair by the fountain while I sat on the circular stone bench under the purple clematis and we reminisced and talked about this and that.

I decided to tell her about Phil. She said that having a lover was perfectly fine and to leave it like that. She belonged to a generation that accepted that men and women had affairs, but you stayed married. It was called 'an arrangement', she said. Her own love life had been particularly racy. She had had affairs with everyone from the Maharaja of Jaipur to J. Paul Getty and a good handful in between. At some point there was a tempestuous fling with someone at Belton House, the glorious seventeenth-century mansion outside Grantham, ancestral home of the Cust family. Harry Cust being Diana's natural father, she could well have been conceived there. All of this and much, much more Aunt Ursie chronicled in riveting detail in her 2014 memoir *The Girl with the Widow's Peak*, a soubriquet she was given by the British press when she was photographed on the balcony of Buckingham Palace after the coronation of King George VI, where she was a train bearer to Queen Elizabeth, mother of the present queen. Photographs of this stunning black-haired beauty with the pronounced widow's peak went round the world, and Lady Ursula Manners became the Pippa Middleton of her day, inadvertently stealing the limelight from the main event.

The funeral was held at her home in West Wratting in Cambridgeshire, where she had lived since the death of her husband, and where her eldest son Henry now lives. It was a very emotional day, most obviously because she had meant so much to me. It was Aunt Ursie who had hosted the family lunch party where the Manners family got their first glimpse of David's intended. Although I arrived incredibly on edge, she had calmed my nerves with her standard remedy of a glass of champagne, and over the years she became my champion. But during the service, sitting there among this throng of Manners, I reflected on how I had let the family down by not holding my marriage together.

Noticing how emotional I was, Ursie's daughter Louisa was particularly sweet to me, as was her youngest son Dickie, who now lives in LA. He subsequently gave the American Foundation £150,000 to restore the silk hangings in the Chinese bedroom in memory of his mother. So, just like the other chatelaines of Belvoir, Ursula's legacy will live on there for ever.

Lady Ursula Manners was the eldest daughter of Kathleen Tennant (Kakoo), who married Violet's son, John, the 9th Duke, who was the spare, the heir, Robert, having died. She was also my father-in-law's older sister, but not by much.

That marriage between Kakoo and Violet's son John

sounds much more promising than his parents'. Kakoo's father, Francis Tennant, in common with Violet, was a member of the Souls, and no doubt, like most daughters, she chose to follow his lead and fell into the artistic camp. John certainly sounds as if he took after his mother rather than his father. He went to Eton and Oxford where history and medieval art became his passion, and then into the diplomatic service, so on paper at least they sound an exceptionally good match.

When the First World War broke out in 1914, John was twenty-eight and as yet unmarried. He served part-time in the local regiment, the 4th Leicesters, and in February 1915 was sent to the Western Front. He did not see active service, however. Violet had lost one son and she wasn't about to lose another, and so did her utmost to protect him. 'I must fight,' she wrote to a friend. 'Other mothers do nothing. What do they get for their bravery? The worst.' Her fighting involved putting pressure on both Lord Kitchener, Secretary of State for War, and Sir John French, then Commander-in-Chief. In her memoir, Violet's daughter Diana writes, 'To get my brother to GHQ was my mother's obsessing hope.' It worked. By 1916, John was back at Belvoir, and while the war was still raging across the Channel, he married Kakoo, three days before her twenty-second birthday in late January.

The lives of those who survived the Great War were not easy from an emotional perspective. John certainly seems to have been racked with guilt; not only did he not fight, but he appears to have allowed his mother to fraudulently claim he was unfit to serve. The percentage of officers who lost their lives was very high compared to other ranks, and a whole generation was decimated. Nine months after they were married, Kakoo's elder brother Mark was killed in action.

John inherited the title on his father's death in 1925, and from then on, the new Duke and Duchess devoted their lives to restoring Haddon, which had been largely abandoned for the past two hundred years. He also embarked on an archaeological dig at Croxton on the outer edge of the Belvoir estate and rooms were set aside in the castle for his finds.

In the 1930s the country was engulfed by a constitutional crisis when the Prince of Wales became involved with the American divorcee Wallis Simpson and threatened to abdicate if he wasn't allowed to marry her, which at that time was forbidden. Things came to a head on the death of King George V in January 1936.

Kakoo was a close friend of the Duchess of York and thus was violently opposed to the relationship. If David, as he was known by the family, did abdicate, then the next in the line of succession was his brother, the Duke of York, something his wife, Elizabeth, was desperate to avoid. Her husband had never been strong physically and she was convinced that the stress involved in taking on the role of sovereign would kill him. Kakoo's sister-in-law Diana, by then married to Duff Cooper, Secretary of State for War, was more sympathetic to the couple. Her husband advised Edward VIII, as he was by then, to wait until after his coronation before marrying Mrs Simpson, as she would then be accepted, he believed.

As we know, the as-yet uncrowned king did not take this

advice, and the Duke of York was crowned George VI on 12 May 1937. Kakoo was one of the four duchesses who held the canopy that covered the new queen as she was anointed by the Archbishop of Canterbury, while her 21-year-old daughter Ursula was one of the six maids of honour who carried the train.

In September 1939, Chamberlain declared war on Germany. Roger was still at school and John was at Oxford, but Charles was quick to join up as a 2nd Lieutenant in the Grenadier Guards. Did the 9th Duke hope that his son might salvage his tarnished reputation? Or was he, like any father, simply wanting him to survive? The archives have nothing to say on the matter, so whatever thoughts he may have had went with him to his grave. He died seven months later in April 1940, nine days after catching pneumonia. He was fifty-three.

When news came through of his father's death, the 10th Duke of Rutland was given leave of absence to attend the funeral, his commanding officer saying that, after all, if he needed him, he 'knew where to find him'. Just a month later, any sense that the war was going to fizzle out or be 'over by Christmas' came to an abrupt end with the German invasion of France and Belgium.

When I think back to our early days in the castle and how little preparation David had before he took over the reins, it's hard to imagine that Charles would have been better prepared, particularly as his father had died so unexpectedly, so quickly and so young. For all that he was now the 10th Duke, Charles was a serving officer in His Majesty's Army and in no way could he oversee the running of the estate, so inevitably it fell to Kakoo to keep things ticking over. But he clearly had complete trust in her ability to do so.

In January 1941 he wrote to his mother saying, 'I don't know what I should do without you, you are the one anchor which makes me hang onto hope these days'. Later that year he sent her a handwritten will, fully expecting to die during the war. Perhaps it was prompted by the news that his uncle, Kakoo's brother Lt Col. John Tennant, had been killed in action in a flying accident on 7 August 1941. He was fifty.

The following year, in 1942, her beloved father Francis also died. Then, just two months later, came news from Charles that she had been dreading:

> Now to come to a most unpleasant and nasty subject, the possibility of my going abroad and how it would effect running things. Naturally I want to leave you sole decider of any problem, with the best adviser to help, of course the actual Estate management would be carried on by the agents, subject to them letting you know periodically the news, and getting you to decide points, as they do with me now.

Meanwhile, John had left Oxford and had signed up with the Life Guards, and in 1944 was recruited by his friend David Sterling to join the 'L' Detachment of the Special Air Service Brigade which Sterling was setting up, later known as the SAS. John was involved in four major operations and was twice parachuted into France. His final posting of the war was in Bergen, Norway, rounding up collaborators.

Their father, the 9th Duke, as somebody who was passionate about both art and history, had early on seen the danger of Hitler's rise to power and had offered Belvoir to the government as secure storage. The offer had been accepted. In 1940, Winston Churchill famously said of the country's works of art: 'Hide them in caves and cellars, but not one picture shall leave this island.' Many were hidden in quarries in Wales, but damp conditions were not suitable for the most fragile. So unlike Castle Howard and Chatsworth, both of which were requisitioned as girls' schools, Belvoir acted as a stronghold for the nation's cultural treasures, among them the Magna Carta. To avoid any risk of damp, the castle remained heated throughout the war, a huge boon for the few people who lived there. In addition to Kakoo, that included Isabel (now Guinness) and her two babies, William and Lindy, who were put in the care of Nanny Webb, who presided over the nursery. Ursie was close by in Grantham, where she was working in an armaments factory (BMARC) managing a workforce of 2,000 women and also having an affair with the managing director, William Kendall. Charles expressed his concern in a letter to his mother in April 1942:

I am very worried about Ursula, the whole matter seems to be going from bad to worse, it would be much better for her to get away from that man, after [all] that sort of thing has been done before frequently, people do fall out of love in time, I have a sort of sneaking feeling that you secretly think it might be a bad thing, if he did get his divorce and marry Ursula, I am quite convinced it would be an appalling thing, and I am quite convinced he is a real whole hearted cad, of the worst type.

In 1943, after a spell home on leave, Charles wrote,

*You are always so wonderful about it, and make
everything so nice, I don't know what I should do
without you, or for that matter, any of us. Believe me
mother dear, you may not realize just exactly what you
do mean to us, I tell you. It is everything, we all feel that
terribly. I daren't think what would happen if anything
happened to you or if you left Belvoir. As far as I am
concerned, it gives me the greatest feeling of security and
pride to know that you are holding the fort at home
during these bloody days.*

Having lost one brother in the First World War and a
second in the Second, Kakoo's fear that she could lose one
of her sons was hardly irrational and, just like her mother-
in-law before her, she was prepared to move mountains to
get Charles back at Belvoir. But Charles was clearly not
happy with the idea.

In January 1944 he wrote, 'When the War in Europe is
over . . . That will be the time when you will have to start
pulling strings to get me out, on the argument that I have
a full time job running my Estates and taking part in the
House of Lords.'

By 1945 all three of Kakoo's sons were in uniform, with
Roger joining the 6th (Armoured) Brigade, where he saw
action in Germany before the war in Europe officially ended
on 8 May 1945, VE Day. In my lifetime, although British
soldiers have been killed on active service – notably in
Northern Ireland and Afghanistan – we have lived through

an unprecedented period of peace and it's hard to imagine what it must have been like for Kakoo, with all three sons fighting somewhere in Europe, never knowing where they were, or whether they were alive or dead.

My generation's equivalent of life being put on hold, that sense of being cut off from normality, of lists of daily casualty figures and not knowing how long it would go on, or even if you or your loved ones would even come out of it alive, was Covid.

Living above the shop does have its advantages – particularly if the shop is in the middle of thousands of acres of some of the most beautiful countryside in Britain. And for me personally, lockdown couldn't have come at a better time. I was able to reconnect with my children in a way that would have been unthinkable even six months previously. They were now grown up, unrecognizable from the little people who had raced along the castle's corridors and driven the staff mad with their water pistols and paper aeroplanes. All five came back to Belvoir, and for the first time in years we lived as a proper family, sharing the cooking, going for walks, and just talking. On winter evenings, after a day spent chopping up fallen trees and exercising the birds of prey with David, there would be chess and backgammon tournaments. And when the snow really hit, tobogganing down the terraces.

The farm element of the estate continued as usual – key workers as in the war – whereas in the castle there was just a skeleton staff to keep things ticking over. The gardens weren't considered essential, however, and to a degree they were left to run wild, but we decided to open them to the local community so they could enjoy them as we could.

When Covid first hit we were all in shock, but as time went on it became increasingly clear that people were both desperate to get out into the countryside and to eat something they hadn't cooked themselves. I began to think what might be possible and within the distancing regulations.

A year before Covid hit, we had opened the Engine Yard, a 'retail park' just outside the main gates with a restaurant and a handful of specialist shops. I had never forgotten the days we used to spend at the farm between Heartsease and Knill and the fun we had playing on old farmyard machinery, and I had been determined to do the same thing here, where children could just clamber around and pretend to be driving a tractor, and we did.

The newly opened Engine Yard already had cooking facilities at the Fuel Tank, so we started doing take-away coffees and fish and chips. Then the boyfriend of one of the girls, who was locked down with us, suggested getting the pizza oven going. This had been built shortly before Covid struck but had never been used.

In times of adversity there are some personalities who come into their own, who can see opportunities. Not one of us had ever cooked pizzas before but thanks to YouTube videos we eventually got the show on the road.

Everyone joined in and it gave me such pleasure seeing them all working as a team. The girls were responsible for taking orders while the boys mainly did the cooking – even David took his turn. They would go down in the mid-afternoon, prepping and getting the oven up to temperature, and then the cars would start to arrive. The field opposite the Engine Yard – earmarked by Capability Brown for haymaking – was overflowing every night, people were so keen to get out and, as restrictions began to lift, they would come from as far afield as Peterborough. They ended up selling over a hundred pizzas a night. It was a complete triumph.

There was such a tremendous feeling of camaraderie. People would come and walk in the gardens, pick up a pizza or a bag of chips and a coffee, and if the Dunkirk spirit can be said to still exist, we had it there.

When I was young, I remember friends of my parents' generation saying so-and-so had 'had a good war', and I would think, how was that possible? How could a war ever be good? Now I understand what they meant: I 'had a good Covid'.

For me, those months of lockdown were a last hurrah. Yes, of course there will be birthday parties and Christmases when we will celebrate as a family, but we will never again be together over such a long period, and I do feel blessed.

For now it's back to business as usual and there is work to be done, most of it essential, because although we're only the guardians of Belvoir, it's our duty to keep it in good repair for the next generation, and the generations after that, and there's a lot still to do.

However, I do also have a wish list. One element of the Capability Brown landscape still needs to be restored. The Chase was originally a hunting ground that ended at the site of the demolished abbey at Croxton. A carriageway – now overgrown – linked the castle to a Palladian house built by the 3rd Duke where Elizabeth and her entourage would stay while enjoying a few days racing on the private racecourse above the ancient fishponds. The house is now a ruin, but it's shored up with scaffolding to prevent further damage and, if funds ever allow, I would love to restore both it and the avenue, which is independent of all public highways. The three uppermost ponds are now dredged and, if the authorities are willing, it would be wonderful to restore the other five. Finally, in researching the history of Croxton, John Phibbs, the Capability Brown expert, has discovered that it is the oldest deer park in Europe. Recently I was out for a morning run when I came upon three dappled roe deer, quietly cropping the grass beside the track. They raised their heads, looked at me without fear then, with a flash of their white tails, were gone, almost as if they were telling me they wanted to come back.

My five are now grown up, but I know that at some point they too will have children and the cycle will continue. I have always been someone's daughter, someone's wife, someone's mother. Now, I am looking forward to being someone's grandmother, to taking him or her out in that ancient Rutland perambulator, visiting the hound puppies, building sandcastles, going crabbing and, above all, teaching them to ride and taking them on treks across Radnor Forest.

Acknowledgements

A book is never a solo effort and I owe eternal gratitude to the many people who have guided me, held me upright and, at times, saved me from becoming my own worst enemy. These people know who they are but I would particularly like to salute my extraordinary 'ghost' Pepsy Dening. As a lifelong sufferer of dyslexia, my need for someone to do the heavy lifting was critical. She picked me up and, with heroic determination, plus a bit of magic, helped me to deliver my story. This book has been a true collaboration.

My darling Robin, who has held all our hands through some difficult moments but always steers us to a gentle landing.

Mum, words will never convey the joy and pride I have felt throughout my life being your daughter. Thank you for sharing so much of your own family history – some things I have learnt for the first time during this sometimes arduous process.

Dad, although not on this side, kicking me on from the other side.

David, my heart fills with pride at all that you have achieved and I thank you for your unconditional support and for the enormous help that you and Vicki Perry have painstakingly given me, digging deep into your beloved archives.

Darling Phil, thank you for the history of Croxton and for your creative eye that has helped sculpt and lay out the land as Capability Brown planned over two centuries ago.

My patient publisher Ingrid Connell and my agent Caroline Michel without whom this book simply had no legs.

Lastly, and most importantly, the support of my wonderful children. Eliza for encouraging me to tell my story and then standing firm. Vi, you are wise beyond your years and, as the oldest sister, you have many times stepped up to the plate and I truly thank you. To Alice, if roles were never sacred, she would have been my mum. Al, I've never been an easy mum for you – thank you for accepting me. My boys – well they speak for themselves, they will be mates forever! Keep up the singing!

This book has been rather like giving birth, and at last it has been delivered.